ARKANA

THE PARTICIPATORY MIND

Educated in Warsaw and at New College, Oxford, where he received a
D.Phil. in 1964, Henryk Skolimowski has been actively engaged in
healing the planet for the last fifteen years. He is the creator of
eco-philosophy and the director of the Eco-philosophy Center. His
book *Eco-philosophy: Designing New Tactics for Living* was the first in
its field and has been translated into twelve languages. He runs
workshops on eco-philosophy and eco-yoga during the summer at the
village of Theologos, on the island of Thassos in northern Greece. He
has published sixteen books and over 300 articles; his book *Living
Philosophy* is also published by Arkana. He is Professor Emeritus at the
University of Michigan, Ann Arbor. In the autumn of 1991 he was
appointed to the Chair of Ecological Philosophy (the first in the
world) at the Technical University of Łódź, in central Poland. His
main interests are eco-philosophy, eco-ethics and evolutionary
epistemology.

The Participatory Mind

A new theory of knowledge and of the universe

HENRYK SKOLIMOWSKI

ARKANA

PENGUIN BOOKS

ARKANA

Published by the Penguin Group
Penguin Books Ltd, 27 Wrights Lane, London, w8 5tz, England
Penguin Books USA Inc., 375 Hudson Street, New York, New York 10014, USA
Penguin Books Australia Ltd, Ringwood, Victoria, Australia
Penguin Books Canada Ltd, 10 Alcorn Avenue, Toronto, Ontario, Canada m4v 3b2
Penguin Books (NZ) Ltd, 182–190 Wairau Road, Auckland 10, New Zealand

Penguin Books Ltd, Registered Offices: Harmondsworth, Middlesex, England

First published 1994
1 3 5 7 9 10 8 6 4 2

The artwork for the figures in this book
was prepared by Nigel Andrews at Capricorn Design

Set in 11/14 pt Monophoto Garamond
Typeset by Datix International Limited, Bungay, Suffolk
Made and printed in England by Clays Ltd, St Ives plc

Contents

CONTENTS

Acknowledgements

Grateful acknowledgement is made to Susan Gorka for her drawings for Figs. 1, 2 and 3 in Chapter 7; to Pierre Le Neuve for supplying the photographs reproduced as Figs. 4 and 5 in Chapter 7; and to Christie's, London (photo: Bridgeman Art Library), for supplying the photograph reproduced as Fig. 6 in Chapter 7.

This book is dedicated to
Heraclitus, Anaxagoras,
Pierre Teilhard de Chardin
and all those who take
evolution seriously

Throughout this book, when I mention concepts of 'man' I mean of course concepts of the human person. Traditional usage makes it more idiomatic to say 'man is a rational animal' than 'the human person is a rational animal'.

Introduction

The dream of absolute knowledge that Isaac Newton and his followers cherished is shattered. It is all in pieces – all coherence is gone. We need to reassemble our world-view in a new way. We need to create new perspectives and visions to comprehend afresh this fabulous universe of ours. We need a deeper and better understanding of the subtle expanses of our inner selves, of our complex relationships with all other forms of creation in this cosmos.

This book outlines a new theory of mind which is the key to multifarious forms of new understanding. The Participatory Mind, conceived as the herald of the unfolding universe, is offered here as a form of liberation from the shackles of the prevailing mechanistic world-view. The same mind also offers itself as a significant healer, since our world needs healing on a vast scale.

Academic philosophy of our time is written by pure brains. It has become unreadable to ordinary persons and even well educated ones. It stands out as a curious marred monument abounding in intellectual labour and yet leaving us totally dry and uninspired. This *philo-sophia* has renounced all claims to *sophia*.

As an antidote to this inhospitable dryness and aridity, a new genre of books has appeared – filling the gap that professional philosophy has left in its wake. Many of these books are written out of pure emotion. They deliver an emotional salvation but only for a weekend. They do not go deep enough. They do not take the human condition seriously enough. They stroke and appease rather than try to reconstruct and break new ground.

Our world needs mending and healing; so does our psyche, which has undergone an unprecedented battering in the twentieth century. This fundamental healing cannot be accomplished through pop philosophies that provide a temporary psychological fix. Nor can it be accomplished by professional philosophical treatises full of inscrutable formulae which dissect language until it becomes a dead tissue.

This healing can be achieved by the development of a new philosophy. This book attempts to provide such a philosophy. It provides a new rendering of reality and a new concept of mind, and by simultaneously reinterpreting the two arrives at a new notion of mind/reality. The philosophy offered here fuses Logos with Eros and shows that the right interpretation of the mind – in its evolutionary unfolding history – not only does not pit mind against emotion but demonstrates that they are two different parts of the same spectrum, the spectrum of human (and evolutionary) sensitivities. The healing of the world (and of ourselves within it) and a new understanding of the universe are complementary aspects of the same process.

The time has come to attempt a new unity. This unity will not come about by reshuffling the existing pieces. We must evoke the pioneering spirit of the pre-Socratics and by bold strokes of imagination remould the universe into a new shape until we gasp in wonder and say to ourselves: why haven't we thought about that before? The key to our reconstruction of the universe is the mind. When we grasp the meaning and place of the mind in the cosmos, we shall be astonished to discover that other things are falling into their places much more readily than we expected.

Against the prevailing trend of empiricism, which has claimed: 'There is nothing in the mind that has not been previously in the senses,' participatory philosophy announces: 'There is nothing in the senses that has not been previously in the structure of our mind.' What we are witnessing in our era is not only the collapse of classical empiricism (which is predominantly an epistemological theory) but the collapse of metaphysical realism which maintains that the world is as it is, and that science describes it as it is. Various and often desperate attempts to recover both empiricism and (metaphysical) realism have invariably failed. What we need is a new metaphysics and a new epistemology. Participatory philosophy provides both.

The idea of the Participatory Mind asserts the centrality of mind in designing our cosmologies, our ontologies, as well as the variety of other products of human culture and spirit. The great luminous insight of Anaxagoras that all is *nous* – mind – needs to be rediscovered and *celebrated*, for it is an astounding anticipation that mind not only beholds but shapes all. From the mind springs the multitude of things comprising all understanding. Without it there is no understanding. Parmenides said, still anticipating Anaxagoras: 'No mind, no world.'

From the central idea of the Participatory Mind grows a whole tree of new understanding – a new epistemology that engenders a new ontology. The Participatory Mind also illumines the paths of individual human destiny. It outlines a new concept of man – as a being endowed with manifold sensitivities. Life is a growing tree of sensitivities. We have as many windows onto the world as sensitivities we have evolved and refined. All human culture is nothing but a monument to our flowering sensitivities. The ascent of evolution is the ascent of sensitivities.

Martin Heidegger was right in turning to the pre-Socratics when attempting to renew philosophy in the twentieth century. But in a sense he followed a wrong trail – Being. Heidegger's discourses on Being have brought much illumination to our understanding, but also much confusion. We shall insist, throughout this book, that the renewal of philosophy must lie in our new understanding of the nature of Becoming. All universe is the flowering of becoming. The mind itself may be seen as the evolution of cosmic dust into sparks of understanding, into visions that far exceed the horizons of the eye.

The twentieth century is like the sixteenth – one of hope and confusion. Above all it is a century of transition: the old is crumbling and the new has not yet sufficiently articulated itself. For all its defects the old mechanistic reason is still holding strong, and it is tenacious. Mechanistic or secular reason was a form of liberation in the seventeenth century, enabling men to free themselves from the shackles of constraining religious orthodoxy. However, in time this reason has itself become a form of tyranny. Secular reason has become so paranoiac vis-à-vis all spiritual teaching that it has blinded itself against its own deficiencies, and in the process blinded us and made us accept a myopic conception of the universe which we have considered for the last three centuries as the only rational one. But as we approach the twenty-first century the incompleteness of the scientific world-view (based on Newtonian mechanics) is all too obvious. We can no longer believe in the primacy of physical facts. Physical facts, eg subatomic particles, have left the realm of palpable, 'hard' reality and ascended to the elusive realm of energy waves.

Tired of the staleness of the religious mode of life, the

seventeenth century rediscovered the physical. Tired of the triviality of the material mode of life, we are rediscovering the spiritual. Indeed, the rediscovery of the spiritual is the hallmark of our time, as we approach the twenty-first century. This rediscovery is manifesting itself in physics, as physicists no longer shy from the intangible and the religious; in psychology, as we no longer try to reduce the human being to behaviourist schemata; in our search for meaning, which par excellence includes the spiritual dimension.

Over and above specific inquiries, this book attempts to show that our world-views and our lifestyles are intimately connected, so that the mechanistic conception of the world implies and necessitates – in the long run – a human universe that is cold, objective and uncaring. As a consequence, human meaning is reduced to quantity and consumption. On the other hand, it becomes clear that if we strive for human meaning that is rich and versatile, that above all contains a spiritual dimension, then this form of human universe implies and necessitates the recognition that the cosmos itself is pregnant with spiritual forces which cannot be reduced to the mechanistic schemata of classical science. Paraphrasing T. S. Eliot we can say that a wrong conception of the universe implies somewhere a wrong conception of life and the result is inevitable doom.

Genuine philosophy for our times must help us to understand the universe in a new way and help us to live in it. It must address itself to the total person, his quests for understanding, for meaning, for consolation. In the words of Euripides: 'Vain is the word of the philosopher if it does not heal any suffering of man. For just as there is no profit in medicine if it does not dispel the disease of the body, so there is no profit in philosophy either if it does not dispel the suffering of the mind.'

We need philosophy connected with life and serving life, philosophy that is not afraid of treading where angels fear to tread. The participatory philosophy developed in this book is not pouring old wine into new bottles but an invitation to a new kind of a participatory 'dance' in the course of which we shall change our destiny.

As regards the content of particular chapters:

Chapter 1 outlines the boundaries of the Participatory Mind. It argues that the notion of the Participatory Universe is incomplete unless we simultaneously introduce the notion of the Participatory Mind and of Participatory Man. Each of these large concepts defines the other. The chapter introduces the three minds: Mind I, which is equivalent to the present analytical mind: Mind II, which is equivalent to the sum-total of all sensitivities that evolution has developed in us; Mind III, which is coextensive with reality. This chapter also outlines a new conception of man, who is defined by the range and power of the sensitivities through which he or she expresses his or her individuality and uniqueness. The chapter also introduces the notion of *noetic monism*, a new form of non-dualism which reinterprets reality as a form of mind and vice versa.

Chapter 2 argues that the Western mind has travelled the whole circle, from the early holistic unity of the pre-Socratics and Plato, via the period of fragmentation and atomization of the empiricist era, to a new wholeness based on evolutionary unity, which is reminiscent of early Greek philosophy, but which nevertheless is not a return to the original starting-point. We have not travelled in a straightforward circle, but in a spiral. We have come to recognize the validity of many tenets of Eastern philosophies. But we do not totally submit ourselves to these philosophies; rather, we absorb them into our own frame of reference, and give them a new coherence and meaning.

Chapter 3 argues that there is a close and inevitable relationship between the view of the cosmos of a given people (cosmology) and the system of knowledge of a given people (epistemology). One recapitulates the other, and is in the image of the other. Thus *the outer walls of the cosmos are the inner walls of the mind*. The inner walls of the mind I call *the spiral of understanding* – which is one of the central categories of the system of participatory philosophy presented in this volume. The chapter also argues that the recognition of mankind's creative nature necessitates the universe which is open and mysterious. And conversely: the open-ended, evolving universe requires and demands the recognition of man's creative nature.

Chapter 4 argues that Teilhard de Chardin's cosmology is essentially incomplete. The epistemological dimension is missing in Teilhard. The thesis of complexity/consciousness (which gives an account of how the world has developed in the ontological sense) must be supplemented by the thesis of simplicity/comprehension (which gives an account of how the mind participates in this development). If the cosmos is infinitely complex, and there is no reason to assume that it isn't, the mind does not have the capacity to deal with that complexity. Thus it must simplify – in order to comprehend. *Understanding is simplifying. Every act of comprehension is an act of simplification.* Specific systems of knowledge are specific patterns of simplification, in accordance with the prevailing view of any given culture concerning the nature of the cosmos.

Chapter 5 demonstrates that a specific cosmology originates its specific logos, and vice versa – a new logos brings about a completely new cosmology. The chapter argues that the Western mind (Western forms of logos) has been changing within historic times, and has gone through four major cycles: mytho-poetic, Greco-Roman, medieval and mechanistic, with the distinctively different logos shaping human sensitivities, perceptions, visions and eschatologies in each period. I postulate, at the end of the chapter, that we are at the threshold of a new logos which I call *Evolutionary Telos*, and which is subtly but inexorably organizing the new emerging civilization.

Chapter 6 articulates some of the aspects of Evolutionary Telos, particularly as expressed in the tenets of the methodology of participation, which in a fundamental way challenges the narrowness of the methodology of objectivity. 'Objectivity' has become a myth which is pernicious and which we need to transcend. When we change the logos of an entire civilization, not only new visions are needed, but also new methodologies, new cognitive strategies, new forms of thinking, new forms of justification. Thus the methodology of participation presents itself as a large-scale tool to help us to articulate a new cosmos and ourselves in the process. Participation becomes our new rallying point.

Chapter 7 argues that the origin of all structures is the process of the articulation of life. The evolutionary ascent has been carried through organized wholes, whose names are structures. When human life began to articulate itself, it burst into symbols and symbolic structures. Symbols continue the odyssey of structures on the level of cultures. We devour symbols and our lives are shaped by them. The deeper the mind, the deeper its symbols. The deeper the symbols, the richer the universe. Symbols and structures ought to be seen within the context of participatory evolution.

Chapter 8 carries the discussion of earlier chapters to some specific conclusions. It argues that *becoming* is not a logical process, but a contingent and a creative one. To be in the process of becoming is invariably to experience creative pains. On another level, the chapter argues that our individual spiral of understanding, although it has been shaped by overwhelming evolutionary and cultural forces, is uniquely and irredeemably our own. This requires the recognition of personal knowledge and personal truth – which, although they are subtle and frail entities, when handled properly, can be accommodated vis-à-vis universal knowledge and universal truth.

Chapter 9 explains why different cultures slice reality differently and why people of a given culture have great difficulty in comprehending the world-view of radically different cultures. We are conditioned to think that our culture knows best. The chapter also demonstrates why the guardians of the status quo are not only unable but positively unwilling to see the new evidence that threatens the views of the status quo. The chapter also presents arguments why the computer, and other deterministic automata, *cannot* perform all human functions without violating the meaning of the term 'human', and also discusses the predecessors of the theory of the participatory mind such as Bateson and Gebser.

Chapter 10 argues that as we have witnessed the collapse of metaphysical realism, we must therefore be prepared to re-examine the traditional concept of truth, especially the classical, or the correspondence theory of truth. The crisis of the correspondence theory has led many to switch over to the coherence theory of truth. But this is mere hiding. We need a new concept of truth, which would be congruent with the participatory nature of the universe. In this chapter I announce and articulate the participatory concept of truth. Participatory truth is species-specific, culture-bound, and evolving. It is not absolute, but it is not subjective. It is inter-subjective within the culture, within the accepted discourse. There is Absolute Truth: it is one gigantic truth about the whole universe in its transformation and unfolding. Depending on the context, we can distinguish various forms of (participatory) truth: religious, cultural, physical, formal, existential and practical.

Chapter 11 examines the Great Circle of Reality–Knowledge, and proposes a new grand theory. In the process we examine the nature of experience – at once a very simple and an exceedingly complex concept. For millennia we have been asking: What is the role of experience in acquiring knowledge? This chapter provides new answers to this question. It also argues that the *axis of reality*, the one enshrined by the methodology of science, and the *axis of contemplation*, the one favoured by the phenomenological method, are each incomplete. They are to be combined within the all-encompassing *path of becoming*, which alone can make sense of the nature of experience, of the notion of knowledge, and of the transition from one reality to another.

Chapter 12 outlines the tenets first of some ultimate philosophies and then those of Participatory philosophy. Participatory philosophy declares that to be a person in the Participatory Universe entails the recognition of the all-important bond of Participation. The metaphysics of Participation is a new key to the universe. *I participate, therefore I am. I do not participate, therefore I am not.* In the process of outlining Participatory philosophy, the rudiments of Participatory ethics are also provided. Participatory ethics is a version of ecological ethics. To participate in the highest realms of human experience is to participate in the sacred. This form of participation has been traditionally called religion. Although Heidegger contended that philosophy is dead, we defy this pronouncement by resurrecting it while testifying to our spiritual rebirth.

CHAPTER I

Outlining the Participatory Mind

1. Mind and life

In great spiritual traditions of the past, the right understanding of the mind is a prerequisite for following the right path. The premise is that to understand life is to understand mind; to understand mind is to understand life. Therefore, a deeper understanding of the mind invariably means a deeper understanding of the self, and of the cosmos at large. Thus an indepth understanding of the mind invariably means deepening one's own life, making it richer and more meaningful.

All this changes with modern philosophy. Since Descartes, since the mind was separated from the body, and furthermore mind and body from the soul; since the moment when the mind was conceived as a ghost in the machine, the study of the mind has increasingly meant the study of the brain; and the study of the brain has increasingly meant the study of the neurophysiology of the brain. Thus, understanding of the mind has been replaced by the knowledge of the chemistry of the brain cells. However, no amount of this knowledge can help us to understand the self better, and to make our lives more meaningful through this knowledge. Hence the sad dilemma of our times: we possess an abundance of knowledge of the brain and very little understanding of the deeper mysteries of the mind. It was just the opposite with ancient spiritual traditions.

We have reached the limit of atomistic understanding and

we no longer believe that more knowledge of the chemistry of the brain cells will resolve the riddle of the mind for us. A Nobel Laureate, Albert Szent-Gyorgyi, epitomizes our dilemma perfectly. He wanted to understand the phenomenon of life. So he first studied organisms in their environment. The subject proved too complex. He then studied the structure of cells. The subject proved too complex. He then studied the chemistry of proteins. The subject proved too complex. So he finally decided to study electrons in order to see whether they could be the harbingers of life. But electrons are electrons, he tells us, 'lifeless creatures'. Somewhere in the pursuit of life, 'life itself has slipped away from my fingers,' he confesses. And so it is with the attempt to understand the mind via the chemistry of the brain cells: we end by knowing more and more chemistry and understanding the mystery of the mind not at all. The mind is a mysterious phenomenon indeed. To acknowledge this mystery is not to mystify the mind but to express our recognition of the exquisite complexity of the universe.

We have a relentless urge to understand. So great is this urge that sometimes we persuade ourselves that we understand when in fact we don't. This is not an act of hypocrisy, but a craving for security in this uncertain world of ours. This drive for existential security via an intellectual understanding has been much more pronounced in the Western world than in other civilizations. People from other cultures have been much happier to live with mystery than we have been. We demand clarity and complete explanation where often none can be obtained. We have a strong but unfounded faith in our linear discursive reason. We want to know all and, like Oedipus, destroy ourselves by our own hubris.

Reason and mind are splendid attainments of evolution and nobody would wish to downgrade them. No one would wish to return to obscurantism and obfuscation when clarity and light are possible. Yet mystery prevails in the universe. We can understand, but only so much. To pretend that we understand more is hubris. To accept our limits is right humility. To try to transcend these limits is to help evolution in the process of becoming. Finally to accept and acknowledge mystery is part of the process of understanding in a deeper sense.

Everything there is, is filtered by the mind, chiselled by the mind, sculptured by the mind. When the universe wanted the human to co-create with it, it invented the mind. And why would the universe do such a thing? Because we are part of the universe evolving itself. To contemplate itself, to see itself, the universe had to develop the eye and the mind; and then the human eye and the human mind. We are the eyes through which the universe contemplates itself. We are the mind through which the universe thinks about its future and its destiny. This is not a form of rampant anthropocentrism, but just the contrary: submitting the human to the overwhelming flow of cosmic evolution. We are not anthropocentrizing the cosmos. *We are cosmologizing the human.* Indeed, the cosmological and the anthropocentric are two aspects of each other. How could it be otherwise?

We increasingly perceive everything as evolving: the continents (geological evolution); the species (biological evolution); the mind and its knowledge (epistemological evolution); finally, our images and the very being of God (theological evolution).

Evolution is a wonderful and divine agency. Whether it itself is God may be too difficult a question for us to determine. But it certainly is divine. As it proceeds, it brings more light, coherence and order to the original chaotic cosmos.

Evolution means also a continuous evolution of science. Science unfolds all the time and sometimes brings such new light that it blinds our eyes and dazzles the human imagination. What happened during the first one-billionth of a second? Why did the Big Bang occur? What is the nature of those forces that created galaxies and then the human imagination? And finally the question we have contemplated so often: what is the nature of this strange, wonderful world around us? Though the question may seem an ancient one, it is now a new question, *our* question. For we ask it in the context of our consciousness, our existential traumas, our discoveries and insight.

If evolution is all-devouring and all-transforming, then *nothing* is out of reach of its wonderfully transformative flow. If all human knowledge is evolutionary (and none is absolute, fixed and unalterable), then our knowledge of theology, of heaven, of God is *also* subject to evolution. If so, then not only our images of God, but the very nature of God is evolving.

Thus, God is an evolutionary being. We cannot return to our old anchors and dogmas. We cannot cling to old images of religion and God. We now live in a new world. Thus, we must not cringe and sheepishly insist that God who is a perfect being cannot be conceived as evolving. He can! If God is perfect, we cannot deny to Him any attribute we think worthwhile. *An evolving God is more perfect than a static one*. To understand this, we need to broaden our thinking and truly embrace the evolutionary perspective. We must start thinking evolutionarily, open our minds to the wonderful flow of evolution. What will help us in acquiring this mode of evolutionary thinking is a new concept of the universe and a new concept of the mind, Participatory Mind.

With the Participatory Mind in the background, we can see

that we have unhinged ourselves from all past dogmas: cosmological, religious, scientific – and we are floating. The older dogmas were our anchors *and* our chains. We were very much tied to the ground and we were used to crawling. The floating universe is not for crawling but for flying. The expanding, all-open universe is not for obedience but for freedom.

Thus in this participatory universe we are creative and free. Our essential freedom and creativity are not little gifts added to our humdrum existence but the very prerequisites of our existence in the new evolutionary participatory world. We are doomed to freedom. We are doomed to creativity. But not in the old sense of existentialist philosophy, where our freedom meant a choice of absurdity because we had to live our absurd lives in our absurd universe. We are doomed to freedom in the participatory world, pervaded with divinity – if we are to escape the absurdity of self-destruction, or slow death by being tortured by our absurd mind or our trivializing technology.

Let me now come to a main point: it is because of the limitation that is inherent in the mechanistic cosmology, and in scientific rationality, that we cannot successfully cope with many problems in society and in the environment. We have tried all the rational strategies available to us. It has not worked. The piecemeal, atomistic, analytical approach, which so often goes in conjunction with the 'technological fix', does not work in relation to complex wholes such as the human being, society, the ecological habitat. What is needed is a new conceptual framework, a new cosmology from which a broadened and more enlightened rationality would follow.

Numerous books have been written on the subject of the inadequacy of the scientific-technological world-view derived from Newtonian mechanics. So I shall not belabour the point.

What should not escape our notice is the fact that we cannot be rational people and at the same time so hopelessly unable to manage our lives and our environment.

True and comprehensive rationality must help us to live, must connect life with knowledge, knowledge with wisdom, must illumine the paths of our individual destiny and connect us with the cosmos in a meaningful way. As it was in great spiritual traditions of the past, so it will be in the future: a deeper understanding of the mind and of human reason must bring about a deeper understanding of the self and of the cosmos at large. To this end the Participatory Theory of Mind is presented.

2. From the minds of amoebas to the mind of Einstein

We should aim at such a theory of mind as is able to explain the mind of the amoeba and the mind of the Buddha; and in between the minds of Einstein, Copernicus and Newton; as well as the mind of the Australian aborigines and the mind of the Masai of Kenya. How are these forms of mind related? They are related by the phenomenon of life.

The architecture of life is the architecture of mind. Understanding of various forms of life is ultimately understanding of various forms of mind. Thus we need to construct a theory of mind that is both comprehensive and at the same time discerning, so that it includes all forms of mind and enables us to differentiate among them.

When we talk about the mind of Einstein (because of our present cultural conditioning) we so often think about his mathematical genius – his abstract mind that could conceive the theory of relativity. But this is not the whole of Einstein's mind: it is only a slice of it. For Einstein's mind was also the mind of a mystic:

The most beautiful thing we can experience is the mysterious. It is the source of all true art and science. He to whom this emotion is a stranger, who can no longer pause to wonder and stand wrapped in awe, is as good as dead: his eyes are closed.

What is impenetrable to us really exists, manifesting itself as the highest wisdom and the most radiant beauty which our dull faculties can comprehend only in their most primitive forms.

Let us draw the first conclusion: it is bad logic to limit the total mind to its abstract computational aspect. That there is such a tendency in our culture, there can be no doubt. That this tendency is unjustified, there can be no doubt either.

For consider the minds of Socrates, Plato and Aristotle; and of the Buddha and Jesus. If mind is limited to that aspect of our intellectual activity which results in hard science, then these illustrious men would have to be considered mindless, which is absurd.

Consider the Masai, who are still happily roaming Kenya. They are said to be one of the most 'primitive' tribes that inhabit the planet. They cut statuesque and splendid figures when you see them in their native land – when they suddenly surround you on an empty desert road, coming as it were from nowhere. They look like characters from a movie. But they are real and can pierce your chest with their spears if you take their photograph without their permission, and then refuse to pay for the privilege. The Masai could not follow our computerized wonders, nor even grasp the meaning of physical laws mathematically expressed. Are they mindless savages?

Until the beginning of the twentieth century, Kenya was full of lions. It was a tradition among the Masai that after reaching the age of manhood, the age of fourteen, the young man, after an appropriate ceremony, would be sent into the night to hunt a lion, with his knife and spear only. To hunt a lion is not a joke. It takes more than courage. It takes skill and dexterity and, indeed, a form of mind that is so quick, subtle and cunning that we Westerners can only gasp in admiration.

Consider also the Australian aborigines who can find food and water in the most inhospitable deserts. In such severe environmental conditions Western man would be lost and wasted in no time. Do these aborigines find the clues and signs that lead them to food and water because of their mindlessness? Or might it be the case that they have very subtle and sensitive minds although organized in a different manner from Western man's?

The second conclusion that we should draw is this: we must find an idiom, a coherent way of explanation whereby the mind of the Masai and the mind of the Australian aborigines, and the mind of Einstein-the-mystic can be fully acknowledged as minds in the proper sense. Let me start to outline the Participatory Mind by distinguishing Mind I and Mind II. Mind I may be designated as that abstract coconut which revels in computation, abstraction and scientific calculation. This mind roughly corresponds to the neo-cortex. Let us pause for a while and take in that our brain is not one homogeneous entity. There are at least two brains built on top of each other. There is the 'old', reptilian brain; and there is the 'new' brain, known as the neo-cortex. Since we have no difficulty in recognizing two brains within each of our heads, we should have none in recognizing two or three minds interlocked with each other within our splendid skulls. Actually, the minds that we possess are not limited to our skulls only; they are distributed throughout our entire wondrous bodies.

Mind II is an altogether different entity. It corresponds roughly to the 'old' brain, but only roughly. We can define Mind II as *the sum-total of all the sensitivities that evolution has developed in us.* By sensitivities we mean all the capacities through which we live our lives, thus sensing, seeing, intuition, instinct; the capacity to make love, to make poetry, to dance, to sing, to contemplate stars; as well as the capacity for moral judgment, the aesthetic sense, the sense of empathy – the whole orchestra of different powers through which life is expressed, apprehended, and sculpted into recognizable shapes.

Life always takes distinctive shapes and forms. These forms are moulded not by the cold intellect but by the variety of sensitivities – which are the sculptors, the transformers, the transmogrifiers of reality; the incredibly accurate registers of the changing seasons of nature and of the changing moods of human beings, of grief and sadness, of joy and ecstasy; the silent witnesses which can hear the stars singing as well as the cries of human hearts. Sensitivities are the artists which receive and transform, which nourish us aesthetically and inform us intellectually; they are the countless windows through which we commune with reality. This is what Mind II is comprised of.

Mind I and Mind II are not separated from each other; they are parts of each other. Mind I is situated within Mind II, and completely surrounded by it. Mind I can be considered as a form of crystallization of Mind II – just as the neo-cortex is an extension and a specific refinement of the 'old' brain.

It is sometimes contended that pure logical reasoning and intuitive thinking exclude each other. This contention is wrong. Even while proving new mathematical theorems, their creators constantly rely on their intuitions, and so often have the intuitive feeling of the proof first before they can envisage the discursive one. On the other hand, our intuitive hunches do not exclude logical reasoning but constantly rely on it as we test and check (often with great speed and subconsciously) the veracity of our intuitions by reasoning: if that is true, then this and this should follow, if it does not, let us try another hunch.

Thus the two minds constantly dialogue with each other, inform each other, even if at times they are at odds with each other; as happens in every family. The two minds are of a family. If only we have enough patience to watch them in action, we shall be astonished to see what a supportive team they make together.

3. Sensitivities – consciousness – mind

Let us focus our attention on the meaning of 'sensitivities' in a specific historical setting – evolution itself. Sensitivities are part of the legacy of evolution, an essential portion of evolution's endowment. As far as the evolutionary process is concerned, sensitivities are precisely those articulators through which evolution acquires new shapes and characteristics. Whenever the evolutionary process increases its scope and powers, it does so by generating new sensitivities. The meaning of sensitivities is intimately connected with the meaning of evolution.

Pierre Teilhard de Chardin (1881–1955) maintains that evolution – as an ongoing process – can be best understood when we realize that it is the process of the augmentation of consciousness.[1] This is an important insight, although it is expressed in a vague way. After the insight is absorbed, we want to know how the growing consciousness is being augmented and expressed. How can it be expressed if not through the human powers we possess? It is thus expressed and articulated precisely by the acquisition of new sensitivities. *Sensitivities are articulators of the growing consciousness.*

The participatory theory of mind accepts many basic insights of Teilhard and Bergson, as well as evolutionary thinkers of our time such as Theodosius Dobzhansky and Gregory Bateson, and builds on these insights.

Our ideas of evolution have been indeed evolving. Darwin took a step, but his theory is only a rough approximation of what is going on in evolution. Actually, Darwin should not be credited with the first step. That credit must go to Charles Lyell who, in his epochal work *Principles of Geology* (1830–33), first conceived the idea of evolution by showing that continents have been evolving. That was the application of the idea of evolution to geology.

Darwin went a step further and applied Lyell's idea to biology by showing that species have been evolving. In the twentieth century we have applied the idea of evolution further still by demonstrating that evolution is continuously creative and that spiritual and cultural forms of human life are part of the flowering of evolution: as evolution unfolds, matter is becoming spirit.

Teilhard de Chardin takes a lion's share of credit in the elucidation of this idea. But Teilhard builds on Bergson.[2] Henri Bergson was born in 1859, the year Darwin's *Origin of Species* was published. By the time Bergson achieved maturity, the Darwinian story of evolution was not only absorbed, but could be creatively transcended. This is what Bergson did in *Creative Evolution*. Bergson does not deny the idea of evolution. He only gives it wings and a creative potency. For Darwin and Neo-Darwinians, evolution is an almost dreary process of chance and necessity (see especially Jacques Monod, *Chance and Necessity*). For Bergson evolution is an exquisitely creative process. This was the first step in liberating evolution from the dreariness of the semi-deterministic and at the same time semi-incomprehensible framework; incomprehensible because it is impossible to explain the transition from lower to higher forms.

Teilhard took another step, showing creative evolution to be all-pervading and leading from matter to spirit. He considered evolution not only creative but also spiritual in character. He demonstrated that there is no inconsistency in considering evolution to be both scientific and spiritual in character, obeying the laws of science and the laws of the spirit. And for a good reason: if evolution embraces all, it lends itself both to scientific and to spiritual interpretations. Cosmogenesis is both a material (physical) and a spiritual process: matter is transformed into matter, but matter is also transformed into spirit.

As Bergson transcended Darwin, and as Teilhard transcended Bergson, so we may seek to transcend them both, for such is the law of evolution; evolution means continuous transcendence. The very least we can do is to fill various missing dimensions in Teilhard and Bergson.

Let us now return to the question of sensitivities. We said that the meaning of sensitivities is intimately connected with the meaning of evolution. That which holds for evolution at large also holds for the individual human life. Its depth and breadth are delineated by the range of sensitivities it contains and expresses. We are quivering bundles of a plethora of different sensitivities. We shall now examine how the evolutionary process has operated through the acquisition of new sensitivities. Then we shall show this process with regard to human beings.

When the first amoebas emerged from the primordial organic soup, they were victorious because they acquired a new sensitivity enabling them to react to the environment in a semi-conscious manner, which was the beginning of all learning. For learning is above all a capacity, a sensitivity, to react to environmental conditions. The glory of evolution starts when organisms begin to use their capacities, thus their sensitivities, in a conscious and deliberate manner to further their well-being.

From the organic soup via the amoeba to the fish; from the fish via reptiles to primates; from primates via the chimpanzee to man – this has been a continuous and enthralling story of the acquisition and refinement of ever-new sensitivities.

When matter started to sense and then evolved the eye (as the organ of its new sensitivity), this was an occasion of momentous importance, for reality could now be seen, could be articulated according to the power of the seeing eye. *No eye to see – no reality to be seen. It is the eye that brought to reality its visual aspect*. The existence of the eye and the existence of visual reality are aspects of each other. One cannot exist without the other. For what is the seeing eye that has nothing to see? And what is the visual reality that has never been seen?

The seeing of the eye is a form of sensitivity through which we articulate reality around us. Seeing is one of many sensitivities which are all products of the articulation of evolution. But they are not just passive repositories of the evolutionary process. Through them we slice, apprehend and articulate what we call reality. There is no more to reality (for us) than our sensitivities can render to us. Sensitivities are articulators of reality. The emergence of every new form of sensitivity is a new window on the world.

It is hard for us to conceive that there was a time in evolution when there was no eye. This does not seem right, for we are used to apprehending reality through our visual powers. Should we ever be able to convey our reality to creatures that have never developed the eye to see? The story of the evolution of the eye is pregnant with meaning and points to some truly amazing possibilities. We have not only evolved the eye to see, but also to apprehend reality aesthetically. For the eye is the receptacle of beauty. Furthermore, if vision through the eye was one of the possibilities latent in evolution, what about other forms of vision through some (hitherto) hidden inner eye? What if one day some new 'eye' is opened to allow us to apprehend some of the new aspects of reality which so far are beyond our comprehension? Are not some of the extrasensory powers possessed by some persons an indication that some 'new eye' is in the process of being opened?[3]

All sensitivities could be considered as forms of seeing. We have developed a great many of these forms. Is it reasonable to assume that evolution has exhausted the stock of its possibilities? Or is it more reasonable to suppose that other forms of seeing are in store for us and, if they become part of our natural capacities, we shall be able to reveal through them new aspects of reality? If this happens, then part of the magical will become part of the natural. Perhaps this is the way we should look at evolution – as transposing that which is in the realm of magic into the realm of the natural. Evolution is the unfolding of natural magic.

With new sensitivities we articulate the world in new ways; we elicit new aspects from the world. The power of sensitivities is the power of co-creation. No aspect of reality imposes itself on us with an irresistible force; we take it in and assimilate it only when we acquire a way of seizing and comprehending it; when we come to possess an appropriate sensitivity that is able to process it for us.

The power of creation is the power of articulation. This is the simplest expression of how evolution unfolds – by endlessly articulating. Such is the story within the human universe. By acquiring new sensitivities we acquire new powers of articulation, thus we acquire new powers of creation. Sensitivity, therefore, holds the key, not only to our understanding of evolution, but to the understanding of ourselves.

When the first amoebas started to articulate themselves from the original sea of the organic soup, this was at once a triumph of life ascending and a triumph (still muted at the time) of consciousness arising. For amoebas started to react to the environment in a deliberate and semi-conscious manner.

From this point on, the evolutionary tale is one of augmentation of consciousness and the continuous acquisition of new sensitivities through which organisms react to the environment in ever more knowing and purposeful ways. *As their sensitivities multiply, organisms elicit more and more from the environment. They draw upon reality in proportion to their ability to receive it and transform it.* At this point we can see that their reality was outlined by the nature and scope of their consciousness and their sensitivities.

There is, therefore, an intimate relationship between our total evolutionary endowment in terms of consciousness, and all the knowing powers we possess, and the nature of reality we construct, receive and recognize. We simply cannot find, see or envisage in reality more than our senses, our intellect, our sensitivities, our intuition (and whatever other evolutionary endowments we possess) allow us to find and see. The more sensitive and knowing we become, the richer and larger becomes our reality. When we say 'our', we do not mean in the sense of the idiosyncratic, subjective perception, but in terms of the capacity of the species. What is beyond the species and the mind of the species may be reality *in potentio* but not reality as we know it; our concept of reality is reality as we know it.

In receiving reality or any aspect of it, the mind always processes it. In processing it, the mind actively transforms reality. Let us reflect on the meaning of the two phrases 'processing reality' and 'transforming reality'. They are both fundamentally inadequate. For they suggest that there is such a thing as an autonomous reality 'out there' to which the mind applies itself and on which it works. Such a picture is fundamentally misconceived. There is no such thing as reality as it is, which the mind visits and on which it works. *Reality is always given together with the mind that comprehends it*. We have no idea whatsoever what reality could be like *as it is* because invariably when we think of it, when we behold it (in whatever manner), reality is presented to us as it has been transformed by our cognitive faculties.

The organism's interaction with reality is a dual process of being in it and articulating it: by grasping onto any aspect of reality the organism invariably articulates it. Reality is never given to the organism (human or otherwise) except in forms of interactions; that is, in the form of continuous articulations and transformations specific to a given organism. We never just receive reality. Even a mirror does not photograph reality: it only reflects some of its features according to its limitations and its specific capacities for reflection.

These are some of the main contentions of the theory of the participatory mind.

Mind is part of the real. It is a fragment of evolution unfolding itself. But rather a special fragment: once it has emerged, it acts as a refracting instrument. It 'bends' reality according to its peculiar laws, propensities and faculties. Mind is that particular part of reality which is both a part of reality and also apart from reality.

This double nature of mind makes it difficult to talk of mind as the stuff of reality. By saying that it is 'of reality' and 'within reality' we expect to find a slot whereby the mind can be shown as existing 'objectively' among other things. But mind is not this kind of thing. Any situating of it in reality is really situating reality within it. Hence the participatory mind is at the same time an interactive mind, a co-creative mind. Reality and mind constantly interact with each other. There is no other way of grasping reality but through the mind. As has just been stated, there is no reality given to us except together with the mind.

The rise and development of the mind is essentially the story of dim light reflecting upon itself and becoming brighter light. In its evolutionary development the mind has not only been continually transformed but continually transforming. The mind, as I have argued throughout, is not to be limited to its one layer embodied in our abstract logical capacities, but must be seen as the total capacity of the organism to react intelligently and purposefully.

Reality for the amoeba has been something less than for the fish, and still less than for the human being. It is not fanciful to talk about reality for an amoeba. After all, the multitude of living beings come from amoebas. The richness and multifariousness of the experience of reality is in proportion to the organism's capacity to receive and decipher it, to emphasize the point. The more primitive the capacities, or to put it in another way, the more primitive the mind, the more primitive the furniture and experience of reality. The more versatile and subtle the mind, the more versatile the reality, and the richer the experience of it. *The organism receives from reality as much as it puts into it.*

The wonder and mystery of the mind in evolution is its capacity to enlarge reality as it grows and transforms itself.

The vision and the seeing cannot be separated from the eye. What the eye is to the act of seeing, the mind is to the act of comprehending reality.

4. *A new concept of the human*

When the idea of sensitivities is systematically applied to the phenomenon of man, we arrive at a new concept of man. It is evident from many quarters that our time craves a new perspective on man. Older visions of man are a form of strait-jacket; they do not fit us any more, constrain rather than liberate. Indeed, a right concept of the human is one that captures our essential characteristics and at the same time provides a scope for freedom and a vehicle for further enlargement and liberation of man.

Aristotle defines man as *a rational animal*. This has been a very popular definition in the West. So popular has it been that we have come to deify reason and the rational faculties of the species. Rationality in this context has almost invariably been linked with intelligence. To score low on IQ tests has been deemed an indication of a low status on the ladder of humanity. Actually, Aristotle's definition has inadvertently led us to justify many forms of racial prejudice. We have reasoned (if only subconsciously) in the following way: we are superior because our intelligence is high; our high intelligence is an indication that we are more rational than other people. Since rationality is man's important attribute, the more rational we are, the more superior we are.

Strangely, we do not have a Compassion Aptitude Test. Yet a moment's reflection must make it clear that anyone who is completely void of compassion and empathy hardly deserves the name of 'human being'. There are hardened criminals who, with perfect command of their rational faculties, kill. Their rationality is intact. But their moral sense and their sense of compassion is missing; missing so badly that we feel bound to isolate them from other human beings, ipso facto screening them out of humanity altogether.

What these arguments show is not that rationality is unimportant in the make-up of man; but rather that we seem to have made too much of it. Cold reason often wreaks havoc with impunity because it knows that we have chosen to enshrine it as the most essential characteristic of the human species – for 'man is a rational being.' A lopsided definition of man leads to innumerable consequences, some of which – later – surprise us with their savage outcomes.

Each definition or conception of man is born out of specific circumstances. Aristotle's definition emerged at the time when reason crystallized as a distinctive faculty, of which the Greeks were immensely proud.

In the nineteenth century a new conception of man appeared. Man began to be defined as Homo Faber, or tool-making and tool-using animal. This conception emerged when the Industrial Revolution was in its full swing and we had become intoxicated by our immense capabilities for making tools and using them. But this conception of man was short-lived because it was so obviously inadequate. Small children up to the age of five cannot make tools and are often unable to use them; yet they are human. Chimpanzees can use many tools dexterously and even make some tools, yet they are not human.

Another characteristic of children as compared to chimpanzees is children's comprehension of language and ability to talk. This was perceived by many (Piaget, Chomsky, et al.) as the dividing line between chimpanzees and other animals and human beings. Thus a new conception of man was born: *man as a language animal.* But this definition is not very promising either. It does not enable us to enlarge ourselves. It does not invite us to reflect more deeply on the meaning of human destiny. No doubt the perception that man is a language animal was an important insight. But after we accept it, we want to ask: so what?

Altogether, twentieth-century Western philosophy has been deficient in generating new concepts of man which would help us to live. The most vocal and influential among philosophical schools have produced pitifully small visions of man.

The pseudo-scientific and half-baked philosophical venture known as 'behaviourism' has shamelessly attempted to reduce the human being to simplistic behavioural schemata, the kind of schemata that do not even do justice to the behaviour of pigeons. That we have tolerated this philosophical farce for a number of years as a 'new vision of man' is a wonder which must make us ask: how rational are we? That we still tolerate some of the lingering shadows of behaviourism in social science and in social interaction is another wonder which must make us reflect how gullible we are and how stupid in trying to explain very complex and subtle matters through very crude schemata.

Existentialism is another absurdity, a conception of man which is the fruit of a shrunken vision of the human being. We are the lonely monads doomed to existential anguish and cosmic despair, so existentialism tells us. The only meaning this monad can arrive at is to look aesthetically at the spectacle of its despair and enjoy it in a half-hedonistic, half-masochistic manner. We can commiserate with ourselves on being totally miserable; and in contemplating our misery we can elevate it to the aesthetic realm. If I am making a caricature of existentialism, let it be said that existentialism has made a caricature of the human being. No doubt existentialism has expressed aspects of the profound disquiet that descended upon the Western mind after World War Two. But to celebrate existentialism as a universal philosophy of man is profoundly to short-change ourselves.

Marxism is another prominent philosophy of man of the twentieth century. On the surface it is optimistic to the point of euphoria, on the surface it offers us wonderful perspectives for the future of man. Yet when we scratch the surface we find that its aspirations are not at all far-reaching and its perspectives shallow. In the best of all possible scenarios, we march towards Communism and when we reach it, we have arrived at Utopia. What kind of utopia? Alas, a consumerist utopia. The Marxist vision is predominantly a materialist one, without any sense of transcendence at a deeper level and without spiritual dimensions. We all know that hunger is a terrible affliction, a calamity that is an insult to the dignity of each of us. Filling the stomachs of the poor is very important. But after the stomachs are filled, and perhaps only then, there is a life to be lived, beauty to be experienced, meaning to be fused into relationships with others, the starry heavens to be contemplated.

It should be emphasized that our time needs a philosophy of hope. Neither behaviourism nor Marxism nor existentialism is such a philosophy. The phenomenon of man is made of many subtle fibres. One of them is hope. Hope is part of our ontological structure. Hope is a mode of our very being. To be alive is to live in the state of hope. Hope is a precondition of our mental health. Hope is the scaffolding of our existence.

Hope is a reassertion of our belief in the meaning of human life; and in the sense of the universe. Hope is the precondition of all meaning, of all strivings, of all actions. To embrace hope is a form of wisdom; to abandon it is a form of foolishness.

The logic of hope is the logic of affirmation. The logic of hope is the logic of solidarity. The logic of hope is the logic of responsibility. All these attributes: affirmation, solidarity, responsibility, compassion, courage, are the very stuff of which life is made; that is, life which is alive, life which leads to peace, harmony and wholeness.

Let us now outline the participatory concept of the human. The rudiments of this concept were provided in the last section in discussion of the nature of sensitivities. Man should be conceived as par excellence a self-sensitizing animal, for he is literally made of the vibrant fields of sensitivities through which he maintains his relationships with the world and by which he is uniquely defined as a multifarious being. As already pointed out: man has been defined as a rational being; as a political being; as Homo Faber. Yet what is most important about man is that he is a self-sensitizing, that is, self-transcending and self-perfecting being. New sensitivities are new windows which enlarge the horizons of our world; they are also the vehicles by which we carry on the evolutionary journey, and through which we make ourselves into more human and more spiritual beings.

Through sensitivities evolution is articulated. Through sensitivities the mind of the human being is created. Through sensitivities the scope of our humanity is delineated. Through sensitivities matter is transformed into spirit.

An objection could be raised at this point. If evolution evolves through the continuous process of articulation, then we should cherish the most advanced fruit of this articulation, such as rational thinking and explicit discursive knowledge. In comparison with instinct and intuitive hunches, explicit discursive knowledge expressed through intersubjective language is much superior. And if such is the case, the objection continues, we should not attempt to reduce explicit thinking and rationality to this vague business of 'sensitivities', for this is a step backward in our evolutionary journey.

We shall acknowledge the importance of the objection yet point out, at the same time, that we are not confusing clear thinking and explicit knowledge with this 'vague business of sensitivities'. For *thinking is a form of sensitivity*. It is a form of seeing with an immediate recall of past experiences as stored in our evolutionary layers. Paradoxically, thinking is not the kind of faculty we often think it is. It was not inserted into us, at a certain stage of our evolution, as a gift from somebody who said: 'Now cerebrate.' Thinking nearly always occurs within a larger framework of our experience, and of the experience of the species, and this experience makes thinking much more than mere cerebration. *Thinking is one of the many threads with which the tapestry of our sensitivities is woven*, it is only one aspect of our evolutionary endowment.

In our evolutionary journey, elementary perceptions (of the amoeba sensing its physical environment) give way to illuminations – when human beings created art and religion. Philosophy, art and religion – as well as knowledge, including science – are different forms of seeing.

Let us emphasize that intuition is a form of sensitivity; the moral sense is a form of sensitivity; the aesthetic sense is a form of sensitivity; the capacity for formal deductive thinking is a form of sensitivity. Now this last capacity appears rather late in human evolution, and some cultures are ill at ease with it still. The capacity to see logical implications and formal logical structures is a wonderful capacity indeed. However, it is much more prevalent in Western culture than in other cultures. This sensitivity is thus culture-specific. It is valued much more in the West than in other cultures. Let us be quite clear about that.

All thinking is light that we shed on the objects of our understanding. This light, when it illumines life, becomes reverence for life. Reverence for life is a form of human sensitivity towards it, and at the same time is a form of thinking about it. Thinking so conceived can be seen throughout all traditional cultures. Plato's fusion of truth, goodness and beauty is a manifestation of it.

In the making of symbols we have found another way of augmenting ourselves. For symbols have facilitated a new and important step in our evolutionary articulation. By developing symbolic codes we have brought art, religion and philosophy to fruition. In the process we have articulated ourselves as social, cultural and spiritual beings.

To define the human being as a sensitive animal, as one who forms himself through the acquisition and enlargement of his sensitivities, is to pay homage to the openness of man's future and also pay homage to the attainment of evolution. Only this concept of man is right, which makes sense of man's future while making sense of his past.

The participatory concept of man does not quarrel with earlier concepts of man which, in a limited way, expressed some essential features of man's nature. The participatory concept is all-inclusive and maintains that man is a rational animal, Homo Faber, and Homo Ludens, and Homo Religiosus, and Homo Aestheticus. These attributes are all combined and orchestrated in one dynamic structure which is *the structure of our sensitivities*.

The comprehensiveness of the conception of man understood as fields of sensitivities lies in the fact that it enables us to characterize all forms of beings through their respective sensitivities. Sensitivities underlie the life of amoebas and the life of human beings. But they are different sensitivities. Therefore they outline different forms of life. In so far as we respond to the environment in primordial amoeba-like fashion, we are amoebas.

The participatory concept of man sheds a new light on the phenomenon of Einstein. And not only Einstein-the-physicist, but also Einstein-the-mystic. Playing the fiddle and wearing two socks of different colours (out of sheer absent-mindedness) does not make Einstein less rational as a scientist but more exquisite as a human being. In the phenomenon of Einstein we witness human life in its completeness: sensitivities flowering abundantly; a mathematical genius and a vulnerable, endearing, slightly crazy little man with his fiddle. We salute him for he did not sacrifice one aspect of his life for the sake of another.

Karl Popper maintains that the difference between an amoeba and an Einstein lies in their different capacities of problem solving. This may be so. But his is a trivial way of characterizing the difference between the two. Given its equipment, its form of 'mind', the amoeba solves its problems with a dexterity bordering on genius. What really distinguishes the two is the range, power and expression of their sensitivities.

Arthur Koestler has insisted that evolution has made a mistake by developing our intellectual capacities so much and our moral sense so little. He thought that this would be the cause of our doom. He was in despair over this 'slip' of evolution. We need not be in despair. For it is very likely that the next stage of our evolutionary unfolding will consist precisely in developing this range of sensitivities which will bring about the acquisition of a deeper moral sense, deeper compassion, a deeper understanding of all there is, including human beings.

Above all, the participatory concept of man unifies man with the cosmos, as well as the human world with all forms of life. They are all bundles of quivering sensitivities; and so are we. The participatory concept of man paves the way to holistic understanding of all that exists. It inspires us to celebrate our uniqueness without giving us a licence to arrogance or superiority. Men can be arrogant creatures, but so can lions. However, among all creatures it is we, human beings, that can understand fully and completely the meaning of compassion and can act on it; can take the responsibility for all; can defend the rights of species different from our own. Compassion and responsibility for all life are forms of sensitivities acquired late in our evolutionary saga. Their possession makes us proud to be human. The use of these sensitivities lies at the heart of the evolutionary process.

The participatory concept of man objects strongly to the idea promoted by some trends of ecological thought that we are the cancer among species. We are not perfect. No species is. Not even evolution itself. But we are aware of our imperfections. Awareness is the first step to improvement. We can develop and perfect ourselves. This is now our imperative. Other species are innocent – but stuck in their niches and their unawareness. The eternal dilemma as outlined by John Stuart Mill is: What is better – to be an unhappy Socrates or a happy cabbage?

5. A model of mind as reality: Noetic Monism

In the previous section consequences from the idea of sensitivities for the understanding of man were drawn. In this section we shall draw the *ontological* consequences entailed in the concept of sensitivities. In the process we shall arrive at a new concept of reality, which I call Noetic Monism. While exploring Noetic Monism we shall complete the outline of the participatory mind begun in section 3. The overall point to bear in mind is this: our in-depth understanding of sensitivities not only affects our concept of man but also radically reshapes our basic notion of reality. First, a brief look at various forms of monism in history.

In the history of philosophy we may distinguish at least four kinds of monism:

(1) Materialist Monism (Marx), the doctrine which claims that all is matter; or that whatever exists (in the *real* sense of existence) is a body;

(2) Idealist (or Spiritual) Monism (Plato), the doctrine which claims that what exist in the primary sense are forms (ideas, spirit);

(3) Mentalism (Bishop Berkeley), the doctrine which claims that what exist in the primary sense are our perceptions (*esse percipi*: it exists because it is perceived);

(4) Naturalist Monism (Spinoza), the doctrine which claims that God is nature, and that nature is God. This doctrine is sometimes called Pantheism.

Noetic Monism is a different kind of monism.[4] It claims that both bodies and ideas (spirit) exist. But their existence takes different forms. What unifies these different forms of existence is *the evolutionary matrix*, which explains both the unity of all existence – hence monism – and also the difference within the underlying unity. All forms of being come from the same evolutionary barrel. Yet they represent different stages of the transformation of evolution. *The different stages of the evolutionary becoming are responsible for different forms of existence.*

Noetic Monism is not a version of realism, as it does not support the view that in the outside world things are 'as they are' and our mind (and our knowledge) apprehend them independently of us. It rather maintains that things *become* what our consciousness makes out of them through the active participation of our mind. Anaxagoras called mind *nous*. Hence this kind of monism, which unifies all through the creative power of the mind, should be justly called Noetic Monism or New Advaita.

The quest for understanding the nature of reality is not limited to Western philosophy. Chinese and Indian philosophies present some great chapters in the history of this quest. Taoism is a form of monism. There is only one true Tao, one right way. But this way is beyond words. Poetic and mystic rather than discursive and rational, Taoism is in fact quite close to Noetic Monism. But one cannot say much about this closeness because Taoism eludes words. Among explicit doctrines, that of Advaita of Hindu philosophy and the Buddhist doctrine of Mind Only are worthy precursors of Noetic Monism. Each of them is a well elaborated metaphysical theory steeped in a noble tradition whose understanding requires the reconstruction of their historical context. For this reason we shall not go into details of these doctrines on this occasion. Instead we shall contrast Noetic Monism with the prevailing metaphysics of the West.

The history of Western metaphysics, by and large, has been the metaphysics of *being*. From Pythagoras via Plato and Aristotle, the mainstream of Western philosophical thinking about the cosmos was rooted in the idea of structure and of being – fixed and permanent, whether these were Plato's Forms or Democritus's atoms. This tradition of the metaphysics of being was powerfully reinforced by Christianity – that is, after Aristotle's metaphysics became the backbone of Christian metaphysics through the reconstruction accomplished by Thomas Aquinas.

When science came upon the stage it did not negate the metaphysics of being. On the contrary, it continued it in another idiom: for science is par excellence a metaphysics of being; that is to say, classical Newtonian science.

Now, we Western people, nourished and conditioned by the metaphysics of being, from Plato and Aristotle onwards, and above all, inculcated with the suppositions and assumptions of the metaphysics of science, are walking repositories of the tradition that tends to interpret the world in terms of structure and being. Thus our perception, thinking and language have been thoroughly biased toward the metaphysics of being.

We tend to think of *reality* as 'that object out there'. Hence, we have enormous difficulties in conceiving of reality differently; for instance, as a continuous flux. For this reason we have great difficulty in coming to terms with the findings of quantum physics. These findings, in a subtle but pervasive way, undermine some of the basic tenets of the metaphysics of being. For this reason, also, we have difficulties in accepting the far-reaching ontological conclusions that follow from the notion of the participatory mind. Our cognitive consciousness, moulded and determined by the metaphysics of science, is afraid that it would have to face too much of an upheaval if we unhinged ourselves from the firm anchor of the metaphysics of being.

But this is exactly what we have to do – if we are to take the notion of the participatory universe and the participatory mind seriously. To our aid comes the metaphysics of becoming which, in the Western world, runs parallel to the metaphysics of being. The metaphysics of becoming, although pushed to the margin for centuries, has never died out. It started with Heraclitus, for whom to understand the world is to understand the process of its change. Aristotle did not like Heraclitus. We can see the reason why.

The Heraclitean tradition of the metaphysics of becoming

was continued during the Middle Ages, mainly through the writings of various mystics, such as Meister Eckhart, of whom we know little, since their views were usually declared heretical and thus suppressed. In the nineteenth century this tradition was powerfully reintroduced by Hegel; and then in a different idiom by Karl Marx. What is at issue is not the difference between the respective systems of Hegel and Marx but the fact that the metaphysics of becoming was at the centre of their thinking.

In the twentieth century the metaphysics of becoming has been magnificently restated by Whitehead for whom PROCESS is the crucial ontological and epistemological category. Quite independently, Teilhard de Chardin outlined his metaphysics of becoming within which evolution, as the motor of cosmogenesis, takes the centre of the stage. This, then, is the context for our discussion of Noetic Monism.

The first point to be made is this. When we attempt to justify Noetic Monism rationally, this justification cannot be found within the cognitive structures controlled by the metaphysics of being. Instead, we align ourselves with a different metaphysics – the metaphysics of becoming – within which basic ontological and epistemological assumptions and presuppositions, including the very conception of 'reality', are differently conceived. We are led back to the story of sensitivities.

We are at the mercy of reality. But reality is, in a subtle way, at our own mercy; at the mercy of our minds. Whenever you make sense of reality, you make sense of it by filtering it through your mind. Let us note: 'reality' that you never make sense of is as good as non-existence. *Whenever there is a notion of reality there is a substratum of consciousness within which this reality is grounded.* No consciousness, no reality. To say it once more, within the participatory mind, reality is not given to us on a silver platter; simply, it is not given to us at all. Even if it were given to us, we should not know how to take it. If and when we begin to take it, we do not take it as it is, but invariably and inexorably through our human filters, by processing and transforming it.

At this point, if we are sufficiently cautious and prudent we should notice that such phrases as 'what reality is', or even the term 'reality' itself, are misnomers. Instead of talking about 'exploring reality' (because again, it suggests this thing 'out there'), we should be talking about reality-making. For each exploration is a transformation. Each journey into 'reality' is always a journey into our mind.

Reality-making is thus the new term for describing this process of interaction of the mind with the Participatory Universe as the result of which we obtain first this configuration of the cosmos, then that configuration of the cosmos, according to the powers and patterns of our articulation. In each of these configurations there is the signature of the artist who has co-created it. This artist is our co-creative Participatory Mind. No mind, no consciousness; and thus no reality to behold.

As we have said, reality for the amoeba has been something less than for the fish, and still less than for the human being, and it bears repeating. The organism receives from reality as much as it puts into it.

This point is of great significance. For it simply informs us that the process of eliciting is one of *co-creating*. We do not receive from out there that which we are unable to behold. *In beholding we are articulating. In articulating we are co-creating. In the act of articulation mind and reality merge; reality becomes an aspect of mind.*

We are now ready to complete the model of mind that we began in section 3, for we have introduced the third sphere of

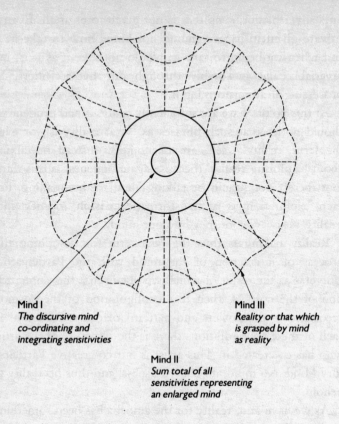

Mind I
The discursive mind co-ordinating and integrating sensitivities

Mind III
Reality or that which is grasped by mind as reality

Mind II
Sum total of all sensitivities representing an enlarged mind

Fig. 1 *The participatory model of the mind*

the mind, mind as coexisting with reality, or Mind III.

Mind I is mind in the narrow sense, the abstract mind. Mind II is the sum-total of all the sensitivities residing within the human species. Mind III is 'reality' – that is, the sum-total of the interactions of our sensitivities with the stuff outside, as delineated and articulated by Mind I and Mind II. Each of these minds is represented by a concentric sphere which is merging with the next. In Fig. 3 these spheres seem to be separated from each other; in fact they are aspects of each other.

Fig. 1 in fact shows the three spheres merging into each other; it is intended to convey the essential evolutionary unity of our cosmology. We are emphasizing here *evolutionary and cosmological unity* but not an ontological homogeneity. Mind I and Mind II are aspects of each other, but at the same time exhibit different stages and different modes of the articulation of evolution. Mind I has provided the material for the making of Mind III; while Mind II makes human sense of Mind I. Noetic Monism does not insist on the sameness of things as Materialist Monism, for instance, does. It insists only on the *noetic unity*, on the unity of comprehension, as based on sensitivities.

Our language, dominated by the precepts of empiricism, is recalcitrant when we wish to express the new cosmological unity, which clearly goes against its grain. I shall therefore call on poets. Thus William Blake:

> But to the eye of the man of Imagination
> Nature is Imagination itself.
> AS MAN IS, SO HE SEES.

The thirteenth-century Persian poet, Mahmud Shabistari, expresses similar insights:

> The world has become a man, and man a world.
> There is no clearer explanation than this.
> When you look well into the root of the matter,
> He is at once seen, seeing eye, and things seen.

And from another poem (*Gulistaneh Raz*):

> You who wander in the desert away from your own consciousness,
> Come back to yourself and find all expertise summed up.
> You are the way and the reality of perfection,
> One in whom the great consciousness of God dwells.

In this section I address the role of the mind in the universe of becoming. The becoming of the universe is inseparable from the becoming of the mind. This insight is in perfect harmony with the new ontological vistas unveiled to us by present particle physics, which has abandoned the rigid, deterministic Newtonian framework and come to recognize that – on the ultimate level of analysis – the observer and the observed merge inseparably.

Moreover, Noetic Monism is this form of ontology, which the New Physics and other holistic paradigms have been groping for but so far have been unable to articulate clearly. It is obvious that we are finished with old-fashioned (metaphysical) realism. It is also obvious that we cannot return to Bishop Berkeley or Plato through the act of simple negation: since realism does not hold, let us return to (metaphysical) idealism. Our problems are new and cannot be handled by old schemes. Noetic Monism offers itself as a new solution. Within Noetic Monism we do not negate the versatility and beauty of the cosmos, including the 'reality' of subatomic particles. Yet we maintain that this beauty and all the 'realities' indelibly bear the imprint of their co-creator – the mind.

No doubt some of the notions here proposed may feel uncomfortable at first. But the history of modern science has been par excellence a story of uncomfortable and indeed incredible notions that have become subsequently built into the floor of our understanding of 'reality'. Ours is the universe of becoming: the universe of emergent qualities, the universe of new forms of understanding, which, although they at first appear as conceptual shocks, after a time resolve themselves as new illuminating insights into the nature of things.

In every culture there is an intimate unity between the concept of reality, the concept of knowledge and the concept

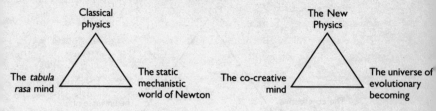

Fig. 2 *Classical physics and the New Physics: co-defining relationships*

of the mind. The three are bound together in a triangular co-defining relationship. This can be observed in Western culture of the past three centuries. If we contrast classical physics with present-day physics we can represent them by two triangles (see Fig. 2).

Within the empiricist tradition the mind is conceived as a *tabula rasa* – a clean sheet of paper on which experience does all the work. There is a congruence between the static (dead) universe that empiricism postulates and its concept of static, entirely passive mind. With the rediscovery of the universe of becoming, which the New Physics supports in a variety of ways, the role of the mind must of necessity be redefined.

We should be aware that in our day the two triangles coexist with each other (Fig. 3), but in a rather confused way, which is causing – through the discrepancies they generate – much conceptual stress and intellectual paranoia; we don't know whom to trust and who is the authority any more.

The participatory theory of mind seeks to transcend this paranoia as it encourages us to take possession of the new freedom in which, unanchored from the shores of determinism, we shall be floating through the new unfolding universe. And aided by new imagination, we shall be discovering new forms of understanding of which philosophers and scientists

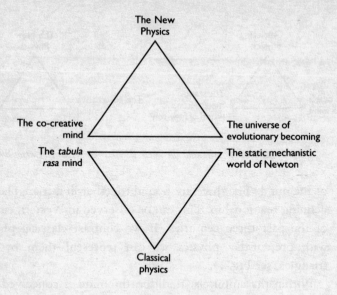

Fig. 3 *Present-day coexistence of two separate triangles
of co-defining relationships*

have never dreamt in their narrowly conceived rational ivory towers of academia.

The emergence of the mind is one of the lasting mysteries. To conceive of mind as a mystery is less mysterious and less mystifying than to take the mind to be a mere brain working according to physiological, mechanistic laws alone; for it is to admit that mystery is part of the natural order of things. Mind and imagination are bound together. The nature of imagination gives us a far better clue to the understanding of the mind than a hundred neurophysiological studies. The nature of imagination is wonderfully mysterious. And wonderfully mysterious is the quality of the universe that mind/ imagination render to us. The unfolding universe is at the mercy of our mind/imagination, for it is our mind/imagination.

Summary

There is no objective reality in the absolute sense, as there is no such thing as objectivity independent of our cognitive faculties. We do not photograph this (purportedly objective) reality in our scientific theories. What is out there is brought about by the alchemy of our mind – which is an inherent part of the real. The nature of our mind is the nature of our knowledge is the nature of our reality. (Try to be an amoeba and 'think' what your 'knowledge' and 'reality' would be like then.)

Different forms of knowledge, different epistemologies, different cosmologies are different ways of articulating the cosmos, different ways of processing and transforming of 'what is there'. What is there can never be separated from the way we obtain it. Extrasensory perception is one form of processing, mathematical equations of quantum physics are another. They are all united by the mind that participates in each of them. No mind, no articulation of knowledge – no quantum physics, no cosmology, no quarks. They are all creative products of the genius of the mind. The participatory mind is one of the chief actors on the stage of the participatory universe.

Through rapid advances in knowledge we have split the cosmos open and are now reassembling it *de novo*. Noetic Monism outlines the matrix of evolutionary unity. In this matrix the mind is not only the mapper but an inherent part of the matrix itself. We always map reality on the map made with the coordinates of the mind. The idiom is again incorrect: map-making and territory are one. As our capacity for map-making increases, our territory becomes larger and richer. *Process, becoming, evolutionary change, transformation* are the basic modes of our reality-making. For every act of reality-making is an act of change, part of the process of transformation. Structure and being are to be considered special cases of the process of becoming.

The mystery of the mind is the key to unlocking the mystery of the cosmos. But in deciphering the cosmos we only look deeper into the mystery of our mind.

CHAPTER 2

Mind in History

1. Empiricists and rationalists – their views of the mind

In Western philosophy theories of mind are as numerous as theories of reality; but with some singular exceptions mind and reality are separated from each other, and viewed independently of each other. Some pre-Socratic philosophers knew better than that. One of them, Parmenides, said: 'No mind, no world.' In these four words a whole magnificent insight is contained. In earlier centuries and millennia we had insufficient knowledge, and perhaps also insufficient courage, to translate this insight into a complete model of Mind/Reality.

Existential and social traumas have often been caused for Western man by the way in which we have split and atomized the world around us. Cartesian dualism, which radically separates the mind from the body and mind from nature, has been at the root of many of our misconceptions and quite a few of our dilemmas. In order to overcome this dualism we must create a unified theory within which mind and reality can be treated as aspects of each other. And that is what Noetic Monism does. Let us take a brief look at some of the theories of mind that have been most influential in the West and that still hold sway.

EMPIRICISM

Empiricism is both a theory of knowledge and a theory of mind. It holds that there is nothing in the intellect that there has not previously been in the senses. Mind is conceived here essentially as a *tabula rasa*, a white sheet on which experience writes its designs. The only active role of the mind is that it allows experience to write on it. Out of rudimentary experiences first impressions are formed. These impressions are transformed into forms of knowledge. How transformations of raw experience and of impression occur has never been satisfactorily explained by empiricism.

On a closer examination, we find that empiricism, as a theory of mind, is a gross caricature of what is going on in the human mind, and what we know about the marvels of human comprehension. One wonders why it has ever been taken so seriously and, indeed, propagated by intelligent people with zeal and commitment. The main reason for the acceptance of this clearly defective theory, in my opinion, has been *ideological*. The empiricist theory of the mind removes human knowledge from the authority of the church and particularly from the church's creeds and dogmas. Empiricism maintains that everything is acquired from the physical universe via the senses, thus instructs us that no authority of any sort needs to be obeyed. The only authority is that of our senses. This was clearly a masterstroke in the process of escaping from the authority of the church.

In the long run, the physical universe becomes the only reality, which we not only explore but also *worship*. All other gods are dethroned. Our senses become not only our authorities but also our deities. A theory of knowledge that sought to overcome the overbearing dogmatism of religious orthodoxies has itself become a sterile dogma: detrimental not only to any quest for knowledge that goes beyond the mere physical surface, but also to the deeper quest for human meaning.

Why is empiricism antithetical to our quest for meaning? Because it claims that there is nothing beyond the physical and beyond the senses. How can we build an edifice of human meaning on such foundations? It seems that the only 'reasonable' outcome is hedonism. And many indeed have accepted this. Yet in the long run hedonism howls empty; for it is not a doctrine of meaning but an *escape* from meaning. Human meaning must have a spiritual dimension. Empiricism is devoid of any spiritual dimension.

We can see at this point that our individual quest for meaning on the one hand, and our cosmological theories on the other hand, although they seem to be worlds apart, in fact are not. They inform each other, influence each other, and sometimes clash with each other.

In spite of its obvious defects, empiricism, which goes under many names nowadays, such as positivism, operationalism, methodology of science or simply scientific method, is still prevalent in our world. Moreover, it is perpetuated as the main underlying dogma in Western universities, which claim to be objective and value-free but support a view of the world in which the physical is elevated and the spiritual suppressed; in which the values of objectivity, rationality and efficiency are constantly upheld, whilst the values of compassion, empathy and altruism are ignored or suppressed. The overall climate created in Western universities is more conducive to moral relativism, cynicism and nihilism than to the search for meaning and the upholding of reverence for life. Such is the consequence of the dogma.

Hence, academia is in a continuous moral crisis, which it tries to ignore by saying: 'We are living in a period of the plurality of values.' In fact, we are living in a period of nihilism and cynicism. In this setting students, who naturally look for some moral guidance, get disoriented, confused, frustrated and often angry – without apparent reason. But the reason is there. In their deeper selves they are dissatisfied with nihilism, which eats at the core of their being.

RATIONALIST THEORIES OF MIND

Rationalist theories of mind predate empiricist ones. To a large degree, they have been eclipsed by empiricism; but not entirely so. It would be truer to say that they run parallel to empiricist theories. Rationalist theories do not consider mind as a *tabula rasa* but, on the contrary, attribute an active role to it. Many of them claim that mind is endowed with capacities and propensities that are inborn, therefore a priori. Among the rationalist theories of mind at least three should be mentioned: Plato's, Berkeley's and Kant's. Plato envisaged mind as active but only in so far as it recognizes ('remembers, recollects') Forms, those ideal, incorruptible, unchangeable blueprints to which all objects of our knowledge and all objects of existence must comply. Objects are what they are *because* ideal Forms, predating their existence, are embodied in them.

So stated, Plato's doctrine seems very dry and abstract. But actually it is much more than that. For Plato wove around it a marvellous conception of man, of human life as a passage from darkness to enlightenment. The human body, in the biological form, is bondage, which the soul must overcome. In overcoming it – its coarseness, limitations and distortions – the soul clears its vision and approaches the Form, which is often identified with Godhead. In this context, the rules of conduct that underlie human behaviour are exactly the ones that enable us to make the transition from darkness to enlightenment, from amorphousness to the beauty of the Form. Plato's theory of mind and reality is far from an abstract theoretical construct; it is a ladder to heaven. In ascending it we build the good life and pursue meaning worthy of human beings.

Berkeley's conception of mind is active in the extreme. Bishop Berkeley (1685–1753) maintained: '*esse percipi*': things exist only insofar as they are perceived. All existence is, in a sense, a figment of our imagination. Things are 'brought' into existence through acts of our perception, and exist only insofar as we perceive them. The consequence is subjective idealism: there is no reality independent of our perception. An ingenious and startling doctrine, particularly when defended by a scintillating mind, but making nonsense of all that we know; and also making nonsense of evolution itself, especially evolution as striving towards greater and greater complexity, attainment, perfection.

The third type of rationalist theory of mind, that provided by Immanuel Kant (1724–1804), comes closest to the participatory conception of mind, and yet is still far removed from it. Kant reversed the whole process envisaged by empiricists. Instead of objects impressing themselves on the mind, Kant claimed that it is the other way round – it is the mind, its specific structure and its specific categories, that is imposed on objects outside, which are shaped according to the categories of the mind. There is conformity between objects and the mind, but this comes about *as the mind imposes its order on things*. We perceive a certain order in the outside world. We structure things with a certain inevitability – because we cannot do otherwise. The structure of our mind continuously impresses itself on the order of reality. The order of reality is really the order of the mind.

Kant claimed that we cannot know the ultimate reality, *das Ding an sich*, 'the thing in itself'. We know only the appearances of things. For we structure (according to the categories of the mind) only the appearances of reality. *The whole conception of reality is opaque in Kant*, one big question mark. There is no room for evolution in the Kantian system. And this was a major reason for the collapse of Kantian philosophy. With the growth of science in the nineteenth century, with the discovery of non-Euclidian geometries and non-Newtonian physics and the acceptance of the idea that time is not absolute (as both Newton and Kant imagined), the 'unalterable' structure of the mind was undermined; according to some, invalidated.

Kant's major shortcoming was to envisage the mind's categories and mind's structure as fixed and absolute. But in postulating an active role for the mind, and in claiming that the world is shaped and determined by the categories of our knowledge, he achieved great and lasting influence.

It should be emphasized that Kant's heritage has been continued (though in a changed idiom) throughout the nineteenth and twentieth centuries. What Kant attributed to the mind – the shaping and determining of reality – various other thinkers subsequently attributed to language. First came Henri Poincaré with his ingenious conception of conventionalism. Then came Kazimierz Ajdukiewicz, Benjamin Lee Whorf and W. V. Quine, who radicalized Poincaré's conventionalism. More recently, Noam Chomsky has crusaded for the recognition of man as a language animal. Each of them has recognized *language as a co-definer of knowledge and of reality*. Each was close to seeing that reality and mind co-define each other.

From these theories of mind, both empiricist and rationalist, we wish to distinguish the evolutionary transcendental theory of mind, which we call the Participatory conception of mind. This participatory mind is much closer to rationalist theories than to empiricist ones. The hallmark of the participatory theory is that it recognizes mind not only as active, but as co-creative, as a shaper of all reality around us. Because the mind is so astonishingly woven into the whole fabric we call reality, any adequate theory of it must also be a rendering of reality itself. The participatory theory is ecumenical. It can accommodate most of the existing theories of mind. They are all partial renderings of the prowess and versatility of mind. Each has attempted to elucidate one particular aspect of mind, and each is a tribute to the mind reflecting upon itself.

The participatory theory of mind is a restatement of Parmenides' seminal insight 'No mind, no world.' One explanation of how it is that these Greek minds could conceive ideas of such depth and beauty is that they lent their minds to the daemon of imagination. And 'daemon' was not a bad word in the Greek vocabulary, but one sublime in tone and denoting extraordinary powers. Yet it has taken twenty-five centuries of reflection and articulation to understand some of these ideas in depth. In particular, we needed to invent and refine the theory of evolution in order to perceive the mind as one of the great evolutionary forces, which articulates evolution and at the same time articulates itself.

That there have been so many theories of mind in history is astonishing. That none of them has proved lastingly 'true' is not astonishing at all. Rather, it is a demonstration that mind's agenda is forever open, that insofar as mind is creative, unfolding and reflecting upon itself, it is bound to transcend whatever structure we impose on it, including that of the participatory mind.

2. The pigeon methodology vs the co-creative mind

Twentieth-century philosophy has mummified our understanding of the mind. Instead of exploring the creative and extraordinary aspects of mind, it has continually attempted to reduce mind to the scope of activities characteristic of pigeons. If you use pigeon methodology, you are bound to arrive at pigeon-like understanding. Let us try to trace the historical circumstances that led to the elevation of the pigeon method-ology as the tool of universal understanding. A termino-logical note: by 'twentieth-century philosophy' I mainly mean the empiricist-bound, analytically oriented philosophy of the Anglo-Saxon persuasion that dominates our present universi-ties and has exerted a considerable influence on our thinking all over the globe in the second part of the twentieth century.

There is a great tension within the framework of twentieth-century scientific understanding. On the one hand there is a tendency to impose the ethos of science, its language and formulations, on all the phenomena of life. This ethos is pursued by some with such an exemplary zeal that human behaviour is reduced to conditioning-response schemata, which are hardly adequate for the study of even the more intricate problems of pigeons. On the other hand there is an opposite tendency: at its cutting edge, physics has been system-atically deserting the positions of Newtonian science for the last eighty years. The general public is more victim of the dogmatic image of past science than beneficiary of the new exciting vistas of physics at the cutting edge.

Now, there were already some serious problems with the scientific understanding of the world in the second half of the nineteenth century. With the discovery of non-Euclidean geometries, space in the Newtonian sense started to totter. Since the absoluteness of space is one of the basic assumptions of the Newtonian system, to learn that space in the universe does not have to conform to Euclidean geometry was impli-citly to admit that the foundations of Newtonian physics were cracking; or at least made uncertain. As a result of absorbing the shock of the realization that many different geometries are possible within which we can describe the physical cosmos, conventionalism was born – an ingenious doctrine developed in the first decade of the twentieth century by Henri Poincaré and Pierre Duhem, who claimed that a system of knowledge does not necessarily describe reality faithfully, in a one-to-one way, but rather that it much depends on the system of axioms accepted at the outset of its development. We have much liberty as to which system of axioms to choose, for instance, in developing geometry. This was an ingenious way of resolving the problem of non-Euclidean geometries.

Conventionalism solved one problem, but it opened up a Pandora's box of many other problems. In particular, it profoundly undermined the very notion of truth as expressed through science; that is to say, it undermined the classical or correspondence notion of truth according to which truth consists of a correspondence between reality R and our description of it D, so that we can claim that science aims at descriptions of reality which are true. Once we admit that the choice of basic concepts and of the conceptual framework is up to us, we so to speak slightly unhinge the classical notion of truth. I say 'slightly unhinge' because at the time when conventionalism was developed it appeared that the classical edifice of knowledge, as presented by science, could be saved by artful modifications of the framework.

The problem of truth is central to science and all learning. We feel that we must have some notion of truth, otherwise how can we assess the validity of our cognitive claims, particularly in science? To put it more emphatically: since conventionalism emerged over a century ago we have not come to terms – faithfully, adequately, unequivocally – with the notion of truth, and with the notion of reality that science purportedly describes. I discount the enormous logical literature on the subject of truth, including Tarski's epoch-making formulation of the classical notion of truth (1933),[1] for all these works are only elegant formulations and reformulations, showing the prowess and the subtlety of our logical apparatus, but not new theories of truth or of reality.

As stated above, big problems began to emerge in science in the nineteenth century. When radioactivity was discovered, the phenomenon was clearly beyond the framework of Newtonian physics. To deal with radioactivity, and a host of other problems, new theories were invented: Einstein's theory of relativity, Bohr's quantum theory, Heisenberg's principle of uncertainty. While those specific extensions of physics were welcomed, we have still not fully realized, let alone absorbed and digested, their consequences as they pertain to our theories of knowledge and of mind.

In putting the proposition that philosophy has not absorbed in depth the new ideas and discoveries of science, we must not forget Karl Popper, who indeed was so struck with the fact that even the most entrenched scientific theories (such as Newton's) finally fall and are falsified that he decided to build a new epistemology on the grounds of this fact. Popper's distinctive philosophy of science takes its cue from Einstein (as the overthrower of Newton) and claims that all knowledge is tentative. But at the same time it attempts to salvage and justify the superiority of scientific knowledge over all other forms of knowledge. Although Popper's epistemology admirably meets the challenge of Einstein,[2] it is ill at ease with regard to quantum theory. Popper's specific work in quantum theory is an attempt to salvage the correspondence theory of truth *per fas et nefas*. The quantum theory represents a wonderfully fluid universe which has been called 'the eternal dance of Shiva.' A most startling aspect of this fluid universe is that observer and observed are so intimately connected that they are inseparable from each other. *Thus the very notion of objectivity is undermined.* When objectivity is undermined, the correspondence theory of truth is undermined. We are then in an altogether new cognitive situation; and we have not yet quite comprehended this situation. In short, Popper's philosophy attempted to meet only Einstein's challenge to Newton. It did not attempt to make sense of the most recent stages of particle physics.

Since the rise of conventionalism, then, we have lost our grasp of the classical notion of truth and also of the notion of reality which science purportedly describes, that is, in the classical sense of the term 'describes'. Even the best of twentieth-century thinkers, men such as Popper, have been unable to resolve the dilemmas that twentieth-century knowledge has posed to our comprehension.[3]

When Newtonian physics could no longer be seen as expressing the unshakable Laws of Nature, many ad hoc theories in science and philosophy sprang up. With Ernst Mach we observe the shift from the correspondence theory of truth to the coherence theory of truth. Since science could not claim to be the guardian of truth, understood as a faithful description of reality out there, scientists and philosophers decided that perhaps we should consider statements and theories as true insofar as they are coherent with the rest of accepted knowledge. However, within the coherence theory of truth we have difficulties in distinguishing fact from fiction, particularly when fiction is coherent (*Alice in Wonderland*).

We are living in an exciting era when science marches from one triumph to another. Yet concealed underneath lie much uncertainty and confusion which even the best minds cannot dispel or come to grips with. To cover up the obvious conceptual shortcomings of our theories, we invent all kinds of ad hoc theories and 'isms'. Some of these 'isms' are no more than hypotheses to save previous conceptions, that is to say, to perpetuate the impression that all is well in the kingdom of science and that science is coping well.

Of the many attempts to make sense of post-Newtonian physics, perhaps the most radical, at least in its conceptual implications, was that of Percy Bridgman,[4] who conceived the doctrine of operationalism. Operationalism was a thorough-going attempt to avoid any metaphysics, and indeed to avoid the troublesome concept of 'reality'. According to Bridgman, physical concepts do not need to have their ontological equivalents in the reality outside physics. The meaning of a concept, Bridgman insisted, is the set of operations we perform with it. 'Meaning is to be sought in operations,' wrote Bridgman in 1934. Then the definitions become increasingly diluted. In 1938 a more liberal definition was provided: 'Operations are a "necessary" but not a "sufficient" condition for the determination of meanings.' This formulation was weakened still further in 1952: 'The operational aspect is not by any means the only aspect of meaning.' A careful reading of the definition of 1934 (the heyday of logical positivism) and the definition of 1952 reveals a complete retreat. It is obvious that Bridgman has given up the idea that meanings are to be sought in operations.

Bridgman's problem is of course well known. I only re-hearse it here in order to make it completely clear that it was a pervading crisis in the foundations of Western knowledge that brought about those pseudo-solutions like operationalism and the empiricist criterion of meaning. These semantic strate-gies were taken at face value and gave rise to a host of new theories, including theories of mind. *The Concept of Mind* by Gilbert Ryle (1949) is a crowning achievement of the whole epoch *bent on attempting to find salvation through semantics*. We shall return to Ryle shortly.

Also putting in an appearance in the early decades of the twentieth century was behaviourism: first in its crude formulation by J. B. Watson,[5] then in its more 'sophisticated' version by B. F. Skinner.[6] Behaviourism was actually a doctrine quite apart from operationalism and logical empiricism (on the latter see the next section). But it had the same purpose: to eliminate everything complex, subtle and human and reduce it to the stuff of pigeons. This is by no means an exaggeration, for the methodology generated by behaviourism was one whose purpose it was to study pigeons. And yet, in all seriousness, it was extended to the study of human beings. The heyday of behaviourism and its methodology is now over. It now appears bizarre that we could have taken such a crude doctrine so seriously. Yet it was taken seriously.

Behaviourism, operationalism, logical empiricism and other forms of positivism were all developed within a larger philosophical framework of the time, which was ontological materialism; often coupled with atheism. The purpose of nearly all the new 'isms' (which somehow signified the Brave New World) was the same: to reduce all layers and aspects of human existence to those of inanimate matter.

To put it all in more human language: a conspiracy has been created against *human beings* – to crucify us on the procrustean bed of one-dimensional philosophies which reduce us in stature, deny us larger horizons, and suffocate our souls. That those philosophies turn us off intellectually and excite our minds not at all is one thing. However, these philosophies have become institutionalized. They are predominant orthodoxies in our schools and academia. When a learned professor tells us that whatever cannot be counted does not count; when our chemistry instructors tell us that all the mystery of life is contained in chemical interactions, this first creates a climate of opinion, and after a while a social reality of a certain kind. We are coerced to follow the 'authorities'. We are each vulnerable to the manipulations of culture, and each culture has a tendency, indeed an urge, to compel and hypnotize us.

Yet there is a limit to the powers of manipulation and the triumphs of one-dimensional philosophies. Euphoria with the Brave New World of science peaked in the 1960s. Since that time we have been on the other side of the wave, so to speak. I see a crucial turning-point with the publication of B. F. Skinner's *Beyond Freedom and Dignity* in 1971. Skinner was a brave man, but not necessarily a wise one. He had the courage of his convictions. If we are just like pigeons and rats; if what matters are our conditioned responses; if intentions, intuition, emotions, love do not matter, *then*, Skinner reasoned, let us take the final bold step: freedom is an illusion, and dignity is an illusion. We don't need them in our brave new world.

Yet they are not illusions; and we do need them. This Skinner discovered very soon after the publication of his book. His thesis was mercilessly crushed from all sides. This was a response to the excesses of 'rational' manipulations – in the name of freedom and dignity. Skinner was so tormented by the negative reviews of his book that he refused to read them. Obviously, he was a man of deep emotions; his emotions were hurt; his offended dignity could surely be taken as a personal refutation of his own thesis.

Ryle's *The Concept of Mind* (1949) is a magnificent book. Yet brilliant as his achievement is, it is but an offering on the altar of the reductionist ethos. Ryle is admirably lucid about his intentions.

This book offers what may with reservations be described as a theory of mind. But it does not give new information about minds.

We possess already a wealth of information about minds, information which is neither derived from, nor upset by, the arguments of philosophers. The philosophical arguments which constitute this book are intended not to increase what we know about minds, but to rectify the logical geography of the knowledge which we already possess.[7]

The rectification of the logical geography of our knowledge about minds becomes a very laboured process, and it finally leads to Ryle's theory of logical types (of mind's activities). The semantic footwork is inventive and brilliant. But the whole venture is simply reductionistic: the idea is not to understand MIND as it is, and as it works, but to reduce it to its observable by-products. Ryle's is a materialist theory of mind. It is also a behaviourist and operationalist theory, as it tries to avoid the problem of mind by studying its outwardly observable behaviour. Thus in Ryle we see a synthesis of materialism, operationalism, logical empiricism and behaviourism. The result is virtuosity in applying the pigeon methodology, which fundamentally obscures a real understanding of the mind.

Ryle marks a pivotal point of the materialist-reductionist-operationalist tradition. His work set the tone for the next decades of endless epicycles on the theme of the semantic-materialist theory. This has now become a tradition and quite an industry, sometimes called 'inquiry into mental concepts'; pretending to be in the domain of the theory of mind and purportedly explaining the life of mind, but actually as detached from it as a dry leaf is detached from a healthy, growing tree.

The tradition here outlined was born of the crisis in the foundations of Western knowledge which is still with us. This tradition, perhaps inadvertently, has created a monumental body of distinctions and semantic refinements which contribute little to our understanding of the world at large. Now if a body of knowledge which obscures rather than illuminates the purposes of our understanding can be called scholasticism, then the semantic empiricist tradition of the twentieth century deserves the name of the New Scholasticism.

3. Karl Popper – a partial liberation from positivism

In the last section we examined the impact of positivism on the theory of mind, particularly its most aggressive, not to say crudest forms such as behaviourism and Ryle's concept of mind. We have tried to show that our times are controlled by simplistic philosophies. Insofar as the jargon of behaviourism, operationalism, physicalism and the like has pervaded (a better term would be 'polluted') daily language, their influence is grave – although we may not be aware of it. For the present we are still steeped in the positivistic-physicalist-behaviourist magma. It will take us a while to extricate ourselves from it. We can do it step by step, however, first of all by being aware of the intellectual territory through which we travel every day. Let us go back to the story of how the horizons of our knowledge have developed since the beginning of the twentieth century.

As we are aware, the intellectual world of the twentieth century has been full of tremors and revolutions – big and small. One of these revolutions was the creation of a no-nonsense philosophy called logical empiricism, by a group of thinkers in Vienna in the late 1920s and early 1930s, led by Moritz Schlick. They called themselves the Vienna Circle, and for this reason their philosophy has sometimes been called the Vienna Circle philosophy. This was a positivism with a vengeance. Whatever limitations of empiricism and positivism were revealed in the eighteenth and nineteenth centuries (and indeed Kant demonstrated how shallow empiricism was), the thinkers of the Vienna Circle decided to forget them and build another empiricist edifice, this time on the foundations of modern formal logic. The edifice was impressive. But *as a philosophy it was a disaster*. Its fall-out has affected our thinking and our mentality to the degree that we have often behaved like positivist morons. Reviewing the decisions made by our policy-makers and all those others who are leading us into the new electronic era, and realizing that these decisions are not enlightened by any deeper values or any larger philosophy and yet are hailed as 'rationally justified' – and proclaimed with pride – we cannot escape the conclusion that *the fall-out from positivist thinking has incapacitated us on countless levels*.

Let us now review some of the historical happenings. As has been emphasized, Kant was astute indeed in postulating that the structure of our knowledge (and thus of our world) conforms to the categories of our mind, and not conversely, as classical empiricism had assumed. But Kant's great insight was marred by one misconception. He made the structure of the mind too rigid and too dogmatic. There is a paradox here, and an epistemological tragedy. Kant set out to liberate Newtonian physics from the strait-jacket of empiricism, and this he did. Yet in the process of the intended liberation, he imprisoned himself in the rigidity of the conceptual universe of Newtonian mechanics.

The genius of Kant consisted in inventing the structure of the mind from which Newtonian physics follows. But this genius also played a part in Kant's undoing. When Newtonian mechanics started to collapse at the end of the nineteenth century, this spelled the doom of the absolute categories that

Kant attributed to the mind. Non-Euclidean geometries were bad omens for Kant's categorical system.

One must be careful here. Advances in geometry (Lobachevsky, Riemann and others) as well as in physics (Einstein and others) did not negate Kant's main thesis concerning the active role of the mind in shaping all knowledge – according to its structures and capacities. What *was* undermined, however, were the *specific structures and categories* that Kant attributed to the mind.

Kant meant to finish empiricism once and for all. Yet, in spite of Kant's marvellous insight into the nature of the human mind, we witness the return to empiricism, wave after wave, as if Kant had never existed. As if Ernst Mach's positivism were not enough, we evolved in the 1930s, under the auspices of the Vienna Circle, a new brand of empiricism – logical empiricism. We are back to our story.

The tools of logic and semantics have simply obsessed the minds of twentieth-century Western philosophers. Through fastidious and exact systems of semantics, logical empiricists (and then analytical philosophers) have hoped to reconstruct traditional philosophy so that it would be on a par with precise systems of exact science. Surely an impossible dream, as science itself is becoming more and more elusive. But philosophy is full of impossible dreams; indeed, thrives on them.

Having worked out elegant and precise semantic and logical matrices, philosophers in the 1930s decided that the structure of the world must conform to the structure of their propositions. Hence, first Ludwig Wittgenstein's *Tractatus Logico-Philosophicus* (1921) and then *The Logical Structure of the World* by Rudolf Carnap (1928, 1962).

Let us clearly examine the nature of the enterprise. The main problem for logical empiricists, for whom Bertrand

Russell was the chief inspiration (particularly his and Alfred Whitehead's *Principia Mathematica*, 1910–13), was how to secure the reliability of human knowledge. Their overall solution lay in structure. In the right logical and semantic structures lies the key to the reconstruction of our knowledge; also the key to the reconstruction of physical reality. In this context, understanding is reduced to understanding via logical structures. This is particularly striking in regard to Russell/ Wittgenstein's logical atomism, within the compass of which negative facts were invented to fit the structure of negative propositions – a preposterous notion which nevertheless was accepted at the time. The positivist epistemological and seman- tic theories worked out in the 1920s and 1930s, under the auspices of logical empiricism, by and large conform to the norm that the logical structure determines all: the process of knowledge, the validity of knowledge, the picture of the world, and, of course, the validity of our language.

Positivism is a tortured philosophy. Seldom in the history of philosophy has such an enormous and sophisticated labour produced so little understanding. Karl Popper, who saw the limitations of the excessively logical approach to knowledge and the world while actually living in the midst of the euphoria of the logical positivist revolution while it was happening in Vienna, was one of the first to call the young Turks of the Schlick School the 'positivists'. In his epoch- making *Logic of Scientific Discovery* (1934, 1959) he showed the importance of the creative agency of the mind. Kant was an enormous inspiration for Popper, yet Kant's influence is quite concealed in his work.

With Popper we witness another revolution in philosophy. To begin with, the main problem for Popper is to understand *how knowledge grows*. Let us state some of the premises of Pop- per's philosophy. To understand the world is to understand the nature of our knowledge. To understand our knowledge is to understand its growth and vicissitudes. Human knowledge does not grow like a pyramid, made of the same kind of stones (physical facts). The shape of the pyramid is continually reconstructed as some parts of it are destroyed or at least significantly changed. The material of which the pyramid is made is also varied – all kinds of things are built into it.

For logical empiricists the chief inspiration was Russell and the *Principia*. Popper's chief inspiration was Einstein and his theory of relativity. Einstein's theory has shown, according to Popper, that no knowledge is absolute. Even such securely established theory as Newtonian mechanics finally gives way. Newtonian physics is not a repository of ultimate and unshakable knowledge, as it was once thought to be. The conclusion that follows is that all knowledge is tentative and conjectural. The best we can do is to play imaginatively with new conjectures (tentative theories), and then submit them to relentless scrutiny. Our rationality, and indeed the foundation of our epistemology, lies in the process of relentless criticism rather than in the process of building an infallible rock-bottom of knowledge out of atomic facts and propositions.

What the *structure* was for logical empiricism, the dialectical *process of continuous criticism* has become for Popper – the cornerstone of rationality and of epistemological worth. There is no question that Popper should be hailed as one of the intellectual giants of the twentieth century, a man who has helped us to liberate ourselves from the strait-jacket of logical empiricism. Yet with the passage of time Popper too has become a new orthodoxy, his followers seeking to monopolize truth and behave as if they had the key to all right solutions.

What was especially liberating in Popper was his pluralism

as he led us away from the one-track approach of logical structuralists. Popper has promoted pluralistic epistemology and open-ended rationality.[8] It was the open-endedness of Popper's philosophy that was so refreshing and promising for the future. To try to make Popper's opus a closed and untouchable system is to do violence to the very nature of his enterprise, according to which *everything* is open to questioning and criticism. It follows therefore that – as our perspectives and problems change – so do our approaches and solutions. And our perspectives and problems *have* changed. During the last thirty years Einstein's theories have no longer been at the centre of controversy, either in physics or in epistemology. Instead, quantum theory or, to use a more general term, the New Physics has been posing the most fascinating and most mind-boggling problems both for physicists and for epistemologists.

This must be admitted: in contradistinction to logical empiricism, Popper acknowledges the active role of the mind. The mind is constantly active, either in generating new conjectures or in ingeniously thinking up new tests of existing theories. But there are firm boundaries within which this process occurs. Reality seems to be given to Popper, and unquestioned. At the centre of Popper's system is the notion of empirical refutability. This notion *assumes* that Nature or Reality is there – firmly and unequivocally established and recognized for what it is; and moreover, that it can shout 'no' whenever we impose on it a theory or proposition that does not fit it. The idea that reality as given is reinforced by Popper's relentless defence of the classical (or the correspondence) theory of truth (discussed in section 2). It bears repeating that the underlying assumption of the correspondence theory of truth is that there is a firm reality 'out there' which we grasp, or at least approximate in our theories. The match between description and reality is based on the notion that there is a 'reality' prior to the description which the description attempts to convey (capture, represent) by means of linguistic symbols. With the recognition of the exquisite powers of sensitivities as co-makers of reality, with the recognition of the main insights of the New Physics, this entire assumption needs to be revised.

Popper's philosophy was unrecognized for quite a while because of the dominance of logical empiricism. Then it was immensely helped by the appearance of Thomas Kuhn's *The Structure of Scientific Revolutions* (1963), which is Popperian in its approach through and through. Popper's philosophy was further popularized by Paul Feyerabend and then Imre Lakatos. The successive extensions of Popper's philosophy led to surprising, if not paradoxical results. By the relentless criticism of the very basis of this philosophy, its practitioners have so much undermined the very notions of refutability and rationality that *the whole epistemological enterprise has become problematic*. The process of the historical reconstruction of science, within Popperian epistemology, has led to the undermining of *every* creed and contention that was ever held about science.

Following this critical approach to its conclusion, Paul Feyerabend has announced that *anything goes*. The enterprise of science, when examined penetratingly, according to Feyerabend, appears to be incoherent and amorphous, and full of question-begging. Feyerabend ultimately argues, in his article 'A Plea for the Hedonist', that a world without science would be more pleasant to live in.[9]

The watershed for Popperian philosophy was the mid-1970s. The colourful and irrepressible Imre Lakatos may have been the man to bring Popper's philosophy to its eclipse mainly because he did so much to popularize it. So intense was their zeal to put Popper on the map that in undercutting

Kuhn, Lakatos and others have undermined the whole élan of conjecturalism.[10] Now, whatever Lakatos' role in extending and therefore in diluting Popper's opus, the fact remains that *Popper's philosophy appears as less and less relevant for the newly emerging epistemological problems of quantum physics, and especially with regard to the conception of reality as coextensive with the mind.*

In the panorama of twentieth-century thought Popper once appeared a bright light.[11] Now this light appears dimmer and dimmer as Popper holds rigidly to his old concepts while new visions, vistas and insights, particularly of the New Physics, open up new horizons. The new light of holistic understanding is dawning on us. The old scientism of whatever variety, with its dogmatic insistence on cognitive knowledge and its enshrining of the empirical and of the physical, is giving way, though slowly.

We may say in summary that logical positivism was the philosophy for the first half of the twentieth century. Popper's was the philosophy for the second half of the twentieth century – the period of transition. Now we need a philosophy for the twenty-first century, a philosophy cognizant of all the developments of the last quarter of the century, and capable of integrating them.

4. The Three Western Projects

It was observed in the last section that the human mind has an astonishing capacity to entertain notions that are odd if not artificial. Indeed, the virtuosity of the mind in defending even preposterous propositions is nothing short of amazing. There must be a deeper explanation of this phenomenon. When we consider such minds as Descartes', Locke's or La Mettrie's we are puzzled as to why, with so much brilliance, they could not *see* any better. My answer is – they did not choose to. They deliberately wanted to view phenomena in a certain way and then employed their formidable intellects to 'prove' what they chose to see. Why would they embark on such strange paths? For a variety of complex ideological and cultural reasons.

Each epoch has its own specific problematics. Take the Middle Ages. Each philosopher of the time was busily constructing his proofs of the existence of God. Were they all *so* interested in the problem? Each one of them? Or was the problem imposed on them by the spirit of the time?

Let us take present-day philosophers. Why are they not interested in providing any proof of the existence of God? Because we are interested in different problems. Why? Because different problems have come to the fore. Why?

We might say that we are interested in certain kinds of problems because others around us are interested in those problems. That is an easy answer and a superficial one. Besides, it reduces us to merely aping what others are doing. To explore a new realm of thought and come up with new, deep insights within it requires a devotion to the subject and a fascination with it. Why would La Mettrie try to prove that man is just a machine in *L'Homme Machine* (1747) if he was not transfixed with the idea? Why would B.F. Skinner devote his best creative energies to a similar idea? They were separated by two centuries, yet possessed by the same fixation. We need to see clearly that they not only shared some common problems but that their *visions* were as close to each other as if they had worked under the auspices of the same deity.

From Francis Bacon and René Descartes, philosophers and ordinary people wanted to see things in a new way, to be liberated from old vistas and visions and from the dogmas and teachings of the church. An entirely new 'project' is under way today. I wish to use the term *project* to denote this overall realm which directs our visions (within a given culture) and guides our inspirations, as well as justifies the ends of our lives. The idea of the project is much larger than that of the paradigm. The project engenders paradigms that serve it. The project is a trans-rational entity. It is a matter of a vision and deep beliefs. After people invest their beliefs in it, they try to justify it rationally.

Thus what we witness in the case of Descartes and Bacon, then Newton and La Place, then Locke and La Mettrie, then Bertrand Russell, B. F. Skinner, Percy Bridgman, Rudolf Carnap et al. is a new journey – the secular project, or the Faustian Project.

This was not the first major project of Western culture; nor is it the last. I propose to distinguish the three main Western Projects. The first was the Greek project, or the Promethean Project, continued from Antiquity roughly to the sixteenth century. In the seventeenth century a new project started to take shape, the secular project, or the Faustian one. The third, the Evolutionary Project, is emerging under our very eyes. It is a holistic and integrative project. Let us go back to where it all started – to Socrates and Plato. We shall view the various projects by concentrating on one of the crucial elements of all cultures: their view of knowledge.

THE FIRST WESTERN PROJECT: THE GREEK

Plato: Knowledge as enlightenment. Knowledge for Plato was in a sense sacred. But it was also an instrument, though no ordinary one. It was an instrument of self-enlightenment. In this capacity knowledge was tremendously important – as the vehicle that enables us to overcome the coarseness of our body, the limitation of our senses, which dim the vision of the soul. The soul is entrapped in the body. The acquisition of knowledge is a slow and painful process of stripping away the unnecessary accretions that muffle the soul. Knowledge is recollection: remembering what the soul once knew. Let us put Plato's perspective in our terms. The basic human project is: *to reach enlightenment and unity with the Godhead*.

When we look at the legacy of Plato, and actually of most ancient Greek philosophies, we see a clear parallelism with Buddhism and Hinduism. In both the Eastern and Western traditions (of the time) we see an enormous importance attached to the mind. In Buddhism, especially, the role of the mind, of right thinking and of right assumptions is particularly emphasized. But this element is also luminously clear in Hindu tradition, especially in the Upanishads.

Here are some quotations from the *Dhammapada*, a basic Buddhist text, the main part of which is attributed to the Buddha:

What we are today comes from our thoughts of yesterday, and our present thoughts build our life of tomorrow: our life is the creation of our mind.[12]

For he whose mind is well trained in the ways that lead to light . . . enjoys the immortal *Nirvana*.[13]

Invisible and subtle is the mind, and it flies after fancies wherever it likes; but let the wise man guard well his mind, for a mind well guarded is a source of great joy.[14]

Hidden in the mystery of consciousness, the mind, incorporeal, flies alone far away. Those who set their mind in harmony become free from the bonds of death.[15]

In a similar vein speak the Upanishads – the basic inspiration for the Hindu ways of thought and life:

... the mind is the organ of thought. It is because of the light of the Spirit that the human mind can see, and can think, and enjoy this world.[16]

Mind is indeed the source of bondage and also the source of liberation.[17]

Let us therefore keep the mind pure, for what a man thinks, that he becomes; this is a mystery of Eternity.[18]

St Augustine and Spinoza. St Augustine (354–430) is a cornerstone of Christian faith and Christian philosophy, one of the chief architects of the Christian world-view. For Augustine, knowledge is very important as well. To possess right knowledge is to be in the right state of being. Put otherwise: one's being is determined by the nature and quality of the knowledge one beholds. For one's knowledge is a form of prayer that leads us to God. You cannot behave badly if you truly possess the right kind of knowledge. If you misbehave and commit evil or criminal acts, then it means you really don't possess right knowledge; you don't understand; it is your ignorance not your knowledge that inspires you and pushes you to evil deeds.

It is important to realize that for Augustine knowledge is intimately connected with life. Right knowledge means right life (or right livelihood, as the Buddhists would say). This is of course a version of the Platonic position. There is, at this stage of European history, no divorce of knowledge from life. The conviction is still held that to possess a superior knowledge leads us to a superior life.

This conviction is still upheld by the Dutch philosopher Boruch Spinoza (1632–77). He died young, slowly suffocated by the glass powder which he inhaled while working as a glass grinder. Spinoza already lived in the age of rising empiricism. He himself insists that virtue is its own reward and that the right cultivation of the intellect is a precondition of the good life. Wise life is good life. Ignorance and stupidity are the causes of calamities, of misery and human suffering.

Thus I have completed all I wished to show concerning the power of the mind over emotions or the freedom of the mind. From which it is clear how much a wise man is in front of the others and how much stronger he is than an ignorant one, who is guided by lust alone. For an ignorant man, besides being agitated in many ways by external causes, never enjoys one true satisfaction of the mind: he lives almost unconscious of himself, God, and things, and as soon as he ceases to be passive, ceases to be. On the contrary, the wise man, in so far as he is considered as such, is scarcely moved in spirit: he is conscious of himself, of God, and of things by a certain eternal necessity, he never ceases to be, and always enjoys satisfaction of the mind. If the road I have shown is very difficult, it can yet be discovered. And clearly it must be very hard when it is so seldom found. But all excellent things are as difficult as they are rare.[19]

But the tide of time is moving from the idea of knowledge as enlightenment. Spinoza is an exception. The dominant cast of the Western mind has changed. The Western Project has changed. It is best exemplified by Francis Bacon (1561–1626) and his new conception of knowledge, according to which *knowledge is power*: power to extricate secrets from nature, power to subdue nature to our wishes, demands and whims, power to make nature serve the ends of humankind.

THE SECOND WESTERN PROJECT

We can see that a new project has evolved in the West. What are the characteristics of the Second Western Project? *To put the universe on a plate and cut it with an analytical knife; then to manipulate it to our advantage.* The analytical knowledge acquired in this manner becomes a tool to harness and exploit nature. This is the first or intellectual aspect of this Second Western Project.

There is also the ideological or religious aspect – secularism. Secularism is a new religion of Western man. It is a religion in disguise. Secularism proclaims that we don't need any religion, any God to bring us salvation. We don't need any salvation. We want fulfilment here on earth. The idea of fulfilment on earth, however, becomes a new form of salvation. We can find fulfilment and happiness on earth through our own effort. We can create a paradise on earth. The paradise on earth becomes a new theology, a new religion.

This is also a challenge to the traditional idea of God. Secularism assumes that we human beings are as powerful as God. In this scheme human reason and human knowledge are elevated to extraordinary heights. Through knowledge, which is power, we shall harness and create a paradise on earth.

Thus we see how the Western Project has evolved: from the idea of knowledge as the instrument of enlightenment and self-perfectibility – resulting in the liberation of the soul and the realization of God within – to the idea of knowledge as power, in order to harness the earth so that we can find fulfilment here and now in material terms.

Let us notice that the ends of human life in the first Western Project are compatible with most Eastern traditions:

Buddhism insists on the right cultivation of the mind in order to reach enlightenment and then liberation.

Hinduism insists on Moksha, which itself is a process of liberation, of merging the Atman with the Brahman.

Taoism insists on following the right Tao, which leads away from illusions and on to the path of serenity and wisdom.

Zen insists on sitting still until enlightenment comes.

This is not so with the second Western Project, which radically separates itself from the major spiritual traditions.

Science as universal philosophy: physics as cosmology. The Second Western Project emphasizes the importance of the exploration of the external world. It also emphasizes the pragmatic aspects of knowledge, namely that knowledge is generated for the sake of the manipulation of the external world. In the First Project, religion is the source of it all. From religion other things follow.

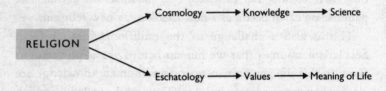

In the Second Project it is science that is at the centre, or rather at the beginning. From science all other things follow.

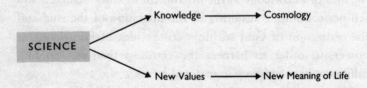

In earlier times cosmology (usually inspired by religion) defined the nature of knowledge. Now cosmology is defined by science and is indeed a branch of it, with all the corresponding limitations.

The Second Western Project has been euphoric, optimistic, promising. It has swayed not only Western minds. The basic assumptions of this project are:

(1) We can know the world. It is ours for the taking.

(2) There are no mysteries. Science will explain all.

(3) Western rationality or scientific rationality is universal. Other cultures must submit to it.

(4) Human progress can be universal if all mankind applies the tools of Western science and technology and the canons of Western rationality.

Within the Second Western Project knowledge and science have been elevated to a religious position. The preeminence of science and the scientific world-view is assured by their perpetuation through Western educational institutions. Western institutions of learning have been able to sway the minds of people of all other cultures. After having received higher education in the West, young people from other cultures invariably become a part of the scientific/rational priesthood. In consequence, they perpetuate the ideology of science and of the Western Project in their own countries. We can see how insidious and subtle are the workings of a powerful project, how it mesmerizes and compels men's minds, and produces types such as Skinner, Carnap and other guardians of the status quo.

Looking more deeply into the phenomenon, we see that the most vital aspects of the Second Western Project are not rational but trans-rational. Basic secular beliefs are not rationally justified. Salvation through consumption was not a rational proposition, yet secularism has had a universal appeal. It has swayed the minds of non-Western people as well, particularly those who have received Western education; they have succumbed to the Western form of salvation.

Such is the general pattern. With notable exceptions. The Hindu mind seems to have been more resilient than the minds of people of other cultures. It seems that the tradition of the Upanishads and the great learning of the Vedas have inspired and guided the Hindu mind and enabled it to see through the limitations of Western assumptions (listed (1)–(4) above).

The end of triumphant secularism. After three centuries of pursuing the scientific-secular project, the Western mind is now reassessing its entire strategy and the ends that have motivated it. The assumptions so dear to the Western mentality, under closer scrutiny, do not appear so universal and indubitably valid as was once surmised. In fact, they appear to us now to be Western dogmas – dazzling but limited, powerful but dangerous. Moreover, the Second Western Project, instead of bringing fulfilment to all people of the earth, has created a nightmarish pseudo-rational reality, with environmental degradation, famines, violence in full abundance.

The present Western mind is confused. *The confused mind is a dangerous one.* It is more than reasonable to assume that this confused mind is the result of the overall fragmentation of values and the fact that there is no centre that holds.

THE THIRD WESTERN PROJECT

There is no doubt that the Western mind is now searching for wholeness, for integration, for values that sustain life, for God-within.

We are slowly abandoning the pretension of the universality of our Western rationality, of our dream of making everybody a success in material terms. We realize more and more that what we took to be indubitable truths (the assumptions (1)–(4) listed above) are only dogmas. This is accompanied by our awareness of the collapse of the Newtonian model of the world as universal and eternal, by our awareness that the New Physics is opening for us far-reaching and often staggeringly novel vistas.

These realizations occur within the context of an intense, though often concealed, search for spiritual values, for the meaning of life which goes beyond material gratification. The Western mind is now prepared to eat humble pie (though still reluctantly) and learn from others and not only *teach* others.

The Third Western Project is not yet clearly defined. Some of its emerging features are:

First, *it is a holistic project emphasizing the unity of all things* – as contrasted with their atomistic separation.

Secondly, *it is a spiritually inclined project* without necessarily invoking any institutional religion or even the notion of God.

Thirdly, *it is an ecologically oriented project*, as ecology provides the key for healing the world and ourselves.

I call the Third Western Project *evolutionary* because we are finally aware of the nature of evolution. By being aware of it, we are responsible for it. In full consciousness we are designing our destiny. In full consciousness we shape the destiny of our minds, which will be the destiny of our world. This knowledge is at times terrifying. Can we assume this awesome responsibility without falling into hubris?

Now some of the attributes of the new Western project are the ones the East has never ceased to hold. Hence we see new grounds for reconciliation.

Yet the fundamental question still remains. How do we accomplish the reconciliation between East and West? Or better still – the synthesis between East and West? This is a problem that has preoccupied many great minds in the twentieth century.

Perhaps the key problem, on which hinges the solution to other problems, is: how to reconcile objective evidence with subjective evidence. Better still: how to demonstrate that 'subjective' evidence and 'objective' evidence interlock, complement each other, represent partial but complementary approaches to ultimate truth. If this is accomplished, then we shall be able to show that:

(1) The Buddha mind and the objective mind are aspects of the same universal/human/cosmic mind.

(2) The objective mind is one extreme articulation of the Buddha mind, and the Buddha mind can also be seen as objective – that is, when we grant the context (and the assumptions) within which the Buddha mind can manifest itself.

(3) The split between the East and the West represents different propensities of the same human mind which can articulate itself, and the world around itself – first in this way, then in that – and each articulation is part of the unfolding of the evolutionary process.

(4) With the rise of the New Physics – when its metaphysical and ethical consequences are clearly spelt out – we have at least the rudiments of the matrix for reconciliation of the West with the East, on a deeper conceptual level, and beyond superficial borrowings.

The matrix of the New Physics informs us unequivocally that:

(a) Objective evidence as such does not exist, for in every bit of the 'objective' evidence a part of our psyche is built.

(b) We are allowed to see ourselves as part of the cosmos not merely in the physical sense but also as Atman participating in the Brahman.

(c) We are allowed to see the entire cosmos as interconnected; moreover, as one magic dance of Shiva.

(5) When all these new metaphysical insights are absorbed and digested, we shall live in a different universe because we shall have created a new universe.

The Third Project of the West is both a peculiarly Western project – born of our problems, vicissitudes and agonies – and at the same time a universal project: the connected, interdependent world requires and demands a common vision, a world philosophy, a platform sustaining us all. The 'ecumenicalism' of the Third Western Project is not born out of our desire to submit others to our will but out of our will to include the perspectives and vistas of others while we seek a universal philosophy capable of sustaining us all.

In a sense the Western world has travelled the whole circle: from early holistic unity of the pre-Socratics and Plato via the period of fragmentation and atomization of the empiricist era, to a new wholeness based on evolutionary unity, which is reminiscent of early Greek philosophy but which nevertheless is not a return to the original point. We have not travelled in a simple circle, but rather in a spiral. Although we have come to re-embrace many points that have been kept as constant stars in the firmament of Eastern thought, we do not dissolve ourselves in Eastern philosophies. Rather, we bring them up to our level, give them a new sense of coherence and meaning. The East and the West are not merging by one absorbing the other, but by each transcending its previous positions.

The role of the participatory mind in this reconstruction, in this process of transcendence, can be seen as second to none. The participatory mind is the vehicle that travels in the spiral of becoming and the imprints of its wheels become the tracks that we call reality. In the following chapters we shall explore the consequences, ramifications and extensions of the participatory mind in the universe of becoming – *the only universe* we live in, if we really live.

Summary

Mind in history is the maker of realities. Understanding this mind is understanding how cosmologies and world-views were formed, and how they have conditioned individual human beings. Individual minds serve the mind of the epoch because they are moulded and conditioned by it. People of various epochs may entertain, with deep convictions, very strange notions. This simply demonstrates that the human mind can articulate reality and culture of a given epoch in a great variety of ways, and sometimes odd ways. This also shows that there is no one prescribed way of articulation. The mind is an artist. And artists are sometimes singularly odd in their creation.

As mind is evolving, it will evolve beyond the moulds of its present articulations. But we need to help mind to evolve. Without changing the direction and structure of our present mechanistic mind, we shall be stuck in our present predicaments. In changing the propensities of the present mind (which is actually the mind of a past epoch), we shall only be following the historical and evolutionary imperative.

CHAPTER 3

The Spiral of Understanding

1. Ontology and epistemology in a circular relationship

The two primary divisions of philosophy are ontology and epistemology. Ontology, the theory of being, is concerned with various forms of being and their specific manifestations. Epistemology, the theory of knowledge, concerns itself with the ways in which we know. How do we know? How can we know? Through which particular faculties can we know? How reliable is this knowledge?

The two divisions are treated separately in some, jointly in other systems of philosophy. Sometimes epistemology is derived from a given ontology, sometimes vice versa; sometimes they are treated independently, as if they did not have much in common with each other.

In Plato's system ontology is primary. The Forms, as conceived by Plato, delineate the basic modes of being. The existence of these Forms necessitates certain cognitive faculties which we must possess in order to apprehend the forms. The theory of recollection is the epistemological doctrine that follows from the ontology based on the existence of the Forms. Plato's theory of enlightenment, as stripping away the distorting influences of the body which prevent the soul from seeing, is another consequence of Plato's theory of being. Our purpose here is not to examine Plato's philosophy in detail. Rather, we wish to show that the epistemological doctrines (modes of knowing) are so devised by Plato as to elicit the existence of Forms, as Plato conceived of them. An ontology has begotten an epistemology – to be supported by it.

In Kant's system, on the other hand, epistemology is primary, while his ontological doctrines are secondary. From the conception of the mind as imposing itself inexorably on the nature of reality, there follows clearly the ontological doctrine that reality (modes of being) is at the disposal of the mind, shaped and moulded by it. The categories of the mind shape only the phenomenal world, the world accessible to the senses. Beyond it there lies the noumenal world, the world of 'things in themselves', independent for their existence on the working of our minds. We do not know anything about this noumenal world.

Among the systems of thought in which ontology and epistemology are seen as independent from each other is science or the scientific world-view. Science assumes, at least classical science does so, that the world exists objectively *as it does*, and that through its 'objective' (scientific) methods, science simply depicts, describes, renders, isomorphizes the world as it is. This is of course an appealing, optimistic prospect. Upon closer inspection, however, we find it far from adequate.

Although science and the scientific world-view seem to consider ontology (the structure of the real world) and epistemology (the right ways of exploring it) as independent of each other, the two are dexterously tied together, feed on each other, and *elicit from each other what they assume in each other*. They are mirror images of each other. Epistemology brings about and illumines what ontology assumes. On the other hand, ontology contains exactly as much as can be ascertained through our scientific epistemologies.

This should not surprise us. In most if not all past and

present cosmologies, what is assumed to be there and how we explore it are intimately linked together. If some societies assume the existence of bad spirits which inhabit human bodies, these societies *must find an appropriate methodology* (an appropriate diagnosis and ritual) which recognizes these bad spirits and then expels them. If some societies, such as ours, recognize the existence (equally invisible to the eye) of entities called subatomic particles, this necessitates a methodology through which these particles can be ascertained. In ultimate terms both methodologies, which reach far beyond the evidently graspable and palpable, are a form of magic.[1] Of course, ascertaining the existence of subatomic particles, even quarks and gluons, is not considered magic in our culture, for we 'know' that they exist. Equally, in societies in which the existence of bad and good spirits (even if they are only forms of energy) is recognized, they are not considered magic, for in these societies it is 'known' that they exist. As we see from these examples, the problem of existence is tough. There are no trans-cultural or, better still, trans-cosmological criteria which inform us about what exists and in what sense.[2]

We thus come face to face with the problem of the reliability of knowledge and also what constitutes *real* existence. In a more subtle way this is also the question of how various cultures understand the cosmos. What is the reason for slicing the universe in so many different ways? This is both an epistemological question and an anthropological one.

If there were one true form of knowledge of the universe, then other forms of understanding of the universe would have to be deemed inadequate, if not false. On the other hand, if there isn't one adequate way of representing the knowledge of the universe, then various systems of knowledge, examined jointly, give us a clue as to how knowledge is formed, and why the universe is sliced or framed in so many different ways. Actually, the idea of 'framing' the universe is quite *à propos*.

What we are discussing is not merely the role of language in the formation and formulation of knowledge. From early conventionalists (Poincaré, Duhem) via radical conventionalists (Ajdukiewicz, Whorf, Quine) up to Chomsky, the role of language, as a unique container of knowledge, has been emphasized and sometimes over-emphasized.[3] But language is only one aspect of the way we apprehend the universe. The translinguistic or non-verbal portion of knowledge of any society is probably much larger and much more important than its linguistic portion. Thus our problem is not only to understand the role of language in rendering the variety of knowledge, but to understand *the role of the human agent in shaping the architecture of the universe.* Furthermore, we must identify the role of the mind in making the cosmos appear to us as it does. What are the rules governing the generation of knowledge within a particular culture? Why do we witness such an extraordinary fit between the ontology of a given culture and its epistemology? We shall address ourselves to the latter question first.

2. The walls of the cosmos and the spiral of the mind

Regarding the Kalahari bushman who uses his senses and his numerous sensitivities which are his methodology (we could even use the term his *epistemology* – ways of knowing and acting in the world) for finding food and his way around his environment, we so often say in a derogatory way: it is just instinct. Yet we should realize that it is a finely tuned knowledge that enables him to survive and to flourish.

When a Western scientist finds a new virus or a new

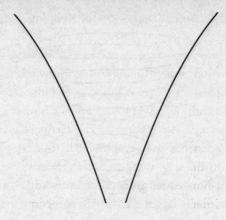

Fig. 1 *The boundaries of our universe*

enzyme, we say it is a tribute to his method and his well-tested knowledge.

In both these cases there is a fit between the given epistemology and the given ontology, between the ways of knowing, on the one hand, and the reality ascertained through this knowledge on the other. This fit is an extraordinary phenomenon, and a bewitching one at times.

Let us remind ourselves of a point that has been established in the preceding chapters: the universe is never given to us as such. The universe is always given to us with our mind contained in it. We often contemplate the notion of a boundless or infinite universe. However, because of the limitations of our understanding, our universe – be it the universe of the individual or of the species – is always limited or bound. Let us present the boundaries of our universe as a cone opening upward (Fig. 1).

Only what is within the cone is the known and the knowable universe. The walls of the cone delineate the walls of our cosmos. They contain our understanding, the sum-total of all

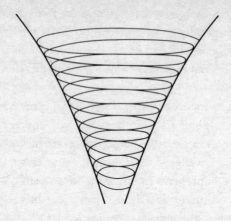

Fig. 2 *The spiral of understanding*

knowledge. Our universe must be supported by our knowledge, otherwise it would be an empty universe. The best way
to conceive how knowledge fills the cone is to imagine that
the cone is wired inside by a spiral. This spiral is what I call
the spiral of understanding (Fig. 2).

The spiral of understanding is our epistemology, the accepted ways of knowing the world; or what we assume to be
the case 'out there'. Let us state some of the consequences.
The spiral of understanding exactly fits the walls of the
cosmos. But we can look at the situation the other way
around. The walls of the cosmos conform exactly to the spiral
of understanding. There is a wonderful fit between the two
of them. And this is so in all cultures. This is the first
conclusion.

Another conclusion is that although the walls of the cosmos
on the one hand, and the spiral of understanding on the other,
can be analysed out as independent entities, they are not
independent of each other. They cannot exist apart from each
other. They are always given together. In any cosmology, the

universe or reality is given together with the knowledge and through the knowledge of this reality. Thus we can say that *the outer walls of the cosmos are the inner walls of the mind*. This insight is of crucial importance. We shall return to it over and over again.

Let us paraphrase our main points. The dimensions of the universe correspond to the spiral of our understanding. It immediately follows that if there is no spiral of understanding to support any walls of the cosmos, there is no cosmos to speak of or comprehend in any way. The cosmos that is not grasped or comprehended in any way is a shadowy Platonic fiction, not a palpable universe for us.

To claim that the universe is as it is, independently of us, is to deny the vital truth that any conception of the cosmos is always given with the spiral of understanding that corresponds to this cosmos, expresses and articulates it. *The unarticulated cosmos is the universe before the day of creation*.

From the crucial dependence of the walls of the cosmos on the spiral of understanding it follows that there is no world given to us outside the categories of understanding that the spiral of understanding delineates for us.

To know is to constitute the world. To apprehend, grasp, behold, seize the world is to embrace it in the tentacles of our knowledge, in the spiral of our understanding. Beyond the tentacles of our knowledge, the world is a buzzing confusion. Actually, to describe the world as 'a buzzing confusion' is to order it, constitute it somewhat. To speak of the world is to commit it to the tentacles of our knowledge, to commit it to the dimensions of our spiral of understanding. To speak of the world is to sentence it to the categories of our knowledge, to embrace it by the spiral of our understanding.

From the dependence of the walls on the spiral, some other important consequences follow. The cone of the cosmos is open-ended, opening upwards, which means that as knowledge unfolds so *the universe enlarges*. However, in extremely rigid cultures and closed societies the lid of the cone can be sealed off. In such circumstances, no alterations to the walls of the cosmos are allowed, no new knowledge is welcome. The culture is in a state of stagnation. Its spiral of understanding is frozen, static and unchanging. Such a culture is ruled by dogma, ritual and often oppressive measures which keep creative individuals under control. We have seen many such societies.

In open societies, on the other hand, as knowledge grows so does the spiral of understanding; so do the walls of the cosmos. To be more precise, the walls do not grow as such. They become adjusted, reassembled, rebuilt, reconstructed. How these reconstructions take place is a fascinating story.

As our knowledge of astrophysics has grown, so have the boundaries of the physical universe. Our universe is now considered to be over fifteen billion light years in dimension, and it is still expanding. Our new discoveries have revealed to us that the universe contains some amazing and perplexing phenomena, such as quasars, black holes, 'strings', 'arcs'. On deeper reflection, we find that it is not the universe that reveals these phenomena to us but our mind.

The universe reveals nothing to the unprepared mind. When the mind is prepared, through its strange magic, it co-creates with the universe. This story of co-creation is one of the marvels of human existence and one of the mysteries of the human mind.

To reiterate, the shape of the universe conforms to the spiral of our understanding. The richness of the furniture of the world is the richness of the mind. As we unravel the relationships between the spiral of understanding and the dimensions of the cosmos some striking paradoxes emerge.

3. How stable is our picture of the universe?

Every culture assumes that its universe is stable and permanent. Each culture is a guardian of the status quo – it inculcates in us the belief that we live in a permanent world, and that therefore the walls of the cosmos are permanent and static. Yet cultures change. Knowledge grows. Our cosmos is continually enlarged; but never without pain, and always with some tribulations and considerable resistance.

Almost every system of knowledge historically known behaves as if it were final. Now let us examine what happens when through new insights within a given culture its knowledge is enlarged to the point at which the old walls of the cosmos cannot contain these insights. Do we simply adjust the walls and that is that? No. The process is usually traumatic. At first the existing walls refuse to budge. That is to say, the guardians of the status quo, who are numerous and powerful in every society, refuse to recognize the new insights. Their argument is, whether stated or unstated: 'We know what is what, and what the world is about. Nobody can tell us that there are things beyond the limits of the world. If there is such a person, he must be demented.' The logic of the argument is correct. The claim that there are things beyond the boundaries of our cosmos (for this is what some of the new insights often assert) will strike most as wild and incomprehensible. Thus the rule is that whenever a radically new insight appears, it is put down. The culture knows best. Its guardians, with due righteousness and support of the culture, act swiftly and unequivocally in holding back potential geniuses, madmen and trouble-makers. The manner of the guardians may be subtle or crude: crude in authoritarian régimes, subtle but nevertheless effective in democratic societies.

The way in which the boundaries of the cosmos of a given society are defended partakes of holy ritual. For a good reason, too. *To question the boundaries of the cosmos of a given culture is to question the identity of the people in that culture. Let us remember that human identity is formed by and anchored in the underlying cosmology.*

In this mental climate, some individuals with wonderful new insights are intimidated at the outset, and their insights are never revealed to the world. We shall never know what wealth of knowledge we have lost in the process. Other individuals, more stubborn and tenacious, refuse to give up. The establishment is invariably hard on people with 'mad ideas'. The lives of gifted and original individuals have been wasted as a result of the establishment's relentless attacks on new insights which are called heresies. Innovative thinkers have ended their lives seized by madness, or have died prematurely. We shall never know how many geniuses have rotted to their death in lunatic asylums because their ideas were derided and destroyed. This is a dark and unwritten chapter in the history of human knowledge. In his play *The Physicists*, Dürrenmatt chillingly touches on it.

Yet some people with new insights persist. They evade all the traps laid for them by the guardians of the status quo. Through their persistence and luck they hammer out their messages until, gradually, they begin to be heard by reluctant ears. It is acknowledged that new ideas are not mad, after all, and may even be right. The new knowledge contained in them indicates that the boundaries of the cosmos must be expanded, the walls of the cosmos must be changed, usually enlarged, to fit the enlarged spiral of understanding.

The astonishing thing is that after such an operation is completed, *the guardians of the status quo behave as if nothing has happened*, as if the walls of the cosmos were as permanent as a rock, and established forever. If they are reminded of the insights that enlarged the existing walls, they say, 'Oh, yes; that little matter; we have taken care of it.'

Another astonishing thing is that *the process of enlarging the spiral of understanding is going on all the time*. However, the culture, each culture for that matter, behaves as if nothing has happened, as if the walls of its cosmos were unchangeable and absolute.

Let us draw some further conclusions. If we reflect on ontology and epistemology in their historical perspective, then we notice that *ontology is always conservative; epistemology is always revolutionary*. Ontology always tries to preserve what is, as it is. Epistemology, on the other hand, by continuous questioning and investigation, always finds that things are different from what we assumed them to be. As long as we allow knowledge to grow, we are, by this very act, revolution-aries, for we allow the universe (including the universe of our culture) to grow and change.

Ultimately we have two choices: either we are truly con-servatives, and by design inhibit and paralyse any growth and change; or we support the growth of knowledge, and then conservatism is unacceptable, for it is incompatible with the imperative of life. *In the long run evolution spells out continuous revolution*.

In order to be alive we must unfold. To unfold we have to articulate the spiral of understanding, which is at the same time the unfolding of the universe and life itself. Thus con-servatism can be seen as a philosophy of small minds which are happy to serve the status quo and confine themselves to established niches, forgetting that the imperative of life is to unfold, to change, to transcend.

4. The peculiarity of the process of understanding

The usual assumption is that the less we know the less we understand; the more we know the more we understand. Thus the more knowledge we possess the better for our understanding. This simplified scheme works but only up to a point. Beyond a certain point it is simply not true that the more knowledge we amass the more we understand. For understanding is an elusive entity. It has laws of its own which defy the crude process of just amassing knowledge.

The process of understanding is a dialectical one. It leads from the simple to the complex and then back to the simple. When we begin to explore a given phenomenon or a given branch of learning, we start with simple precepts. We understand only a little. Then as we acquire more and more information and knowledge, our understanding increases.

But after a while some astonishing things begin to happen: after we have amassed a lot of knowledge of a given phenomenon or a given branch of knowledge, we are less certain about our understanding. We are confronted with some puzzling, unexplained phenomena that do not fit. You can call them anomalies. You can call them aberrations. You can call them inexplicable puzzles. They appear only on a very sophisticated level of understanding when we have amassed a great deal of knowledge. These puzzles are invisible to the mind of the beginner. They are the *result* of our relentless acquisition of knowledge. It is at this level that a curious dialectic occurs.

After we have accumulated a considerable amount of knowledge, our picture – of whatever we investigate – grows more and more complex. More and more things bother us. What we gradually obtain is not growing clarity but (if we are honest with ourselves) growing obfuscation. The simple conclusion is that the relentless acquisition of knowledge doesn't automatically lead to the growing clarity of understanding but, after a certain point, to growing obfuscation. And this is so with any subject-matter.

The more relentless we are in amassing relevant information on a subject, the more surely shall we come to a juncture at which our picture becomes so complex that we are simply lost in it. Understanding we receive no more. Our mind is too perplexed and bewildered, and it cries for help. But it cannot receive any help but from itself. At such points of unmanageable complexity and obfuscation, the mind decides on radical surgery: it cuts across the bewildering complexity and establishes new patterns of simplicity. From this point a new journey begins . . . until the complexity again grows to the point that it is unmanageable.

We need to examine this whole process in some detail, for it presents an altogether different picture from the traditional idea of 'the more you know the more you understand.' Let us first look at the very concepts of simplicity and complexity. What is simple? What is complex? The cell is simple when we consider it as a building block of an organ. If we look into the cell itself, it is amazingly complex: it mirrors the whole universe. How do we comprehend the universe of the cell? By descending to simpler elements, to its molecular structure, until we end up with atoms. Atoms are simple; that is, as building blocks of molecular structures of living cells. But when we look into the structure of the atom itself, it is again amazingly complex. And the more we know about it, the more complex it becomes.

Now let us have the courage to ask ourselves unorthodox questions. Was the atom simple *before we made it complex* – in the pursuit of our knowledge? Was the cell simple, *before we made it complex* – by knowing more and more about it? These questions are never asked. For so often we naïvely presume that we explore things as they are. Let us draw some conclusions.

If the cosmos is infinitely complex (and there is no reason to believe that it is not); if the single cell is infinitely complex (and there is no reason to believe that it is not); if the single atom is infinitely complex (and this may very well be the case) – then we are in trouble, for the mind cannot deal with that complexity. Of necessity – because of its very nature the mind has to simplify. *To comprehend is to simplify*.

Let us restate some of our conclusions. The attributes 'complex' and 'simple' are not objective attributes of the world as it is. Why should the universe bother whether it is simple or complex? *We* bother because we must, because we want to understand. The patterns and configurations of the world are not there independently of mind, but are the patterns of our knowledge through which our minds work. Things do not become either simple or complex – whether they are atoms, cells or galaxies – by themselves. *It is our knowledge that makes them so. It is our mind that makes them so.*

What we consider the order 'out there' is actually the order of the mind. We have to learn to live with this conclusion: our mind is in everything we touch and comprehend. We are woven into the universe we explore. When we unfold the universe, we invariably unfold the mind. This is an exhilarating challenge, that so much of our mind is contained in everything we discover, and that if we allow our creative wings to open up, we can bring about new dimensions to the universe and to ourselves.

Some scientists maintain (Eugene Wiegner, for example) that our knowledge of physics has grown so phenomenally that no single individual can embrace all knowledge of one single field, be it physics or chemistry. This spells bad auguries for our understanding of the physical world. Does it mean that the physical universe is so complex that it is beyond our comprehension? It may be so. Or does it mean that the *picture* we have created is beyond our grasp? I believe the latter is the case. We have made the picture of the physical world unmanageable and in many ways incomprehensible. And this is, paradoxically, the result of our relentless quest to amass more and more physical knowledge.

The mind cannot help imposing patterns of simplicity on the world, in order to understand the world. Such is the nature of our mind. Simplification is the *modus operandi* of the human mind. Expressed in other terms: *simplicity is the methodology of the mind*. Insofar as mind interlocks with reality and attempts to understand this reality, complexity/simplicity is a dual aspect of the world/understanding, or reality/mind.

The present world, as rendered by the categories of classical science, has grown so 'complex' that it is beyond our comprehension; which means it is too complex for the mind; which means the mind will have to devise new patterns of understanding, new patterns of simplicity, new forms of logos, which will be imposed on this bewildering complexity in order to arrive at a new order and a new clarity. This is what mind has always done in history.

Let us state some of the paradoxes of knowledge explicitly.

(1) It is incomprehensible that we comprehend anything; how we comprehend is a big mystery.

(2) The more deeply we explore any subject-matter the more surely we are going to arrive at unexplained phenomena which challenge the entire framework of our quest for knowledge.

(3) The pursuit of knowledge is the pursuit from comprehension to incomprehension. We always start with something we know fairly well and end up with big puzzles.

Summary

The outer walls of the cosmos are the inner walls of the mind. The dimensions of the universe correspond to the spiral of our understanding. To speak of the world is to sentence it to the categories of our understanding, to embrace it by the spiral of understanding.

The recognition of the creative nature of man necessitates the universe that is open and mysterious. The mystery of the universe and man's essential creativity can be now seen as parts of the fundamental structure of the universe. Unless the universe is open and undetermined, we cannot hope for new articulations, new knowledge, the growth of the spiral of understanding. But since the spiral of understanding has grown, we can safely deduce that the universe is open and undetermined.

Simplicity and complexity are attributes of human mind and not of objective reality; and so are all cognitive orders we find in the universe. The spiral of understanding is the key to the comprehension of our knowledge and to the metamorphosis of reality through our knowledge, as well as the key to understanding the mystery and beauty of individual human existence. Cultivate the right spiral and you will dwell in the right universe and will embrace the right mode of life.

'What is impenetrable to us really exists manifesting itself as the highest wisdom' (Albert Einstein). The human agent is one part of the triangle of which the other two parts are the participatory mind and the participatory universe. The presence of the participatory mind immediately implies the existence of the human agent, which is essentially creative, and vice versa. Our creativity is inherent in the structure of the participatory universe.

CHAPTER 4

Teilhard's Story of Complexity: its Beauty and its Essential Incompleteness

1. Teilhard's legacy

The impact of Pierre Teilhard de Chardin (1881–1955) on twentieth-century thought cannot be overestimated. His protean mind shone in an age dominated by tedious atomization. He had the power of exquisite synthesis in an age of shrunken vision. It is much easier for us now, at the threshold of the twenty-first century, to speak of holistic visions than it was for Teilhard in the mid-1930s when he was writing *The Phenomenon of Man*, his most important work. We have all learned from Teilhard the courage to be comprehensive and visionary, the capacity to weave together large cosmic tapestries, the wisdom of including science and religion into our ultimate designs.

The human being is essentially a holistic being who lives in integrated totalities. When the human being is forced to lead a fragmented life, he/she shrinks, is frustrated, diminished and dwarfed. Teilhard's synthesis was an act of restoration. It restored for us the right evolutionary context in which we acknowledge ourselves to be physically small but spiritually significant. Above all, it restored our confidence to live integrally and wholly in an age in which even atoms are split and disintegrate into a myriad of sub-elements whose variety bewilders our comprehension.

Perhaps Teilhard's greatest achievement is his compelling reconstruction of the story of evolution. In Teilhard's rendering, evolution is an epic of unsurpassed grandeur and glory. While following this epic one is humbled and at the same time elevated by it.

Teilhard's genius lay partly in his capacity to weave one huge homogeneous tapestry in which the prehistory of life, life, and the phenomenon of man are parts of one unbroken stupendous flow – all unified by the ascent of evolution. Evolution is not only unifying. It is also creative – in the very similar sense in which we use the term in art and in human affairs. This view is held not only by philosophers but also by evolutionary biologists, such as Theodosius Dobzhansky and Charles Birch.[1]

Teilhard introduced the idea of the *noosphere*, the sphere of the mind or the sphere of thought, as a natural envelope of life at large. He also showed that all life has been groping to articulate itself in the shape of the noosphere.[2] By broadening the conception of evolution, Teilhard also broadened our vision of ourselves in it. This led to the idea that *we are evolution conscious of itself*.

There is no assured scientific or philosophical perspective which informs us with certainty how evolution should be viewed and comprehended – whether as the process of mere chance and brute necessity (Jacques Monod) or whether as a relentless self-articulating process verging on the creative, as Bergson, Teilhard, Dobzhansky and others saw it. In such circumstances we must rely on our deepest intuitions.

The lenses of science are wonderful. But change the lenses, and you change the perspective. Science has often changed its lenses. In such circumstances we cannot expect an ultimate perspective to come from science.[3]

Our deepest intuition informs us that we are a form of life that incorporates all previous forms of life. We resonate with other forms of life. We empathize with earlier forms of life because we have incorporated them into our structures. We are aware of the genius of life because we feel it in our bones, blood and flesh; in our deepest intuitions. We cannot validate our perception of the genius of life by scientific concepts; nor do we feel obliged to do so. This sense of the genius of life, which we all behold, informs us that Teilhard's rendering of evolution is much closer to the truth than the neo-Darwinian rendering of evolution which conceives of it as the blind watchmaker.

When you think of it, the idea of evolution as the blind watchmaker is incomprehensible to human reason, if not absurd. How could something as exquisite as life in all its manifestations be the result of a totally blind force? It makes no sense. The whole metaphor of the blind watchmaker as an attempted elucidation of the process behind evolution appears to be so misconceived as to be offensive to reason. At least this is what our deepest instinct tells us. We shall do well to listen to it because it is a good advisor.

Yet some respectable scientists are so enamoured of the metaphor that they write whole books on it. Richard Dawkins published *The Blind Watchmaker* in 1986.[4] And what a strange book it is! It very skilfully manipulates the available evidence to fit it into the pre-established thesis, namely, that evolution is the blind watchmaker. Dawkins' approach is exemplary in its power of selection and also its power of omission. Teilhard's name is not mentioned even once! It is very strange indeed that one can venture to write a scholarly book on evolution at large at the end of the twentieth century and not discuss Teilhard in some depth. As a result, Dawkins' book reads more like an ideological manifesto than an impartial scholarly treatise.

Dawkins' book is one of many. The chasm is still deep between the narrow Darwinian (or neo-Darwinian) vision of evolution and the creative vision of evolution, in which it transforms matter into spirit. We have to bridge this chasm somehow.

By its inner imperative, the origin of which we do not know, evolution has consistently been trying to make something first of matter, then of life, then the intelligence it has created. For we live in an intelligent universe.

Now when looked at through the spectacles of the 'blind watchmaker' the genius of life is a fluke and an aberration. And so is the phenomenon of man. Neo-Darwinism can be justly called a theory of *evolution* if and when it explains satisfactorily the phenomenon of man, the phenomenon of culture, the phenomenon of religion, the phenomenon of spirituality, the phenomenon of matter becoming spirit – without explaining these phenomena away; otherwise it is only a limited theory of mutation within *some* evolutionary cycles.

2. Is gradualism an ideology or a scientific theory?

What about the gradualist-punctualist controversy? Has evolution been proceeding smoothly by small imperceptible tiny steps? Or has its development been marked by discontinuities and leaps? But who cares? Especially as so often the dispute is merely verbal: the same piece of evidence is seen by some as evidence of the gradualist nature of evolution, by others as evidence of discontinuities and qualitative changes.

It has never been resolved what counts as a gradualist change and what should be considered as a punctuated change.[5] Obviously for determined gradualists nothing counts as a punctuated change for they preclude any possibility of such a change, and strenuously argue that what *appears* to be a discontinuity, a leap of a qualitative nature, was in fact a gradual change – if we take into account the long stretches of time in which it took place. Since every event that occurs in evolution takes such a long time, each can be considered gradualist in nature. The argument is logically right. But it is a barren argument, and a question-begging one: gradualism assumes from the start that everything that happens in evolution happens by small, imperceptible, incremental steps. In this scenario, whatever leaps and discontinuities we come across are explained away.

We could indeed ignore the whole problem by saying: who cares whether the main modus of evolution is gradualism or punctualism as long as it delivers its wondrous works? Yet behind the superficial semantic disagreements there lie some deeper and more important issues.

We shall first notice that the very problem, gradualism vs punctualism, is not a scientific problem but an epistemological one. It cannot be resolved within the domain of science proper because we cannot scientifically determine what is the right meaning of gradualism and of punctualism, and what counts as appropriate *evidence* for each. The problems of meaning and of evidence are epistemological problems. These problems belong to the domain of the theory of knowledge.

Let us be more specific. Neo-Darwinism cannot claim that it has established gradualism on a scientific basis. For gradualism as an idea is outside science; it is an epistemological category as it pertains to the order of knowledge. Science is, by and large, powerless in establishing (in the strict scientific sense) the basic epistemological and metaphysical categories – for they precede science and its practice.

Let us move to more interesting issues underlying the controversy of gradualism-punctualism. One obvious point must be granted. No one denies that gradualism has been part of the modus of evolution. Many changes in evolution have indeed been small, imperceptible, gradual. But this is not the point. The point is rather whether there was some other kind of change which was really most important for making evolution move forward. What we are asking is the following question: how should we look at those changes in evolution which represent the process of *transcendence*, at the end of which some new quality, some new sensitivity, some new form of life is created? These are the non-trivial changes through which the miracle of life is manifested.[6]

There are some thinkers who are unimpressed by the gradualist theory of evolution and adamantly contend that evolution could not have produced new significant variations by just 'tinkering' and making minute steps. To this class belongs the Nobel Laureate Albert Szent-Gyorgyi. He argues that it is quite inconceivable, and in fact absurd, to suggest that an intricate whole such as a living organism could be radically improved or qualitatively changed by random mutation of one link. Would it be possible to improve a Swiss watch by bending one of its wheels or axes, Szent-Gyorgyi asks. 'No!' he responds. He clinches his argument by insisting: to get a better watch, you must change all the wheels simultaneously to make a good fit again.

Another Nobel Laureate, Ilya Prigogine, holds a very similar view. Prigogine has absorbed the import of Teilhard. For him, to understand the nature of evolution is to understand the nature of its complexities. These complexities are stable but only up to a point. Open systems, Prigogine claims, are in a dynamic equilibrium which we could perceive as flowing wholeness. However, there exists an evolutionary stress, which constantly impinges on these flowing wholenesses. When organisms and other open systems cannot take evolutionary pressure (and other forms of pressure) any more, they do not collapse and disintegrate. Most of them, at least the tenacious ones, *reintegrate on a new level of complexity*. This new level is one which is more coherent and more resilient. This process of partial disintegration and then reintegration is uniquely expressed by the idea of *dissipative structures* which is a concept specific to the Prigogine system.[7] This whole process can be seen as *life devouring entropy*.

Teilhard, Szent-Gyorgyi and Prigogine may still be in a numerical minority in our age dominated by the metaphysics of Newtonian science. But the tradition they represent is ancient and noble. This is the tradition of Heraclitus, the tradition of *becoming*, the tradition which was pushed to the margin by Plato's metaphysics of being, but one which was never eliminated from Western thought. This is incidentally the tradition of the Dancing Shiva – of the cosmos conceived in a perpetual state of *significant* change.

Let us look at other pieces of evidence which point out that discontinuous changes are in the nature of the evolving universe. Take the beginning of the universe and the Big Bang itself. This was not a gradualist change! I hope we all agree that at the outset of our universe there was a monstrous convulsive change. The universe started with a magnificent explosion, not through small tinkering changes.

Let us consider the other end of the spectrum – the phenomenon of human life. There is a great deal of plodding and many small changes in our life. But what makes life significant, within the compass of the individual life and within the compass of whole cultures, are those singular leaps, those discontinuities, those qualitative changes, things out of the ordinary when we creatively negate the plodding gradualism and soar on the wings of imagination. We know indubitably that in such moments of delight we have abandoned plodding gradualism. We also know that such moments are singularly important for the life of individuals and for the life of cultures. It is at such moments that real creative change occurs. At such moments real transcendence takes place.

Given the turbulent beginning of the universe on the one hand and the wonderful discontinuities in human life on the other (including the significant discontinuities in the development of science)[8], we have ample evidence in front of our eyes that the universe has developed in a discontinuous way. Heraclitus and other dialecticians were right!

Why do some people so tenaciously hold to the gradualist theory, why is it so important to them? We are changing the focus of our inquiry – from the mode of operation of the cosmos to the mode of operation of some scientists' minds in present times. Anticipating the conclusion, we may say in the simplest possible way: the issue of gradualism and the whole spectacle of neo-Darwinism is much less a scientific issue than a religious issue.

Gradualists and neo-Darwinists are afraid of punctualism because in their opinion it is too close to creationism, indeed may be considered as a form of creationism, broadly conceived. If we allow punctualism, we may inadvertently allow religion and God to enter through the back door of evolution. Such is the fear, although never explicitly expressed.

By and large neo-Darwinists and gradualists are secular humanists; some are devout atheists. Through their views on evolution they defend the materialist world-view, sometimes overtly, as with Monod's *Chance and Necessity* (1971), and sometimes covertly, as with Dawkins' *The Blind Watchmaker*. Deep down in their souls the neo-Darwinians think that gradualism is more scientific than punctualism because it bars the divine intervention from the realm of evolution and the universe at large. So at bottom the debate is ideological and religious rather than scientific.

The main issue is often veiled. But basically it is the old issue of science vs religion; or gradualism vs the inexplicable intervention of the forces that are beyond the power of explanation through human reason and science.

When Darwin published *The Origin of Species*, Karl Marx hailed it as an extension of the materialist view of the world. In his enthusiasm for Darwin, Marx wanted to dedicate *Das Kapital* to him. Darwin politely declined. But there was no question in the minds of materialists and atheists that Darwinism was the water on their mill.

For a century or so, Darwinism and then neo-Darwinism have served as an ideological adjunct of aggressive materialism, atheism and agnosticism. Now gradualism (although in a veiled form) serves the same function: it is a sophisticated form of the defence of the positivist-mechanistic-scientific world-view; and, more often than not, a defence of the secularist and atheist positions. *This is the theological kernel of the gradualist theory of evolution.*

To pit science against religion now is old hat. To regard as unscientific the view of evolution that considers it to be endowed with a creative vector is an old-fashioned dogma. There is no reason why we should not acknowledge that *evolution is both natural and divine*. Only an old-fashioned materialist will shrink from recognizing the awesome beauty and in a sense the divinity of this extraordinarily complex and mysterious cosmos.

Natural divinity is our key concept. In this framework evolution can be recognized as part of a divinizing process – unfolding the layers upon layers of sensitivities through which we can not only articulate the cosmos and ourselves, but through which we also make the cosmos more and more meaningful and ultimately sacred – without at the same time invoking old-fashioned ideas of religion and God.

Willis Harman has argued that we cannot prove as true or false those structures which we call world-views or cosmologies or metaphysics. They are to be assessed not in terms of truth and falsity but in terms of how they serve human ends. It is by their fruit that you judge them. We are at liberty to choose those metaphysical systems that give more support to our total strivings over those which give little. Harman writes:

It is futile to seek through research to answer the question 'What metaphysic is correct?' Research findings cannot test or 'prove' metaphysics. The basic reason is that *the research methodology itself grows out of a metaphysics*, so the research tends to lead us full-circle, back to that metaphysics.

... *Ultimately, each of us bets our life on some picture of reality*, recognizing (perhaps) that in a scientific sense at least, we can never *know*. What is the best way to make that bet?

The Roman Catholic scholar Père A. G. Poulain gave three tests for transcendental experience, which will suffice to test the choice of metaphysics: (1) Does it lead to sound ethical and moral values, to wholesome behavior and attitudes? (2) Is it in accord with the best of tradition – with the deepest wisdom of human experience down through the ages? (3) Does it feel deeply, intuitively 'right' – and does it continue to feel so as time goes on?

We seem to be living at a time in history when vast numbers of individuals are making that choice – and betting their lives – in a way that in the end amounts to a new choice for society.[9]

In the same sense we are at liberty to choose among various views of evolution. I therefore propose that we choose the view of evolution that makes intelligible the whole evolving cosmos, including our place in it, especially that makes sense of human strivings and human meaning, and not the one that makes us *cosmic plodders*, and that reduces the meaning of human life to insignificant dust.

3. The thesis of simplicity/comprehension

To return to Teilhard. The specific focus of his theory of evolution and one of the most original insights in his thesis is his idea of complexity/consciousness. As evolution unfolds the complexity of organisms grows. As complexity increases so also *consciousness increases*. This is an extremely simple and, at the same time, a very far-reaching idea.

The more complex the system, the more performance it is capable of, and therefore the more potential it contains. Thus *complexity emerges as the crucial concept of evolution* – the hidden spring that guides the process of growth; as well as the overall concept that enables us to understand the unfolding of evolution.

The story of evolution, according to Teilhard's complexity/consciousness thesis, is the metamorphosis from the simple to the more complex, and the more complex still; from the first atoms of hydrogen to molecules, to fish, to mammals; from the dim consciousness of the amoeba to the consciousness of birds and self-consciousness of man. This story is beautiful and compelling. But it is essentially incomplete.

Teilhard's reconstruction assumes that there is only one process: that of building up ontological complexity, the complexity of the world out there. Only the ontological dimension is present in Teilhard's idea of complexity. The epistemological dimension (how the mind receives and comprehends this complexity) is missing.

From our earliest discussion it follows that whatever complexity we attribute to 'the real world', it is complexity as received and conceived by our mind. Complexity is an attribute of our understanding. What is complex and what is

Fig. 1 *Evolution with uninterrupted growth of complexity*

simple is a very intricate question. *Nothing is complex by itself but only through the intervention of our mind.*

If the story of evolution were an uninterrupted growth of complexity in the ontological sense, sooner or later this complexity would grow to such a degree that it would be beyond the comprehension of mind, and the world would appear to us as utter chaos (see Fig. 1).

Yet this does not happen. We have the capacity to command immense complexities through simple patterns of our understanding. Why? Because the mind imposes its epistemological order on those otherwise unruly complexities. The mind intervenes and subdues these complexities to the imperatives of its understanding. To understand, as we stated in chapter 3 section 4, is to simplify.

Now the mind is not a set of patterns imposed from the outside on the sea of complexities. The sea and the sailor are one. Whatever complexities or simplicities we perceive out there, the order of the mind is built into them.

We are now ready to complete Teilhard's picture by introducing *the thesis of simplicity/comprehension*. We can express our thesis in ancient Greek terms: Logos is continually organizing the chaotic cosmos. We are back to some insights of the Greeks.

With the emergence of the self-conscious mind, which is creating knowledge as the vehicle of its understanding, the story of complexity/consciousness acquires a new meaning, for it is continually punctuated by the stages of simplicity/comprehension. As we concluded in the preceding chapter, the human mind cannot cope with too many and too intricate complexities. For this reason the mind continually imposes its patterns of simplified understanding. Logos imposes itself on the unruly cosmos. This leads to what I call the metamorphosis of reality.

Thus, the ontological complexity is not independent of mind. In actuality we witness two parallel orders: the ontological order (the order of reality) and the epistemological order (the order of the mind). Complexity on the ontological level and simplicity on the level of our understanding (on the level of the mind) are inseparable companions. We always simplify, in order to understand. Understanding *is* simplifying. Human knowledge represents the patterns of simplicity through which the extraordinary richness of the universe is digested by the human mind.

We are back to the spiral of understanding fitting the walls of the cosmos. We are back to the conception of the cosmos delineated by the spiral of understanding. The dialectics of complexity/simplicity is the reciprocal dialogue between the walls of the cosmos and the spiral of understanding.

When the complexity of the ontological order becomes unmanageable, the mind 'simplifies' reality by imposing a new order on it. A new form of logos is imposed on the

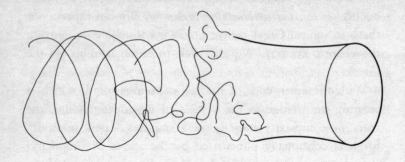

Fig. 2 *When knowledge becomes too complex, the mind imposes a new logos*

unmanageable cosmos. This is what happened around the sixth century BC in ancient Greece, when the mythological conception of reality gave way to a rational conception of reality. A new logos emerged. As I shall argue, this was not a unique event in the history of Western thought but a part of the pattern that was to recur over and over again.

The important point to bear in mind is that the order of the mind continuously shadows the order of reality, and vice versa. At those periods when our knowledge becomes too complex, the mind imposes a new logos on past complexities (see Fig. 2).

To understand this diagram fully we need to remind ourselves that the mind never conceives of bits of reality independent of each other. We always comprehend in large patterns. These patterns are known as cultures, systems of philosophy, systems of beliefs, or the architecture of the individual mind. They render reality in specific ways. This rendering, as we remember, should really be called *realitying*: transforming reality while comprehending it.

We *reality* in specific patterns. These patterns are usually large. We could use the term *paradigm*, although it is an abused term. *Realitying*, or *reality-making*, occurs within paradigms.

When a radically new insight appears, then the walls of the cosmos are ruffled; the surface of the paradigm is disturbed. In some periods of history the new insights are so numerous and so profound in their implications that the entire walls of the cosmos tremble; sometimes they fall down; the paradigm is shattered. At such periods a civilization or a culture collapses and has to be reconstructed.

The collapse of a culture invariably means the collapse of its spiral of understanding and the walls of its cosmos. Let us recapitulate. The spiral of understanding is continually changing. Most of the time it is changing gradually – by accommodating new insights into its existing structure. Sometimes it changes fundamentally, and at such times a new vision of the cosmos emerges. Simultaneously, new ways of looking at it and thinking about it manifest themselves. In the next chapter we shall retrace the major cycles of Western civilization and show how simultaneously we changed our cosmos and our logos at least four times.

What we now witness with regard to Western industrial civilization is at least a partial collapse of its spiral of understanding – some would contend a total collapse – and the corresponding collapse of the walls of its cosmos. It is a serious business. We have tried to patch our spiral of understanding (based on the Newtonian-mechanistic paradigm) in so many ways. It simply does not work. We have to realize clearly that what we are looking for is not only an alternative to hi-tech-based medicine, or an alternative to our atomistic objectifying thinking – but an alternative to our entire spiral of understanding, an alternative to our entire conception of the cosmos.

We are at a seminal juncture of history at which we

attempt to create a new reality. We strive to construct a new spiral of understanding for the whole culture so that our *reality*-making can become compassionate, gentle, cooperative, creative and based on the ideals of solidarity – with all living creatures – rather than on the ideals of selfish exploitation. This is not the description of a new utopia but a specific epistemological programme which will become a reality if we choose it.

Our reality is at the mercy of mind. Our mind is directed and guided by our will and our higher aspirations. Mind in the universe of becoming simply means that we must transcend whatever station we have attained, whatever goal we have reached, whatever spiritual level we have elevated ourselves to. Only then do we do justice to our evolutionary potential, to our cosmic potential, to our divine potential.

What we have said about the mind of the species applies directly to the individual mind – yours and mine. We are guided and conditioned by our respective spirals of understanding which grow and evolve if we grow and evolve. And conversely, when our spiral of understanding grows and evolves, we grow and evolve.

The spiral of individual understanding should not be limited to our intellectual capacities, nor to our abstract knowledge. This spiral includes all the sensitivities we incorporate into the structure of our being, all our spiritual heritage. The spiral is the essence of our being.

Our individual spirals of understanding are as susceptible to influences and changes as is the spiral of understanding of the whole culture, and even more so. Our individual spiral is sometimes inspired by wonderful new insights. However, sometimes we are weary of new insights for the more radical and beautiful the insight, the deeper inner reconstruction it requires. These reconstructions may be joyous – when we are ascending to new spiritual heights. These insights may be painful and agonizing – when we realize that our well-constructed cosmos is disintegrating.

As with entire cultures and systems of knowledge, so with individual spirals of understanding – they may crumble under the weight of new insights. Our universe is then literally in pieces. A deep existential crisis follows. This is not only a crisis of identity but something much deeper: the scaffoldings of our being are falling apart. This means that our entire life needs to be reconstructed, which is never easy, sometimes impossible.

Summary

With the emergence of the self-conscious mind, which creates knowledge as the vehicle of its understanding, the story of complexity/consciousness is punctuated by the stages of simplicity/comprehension. The thesis of simplicity/comprehension is the missing dimension of Teilhard's story of complexity. The human mind cannot cope with too many complexities, especially with infinite complexity. If the cosmos is infinitely complex, and there is no reason to assume that it isn't, the mind does not have the capacity to deal with that complexity. Thus it must simplify – in order to comprehend. Understanding is simplifying.

Every act of understanding is an act of simplification. Specific systems of knowledge are specific patterns of simplification – according to the prevailing views of a given culture and in congruence with the level of articulation a given culture has attained.

All knowledge is species-specific. All knowledge is culture-bound. It was a mistake, and a great presumption, on the part of science to assume that it represents universal knowledge for all cultures and for all times.

In our actual encounter with the cosmos, we are not just its passive observers. The cosmos is continually transforming itself, and so are we. The power of the creative mind signifies the act of logos imposing itself on the cosmos, and the combination of the two results in what we call human knowledge of the world. The role of logos in controlling unruly cosmos is of significance second to none. Without logos, cosmos would be one incoherent mass of confusion – if it existed at all. 'No mind, no world' (Parmenides).

Mind in the universe of becoming means that we must transcend whatever level we have attained. Only then do we do justice to our evolutionary potential, to our cosmic potential, to our divine potential.

Our deepest intuition informs us that we are a form of life that incorporates all previous forms of life. This intuition informs us that Teilhard's rendering of evolution is much closer to the truth than the neo-Darwinian rendering of evolution which can only conceive of its magnificent panorama through the stupid metaphor of the blind watchmaker.

Gradualism as a theory of evolution may be more an expression of an ideological (or even a theological) position than a scientific one. Gradualism is an ingenious way of using evolution to safeguard the old-fashioned mechanistic-secular-atheistic world-view. To pit science against religion at the present time is deeply to misunderstand the essence of both science and religion.

CHAPTER 5

The Four Great Cycles of the Western Mind

1. Recapitulating our position

The theory of the participatory mind we have thus far developed is composed of at least five distinctive but interconnected components:

(1) The theory of sensitivities.

(2) The theory of the three minds.

(3) Noetic Monism.

(4) The theory of the spiral of understanding as filling the walls of the cosmos.

(5) The thesis of simplicity/comprehension.

(*1*) *The theory of sensitivities.* We receive reality by creatively unfolding it through the power of our sensitivities. The organism receives from reality as much as it puts into it. The encounter of living forms with reality is a relentless process of articulation. Articulation is a modus of our being, a code for deciphering reality, for co-creating with it. *All creation is articulation.* The art of elucidation and of explanation is the art of articulation. Articulation can be thus seen as an instrument of knowledge, thus an epistemological category: it marks the transition from non-being to being. More specifically, articulation is the vital process through which the world acquires its shape. *The shape of the world is acquired through a distinctive articulation.* All epistemology owes its existence to the power of articulation.

Our knowledge acquires its distinctive shapes and its specific categories because of the distinctive modes of our articulation. All categories of knowledge, all distinctions and nuances we make within our epistemologies, and within language conceived as an illuminator of reality, are forms and modes of articulation.

We can distinguish primary and secondary sensations. We can distinguish speech acts (Austin)[1] from mere descriptions of language. We can draw the distinction between the analytic and the synthetic. Yet we must remember that all these different distinctions are different forms of articulation of language and then of reality. The distinction between primary and secondary sensations is not in the sensations themselves. The distinction between the analytic and the synthetic is not in the language as such. All these distinctions are products of human ingenuity, specific forms of ordering language and then of the world. All orders are human orders. So are the forms of articulation within knowledge and within the world.

In this scheme of things sensitivities acquire the status of epistemological entities. They are exactly those forms and moulds through which reality acquires specific shapes and dimensions. The fluidity of sensitivities is a fact of life. We adjust to changes in sensitivities in a natural, almost automatic, homeostatic way. Sensitivities prestructure our perception and reception of reality. Whatever comes our way is filtered through sensitivities. This is the first epistemological transformation, even if the results of this filtering cannot be expressed linguistically. Then there is the second epistemological transformation – through the filters of our languages: whatever our sensitivities have elicited is now processed through language and through accepted categories of knowledge.

Sensitivities thus can work on a prelinguistic level. When this occurs, there is an intercourse with reality without linguistic forms. Yet often we *adjust* our sensitivities to the moulds of language. Then we usually simplify the structure of our sensitivities. For language is a great simplifier.

Now, if the structure of our language is rigidly conceived, if the accepted language is brittle and exclusive, limited to cognitive categories of empiricism,[2] then we brutally amputate the flux and web of oncoming sensitivities and out of the prolific flowering let in only prestructured aspects. If, on the other hand, we desire to express the flux, then we are compelled to invent new categories (and perhaps a new language) – so that the officially accepted language does not do violence to the richness of the flux. This is what Whitehead did in his 'process' philosophy. He had to invent terms and categories to express reality as a process.

The road to Damascus is fraught with difficulties. If we are so stringent in our logical demands that we want to consider as valid only knowledge that can be formulated in sharp, intersubjective, cognitive terms – then we *may* do so. We have done so. Various forms of empiricist epistemology are examplars of this form of articulating reality.

Each system of knowledge is only a specific form of articulation. No form of articulation was God-given. No form of articulation is absolute. Each emerges within a certain historic context and changes as the context itself changes. Popper rightly says that all knowledge is tentative. All spirals of understanding and all forms of articulation are historic in character.

Cognitive understanding takes a myriad forms.[3] In one sense, *all sensitivities are forms of cognition*; and all forms of knowledge are packaged sensitivities. We have discussed sensitivities as cognitive entities. We have enlarged the colloquial meaning of the term 'sensitivities' to include all the wonderful instrumentarium of the organism. We have also discussed the term 'articulation' as an epistemological category. We have shown that underlying all epistemologies is the subtle process of articulation via sensitivities; or structuring sensitivities through various processes of articulation. *Articulation* and *sensitivities* are key concepts of the epistemology of becoming and of the participatory mind. All evolution is articulation. All articulation occurs via sensitivities. *As evolution evolves it moves on the spiral of articulation via the vehicle called 'sensitivities'.*

(2) *The theory of the three minds.* We can now clearly see how other components of the participatory mind fit into one comprehensive, dynamic whole. The distinction of the three minds is but a recognition that sensitivities pervade it all – Mind I, Mind II and Mind III (which is reality itself); also an acknowledgement that the mind cannot be limited to the abstract coconut which does the computation and other sorts of abstract and analytical tasks – for such a limited conception of mind is a travesty of our understanding of what mind is and what it does. Mind I and Mind II are in a continuous dialogue with each other; they are one continuous mind. The combined Mind I and Mind II dialogue with Mind III. The result of this dialogue is *reality-making* – receiving reality as a continuous process of transformation.

Thus we have connected the concept of sensitivities with reality via the three minds. The three minds structure is one that elucidates the meaning of sensitivities and the meaning of reality. Thus presented, the three minds appear to be a structure in between the sensitivities and reality – the bridge connecting the two (logos). Conceptually we can *think* of the three minds in this way. In reality all is interconnected. Each of the components is inherently woven into the same structure, or rather into the same process. This leads us directly to the recognition of Noetic Monism, or New Advaita (discussed in section 5 of chapter 1).

(3) *Noetic Monism*. Seen in a proper context, Noetic Monism is a natural consequence of the combined theories of sensitivities and the three minds. Reality is not to be denied. It is not Maya. But it is not to be asserted as something obvious, in a naïve naturalistic way. Our eyes can see but they are always programmed; they see what they are programmed to see. Our vision is always 'contaminated'. The retina of our eyes is wired with all kinds of theories. Our eye has been conditioned by the experience of the species, by the experience of the culture; by our own unique experiences. All reality (more precisely – the process of *reality-making*) is a fusion of our sensitivities and the primordial stuff 'out there'. We have no name for this primordial stuff, for once we have named it, it is no longer primordial; we have processed it, we have fused it with our sensitivities, with our understanding.

Noetic Monism states in ontological terms what the theories of sensitivities and of the three minds assert in epistemological terms. There is one unitary reality. Bodies exist and ideas (spirit) exist. But their respective existences take different forms. What unifies these different forms is the evolutionary matrix: the different stages of evolutionary becoming are responsible for different forms of existence.

What finally makes any existence, and all existence, comprehensible is mind – *nous*. All existence is formed by the mind and through the mind. Mind gives its imprimatur to all existence. What exists is only that which is comprehensible to the mind, that is, prestructured by the mind. *Pure existence is a meaningless term*. 'Being that encompasses all' is beyond words. Whenever we decide to utter the term 'being' or 'Being', in whatever form, we have resigned ourselves to the recognition of mind as shaper and maker of being. Mind shapes all. Mind unites all. *Noetic Monism is the recognition of the quintessentially Noetic nature of all knowledge and of all reality.*

(4) *The spiral of understanding.* Our discussion is incomplete until and unless we explain why different cultures and cosmologies receive reality so differently. Why does reality manifest itself in such a variety of ways? Or why can reality-making occur in such manifold guises? To answer this question we have to apply the idea of the spiral of understanding as fitting exactly the walls of a given cosmos. The spiral of understanding is a specific articulation of a given cosmos. The spiral is not objective in the strict scientific or positivistic sense. It is culture-specific. Within a culture it is intersubjective.

Between the absolute or objective concept of reality, according to which we receive reality in the same way (all of us, at all times, in all cultures), and the relativistic or subjectivist concept of reality, which claims that reality does not exist, or that there are as many realities as minds, there exists a participatory or noetic concept of reality, which is to be conceived as neither absolute nor relativistic but as uniquely woven of the webs of our human participatory understanding. The participatory universe is trans-subjective, for otherwise we could never agree on anything. But it is not objective, let alone absolute. All acts of participation are culture-bound and species-specific. We participate in the way appropriate to our species. Only in this way can we receive reality.

We have to awaken to the meaning and message of evolution. For indeed we should not expect the amoeba and the fox to possess the same sort of knowledge and the same sense of the universe. The knowledge (read *sensitivities*) of the fox is not illusory or relativistic. All foxes have the same structure of understanding. If foxes became lions or mice their structure of understanding would then be different.

The spiral of understanding explains why, on the level of human cultures, our understanding is neither absolute nor subjective. The spiral of understanding is a trans-subjective guardian; it is a historical entity, not a whimsical entity. The spiral of the species is a historical entity, not a whimsical entity. The spiral of culture is inculcated into us. For this reason, within a given culture, we receive reality intersubjectively (we process reality in a very similar way). We are *realitying* in a very similar way. Yet the species changes. And cultures change. Evolution goes on. The spirals of understanding undergo change. Thus the rendering of reality and the shapes of reality change.

(*5*) *The thesis of simplicity/comprehension.* The thesis of simplicity/comprehension is a specific articulation of the spiral of understanding. The thesis attempts to answer such questions as: Why are we not overwhelmed by the growing complexity of the world? Why do systems of knowledge change? What happens during the act of understanding? The thesis of simplicity/comprehension simply reasserts that there are parallel orders running together: complexity/simplicity, cosmos/comprehension, ontology/epistemology, reality/mind.

The mystery of the mind is the mastery of the mind in riding on the crests of extraordinary complexities, the mastery of the mind in simplifying and yet not losing depth, the mastery of the mind in moving across various levels of recalcitrant reality without losing the Ariadne's thread of human meaning.

The five components we have discussed should be seen as

parts of one dynamic structure. We are not creating a number of separate and rigid boxes. Ours is not a linear model, but a systemic one. Moreover, it is a systemic-evolutionary model; and a transformative-systemic-evolutionary model; and a transformative-transcendent-systemic-evolutionary model.

Let us say it clearly: what we have been developing is *a new model of the universe*. Although this description sounds overly ambitious, not to say megalomaniac, we need to have the courage of our visions. The participatory mind is a model of the universe. It not only offers a new conception of mind and of knowledge, but also offers a new conception of the cosmos and of the human person in it. It also redefines the meaning of life and the meaning of cultures; and the meaning of history and the meaning of the future.

No new model of the universe can be complete. Of necessity, it only sketches the main outlines and leaves vast stretches of the territory for others to map out. A new view of the world is invariably the result of many minds working together; it is like a cathedral to which many masons, masters and ordinary workers contribute.

That we need a new model of the universe there can be no doubt. That this model must be comprehensive, participatory, evolutionary and dynamic, there can be no doubt either. The fantastic pace of change in our time, including the changes in the forms of our understanding, makes any static and mechanistic model obsolete from the start.

The models of the past, particularly those based on traditional religions, cannot serve our needs adequately. We must admit that some of these traditional models are marvels of human invention. But we should not expect them to answer the problems of our time. These absolutist models are not suitable candidates for our exploding universe, our exploding knowledge, our new spirals of understanding, if only because these absolutist models refer us back to old spirals of understanding, to old modes of thinking.

In the remaining part of this chapter I shall discuss the transitions of Western civilization during the last twenty-six centuries, and show how the new spiral of understanding, the new organizing logos (different in each case) was responsible for the emergence of a new reality. Behind the tumult of big epochal transitions, invisible to the ordinary human eye, there lurks the all-powerful new logos, which gradually gives a new shape to the multitude of things that were in disarray in old frames of reference.

2. From the tempestuousness of the Homeric heroes to the lucidity of Plato

The spiral of understanding is all-pervading. We can see its manifestations not only in the vicissitudes of particular cultures, not only in the stories of our individual lives but also, and perhaps above all, in the transitions from one culture to another.

We know that even within the limits of Western civilization, we are heirs to various traditions. We trace our ancestry back to the Greek mind, to the organizing power of Greek logos out of which – like Botticelli's Venus emerging from the foam of the sea – we emerged as distinctive Western people. Without any shadow of doubt, our form of reason, our form of perception, our ways of organizing the cosmos are Greek in origin. The Greeks formed our logos, and we in turn have perpetuated their cosmos; with some notable departures, of course.

Let us reconstruct this enthralling story – the story of the emergence of Western mind and its consecutive manifestations;

which is also the story of the spiral of understanding of Western civilization at large: how was it formed, how did it transform itself, and how did it metamorphize that entity which we call visible reality?

The translucent Greek mind did not spring forth as a *deus ex machina*. It is a continuation of the Homeric tradition. Though a continuation, it is also a radical departure. And what a wonderful departure it is!

How did this transformation of the Homeric culture into the Socratic culture occur? How do transformations occur from one culture to another? How does a new cosmology emerge? Is there a rational way of studying the vicissitudes of the ever-changing cosmologies – which are so often at the mercy of the vagaries of different rationalities? We shall attempt to answer these questions by using the model of the participatory mind, and in particular, by analysing the change in the spiral of understanding of the various cultures.

Our main thesis is that *as the logos of a given culture changes so does its cosmos*. The emergence of a radically new culture signifies the emergence of a new logos which organizes the experience of the culture, including its cosmology, in a new way, including the perception of what is visible and what is invisible. The new organizing logos is, in our terms, the new spiral of understanding.

The reality of any people is woven around their spiral of understanding. The spiral provides the foundation, the matrix that defines the reality for us, determines what phenomena are there and how we should perceive them; and also how we should justify them rationally. The ways of looking at reality and of justifying it constitute what we call the rationality of a given cosmology.

There are probably as many different rationalities as there are different cosmologies. Each different cosmology originates the rationality specific to it, originates and develops different ways of justifying its distinctive knowledge and its distinctive ways of looking at reality. The range of perceptions may differ enormously from culture to culture, from cosmology to cosmology. What we perceive is part and parcel of what we assume to be there.

Every culture develops ways of perceiving phenomena which are invisible to the naked eye. In our scientific culture we do not see electrons, yet we 'perceive' them through our instruments, equations and photographic plates – on which they leave the traces of their existence. (How much this existence is independent of us, and how much it is our mind that we see on the plates, is another matter.)

The ancient Greeks of the Homeric period saw in the stories of their lives the visible presence of gods, intervening into their lives from Mount Olympus. The great Greek tragedies are a dramatic manifestation of how the people of the time rationalized their frail condition. In these tragedies myth is rationalized through the vicissitudes of human lives with which we empathize. Greek tragedies present the darker aspects of the human condition. The heroes are exposed to the inexplicable blows of an outrageous fortune. These blows defy human reason. They can only be explained by the continuous intervention of the often capricious gods. On a deeper level, these blows are often seen as the result of negative karma, which came back to haunt people whose ancestors transgressed in a fundamental way.

Let us note, however, that Homeric heroes are rational people. But their rationality is of a different sort from our own. Their rationality was distinctly shaped by their cosmology. Although to us, the continuous interventions of Zeus, Poseidon, Athena, Hera and other gods seem childish if not ridiculous, there was a deep if not sublime reason in the scheme of things whereby gods were allowed to intervene in man's affairs almost daily. The Greeks recognized the fact that we can be masters of our own destiny only up to a point. Beyond this point the world is inscrutable and our lives mysterious. To account for this inscrutable and mysterious human condition, the Greeks invented the intervention of gods – which was a rational act. The gods were responsible for what was otherwise inexplicable and incomprehensible.

There was another scheme at work behind the interventions of the gods. This scheme was related to the law of karma. The Greeks recognized that as you sow, so you shall reap. We gather the fruit of our early doings, even if these occurred in a previous incarnation. If you suffer the slings and arrows of outrageous fortune *now*, it means you have offended some god earlier: you have committed some foul deed for which you are now punished. It is all rational, but in a different sense from that which our rationale allows.

We may say in summary that the underlying form of reasoning of the Homeric people was one based on myths. We shall call this form of reasoning *Mythos*. For a number of centuries the form of rationale based on mythos – and its corresponding cosmology – worked well. Then at the transition from the sixth to the fifth century BC something happened: the Greek *logos* was born. A new luminous light started to be shed from the human mind. New dimensions of reason were discovered. New lucidity was acquired.

In the transition from mythos to logos, we witness the emergence of a radically new form of understanding. As a consequence, extraordinary flowerings in art, philosophy, science, social and political institutions occurred. These new forms of logos exploded on the scene of human history like a supernova. Never in the history of the human mind has the transition from one form of reason to another been more significant and far-reaching. Never before and never since has human thought been capable of exploding with achievements of such staggering dimensions and lasting beauty.

As the result of this transition from mythos to logos, a new sense of reality was created. Indeed, a new reality was created. The lucid logos of the Greeks, of the classical era, created a new cosmology within which things were explained by the natural powers of reason, and without the intervention of gods from Olympus.

The discovery of logos (or was it an invention?) was for the Greeks a completely natural thing. At a certain point, they assumed that the whole world around them was pervaded with *nous*, a coherent and harmonious order of the universe. To be intelligent and rational meant to decipher the meaning of harmony as outlined by all-pervading nous; and then to act out this wonderful harmony through works of art, architecture, and above all philosophy. Logos meant both: understanding the rational structure of nous and acting it out in life through creating ever-new forms expressing the underlying harmony.

We have just retraced one of those momentous transitions in our intellectual history, whereby the new logos created a new cosmos. A new spiral of understanding created new walls of the cosmos. The two, logos and cosmos, go hand in hand, co-define each other. Change one and you will inevitably have changed the other. It is very difficult for any people to behold one form of cosmos and at the same time to use the categories of understanding that belong to (or uniquely fit) another cosmos. If such a thing happens, people live split lives. Their condition is schizophrenic. They know, or at least *feel* deep down, that there is a chasm between the official knowledge given to them and the kind of knowledge that they feel in their bones, in their intuition – which much more adequately explains the world to them. In such a situation the personal logos and the official logos are at odds with each other.

This is just the sort of situation we now face in the West; and on the scale of the whole culture. We are in crisis because we know (within our deeper selves) that the official knowledge, based on the mechanistic metaphor, has collapsed or is collapsing. The whole culture knows instinctively that it has transcended its old paradigm, that our reality is more challenging and more fascinating than we have allowed ourselves to believe. We are in a period of cognitive schizophrenia: the term 'cognitive dissonance' no longer suffices. Our evolving spiral of understanding is piercing through the walls of the restrictive mechanistic cosmos . . . which still tries to hold us back. Where is our solution?

It lies in creating a new form of logos and recreating around it a new reality. Before we attempt to do that, let us retrace some other major steps in our intellectual history.

The lucid logos of classical Greece produced memorable and lasting achievements. It was the light shining through everything the Greek mind touched. Yet around the fifth century AD we witness the exhaustion of the Greek-Roman cycle. The whole civilization collapsed – and with it the Greek form of reason and its distinctive cosmology. A new formation was being born. A different form of reason emerged, ultimately leading to a new cosmology.

Before we analyse this new cycle, let us reflect on the glory of the Greek logos, which was already fading in the third and fourth century AD. We should acknowledge the outstanding achievement of the Roman civilization: it incorporated the Greek logos within its culture and then spread it throughout the Roman Empire as the Pax Romana. It was very fortunate that the conquering heroes, the Romans, allowed themselves to be spiritually conquered by the conquered Greeks. Through this fusion of the Greek logos with Roman power, the logos was carried out to the world at large.

The Roman Empire was resilient, and in many ways magnificent. Yet from the second century onwards, the seed of decay set in. Some mysterious process was going on which we do not understand clearly. It seems that nothing could save the aging giant. Was the fading of the Roman Empire the result of an ecological disaster? Was it because the upper classes drank from lead cups that their minds became dimmed, as they slowly but systematically poisoned themselves? We shall never know. The Roman Empire collapsed in 410, invaded by the Goths and other northern hordes.

In the sixth and seventh centuries, cows grazed on the Capitol Hill of eternal Rome, of so much former splendour and glory. The Roman Empire was no more. A dark period now envelops vast stretches of Western Europe. The seventh and eighth centuries are truly the period of darkness for Western civilization. However, even during this darkness some lights were burning dimly. Very quietly a new form of logos was shaping itself, mainly in the monasteries.

3. From the fall of the Roman Empire to the building of Chartres Cathedral

Out of the ruins of the Roman Empire a new civilization arose. The new logos required about four centuries to consolidate itself. It did so in small monasteries scattered throughout Western Europe, the bearers of the new light, of the new purpose and determination. The monasteries in Ireland should be mentioned especially, particularly as far as the ninth and tenth centuries are concerned. When most of Western Europe was still steeped in darkness, Ireland was already beginning to shine. The Irish Renaissance is still inadequately appreciated for its role in the revival of Western European culture.

From the eleventh century the light was spreading across Western Europe. The haunting sense of doom that was to come with the expectation of the second coming of Christ in the year 1000 released in people an extraordinary amount of energy which has been flowing ever since. The new form of reason, which emerged out of the ruins of the Graeco-Roman logos, I shall call *Theos* – the reason inspired and guided by the monotheistic Judaeo-Christian God. The cosmology that is woven around it emphasizes the transient nature of physical reality and of earthly existence. It is a hierarchical world in which the individual must submit to the preordained plan of God. The individuality of the human person is much less emphasized now than it was at the time of Pericles and Plato. True enough, the medieval troubadours may be seen as the heralds of individuality. But this individuality was very timid. It never tried to change or challenge the existing order. It expressed the longings of the heart, not the yearning for freedom of the mind and soul.

Under the inspiration of the medieval world-view, with God constantly viewing the vicissitudes of the human lot, great new achievements are accomplished; God-inspired energy drives people onward and upward: from the Gregorian chant to Chartres Cathedral, from the poetry of the medieval troubadours to the subtlety of scholastic arguments of the fourteenth-century philosophers, we witness the flowering of a new form of logos, medieval Theos.

To consider the mind of medieval man is to realize at once what a colossal change has occurred within the spiral of understanding. Undoubtedly, some of the elements of antiquity have remained. But basically we witness a different reality, a different conception of man, a different idea of knowledge – within which revelation is considered more important than discursive inquiry.

Medieval man did not consider his way of approaching the world to be irrational. On the contrary, he thought of himself as a pre-eminently rational being. Given his premises about the nature of God, the nature of the world, and the nature of man, his modus of behaviour is both justified and rational. Rationality is always context-bound, is determined by a larger framework from which it is derived.

Medieval man lived in poor economic conditions by our standards. But his world had an exuberance and variety that we often forget. The interconnectedness of human lives in tightly woven communities, and the joy of human interaction, is something we no longer experience. Medieval communities were poor, but they managed to build magnificent cathedrals. Think about our economic riches – what kind of monuments are we going to leave to posterity? What a contrast! Medieval cities and towns competed to build the most magnificent cathedral, and each was a project mobilizing the entire community. It was a celestial competition. To erect a new house of God, and to adorn it with lavish art, the best that was available at the time, were the highest aspirations. People considered themselves the children of God. There was nothing more worthy and sublime they could do than to build a cathedral and the process of building one gave an enormous sense of purpose and coherence.

Coherence is something we should emphasize. For the medieval world was a beautifully ordered cosmos, with everybody knowing his place and serving a purpose. All was woven into a tight hierarchical structure with God at the top, the church and the bishops on the ladder, and lowly peasants at the bottom of it. But it was a celestial ladder. You didn't mind being at the bottom because it was an inevitable order of things. You did not question the order because it was the divine order, ruled by the magnificent, omniscient, omnipotent (and sometimes angry) God. If you started questioning the existing order, you might get burned at the stake. If you got into trouble with the authorities nobody would pity you. Medieval man was convinced it was right to burn the heretics and witches who insulted the all-mighty, all-beneficent God.

In short, the medieval world was completely coherent and it responded to every need of man on every level of human existence. It was almost inconceivable for medieval man to think that things could be otherwise. Again, what a contrast to our own times when all coherence is gone, and when we wistfully wish that there were an order of things on which we could rely and within which we could comfortably settle. *This psychological comfort, of knowing that things were right in heaven and on earth, was a great solace to medieval man.*

Yet eventually the centre began to disintegrate. One contributing cause to the process was the phenomenal growth of the power of the Church. From a merely spiritual seed, the Roman Catholic Church became an empire. Power corrupts. The more power the Church accumulated the more vulnerable it became to corruption. The fifteenth and sixteenth centuries offer an unholy spectacle of the debauchery of monks who have never had it so good (cf. Boccaccio's *Decameron*). Popes appointed their bastard children to important administrative jobs. Anger and ferment slowly brewed. God did not seem to be benign any more, and seemed to have forgotten to look after his children down the ladder. New intellectual difficulties emerged. In the fourteenth century philosophers and theologians began to get lost in the architecture of their theological speculations, and the whole mode of thought became more and more scholastic, more and more remote from people. Proofs of the existence of God became so subtle and obscure that even theologians were lost in their intricacies, spelling bad auguries for a civilization governed ostensibly by the reason of God.

Discontent grew in many different quarters. The Church began to be seen as an oppressor. The slow collapse began. The creative substance of a culture seemed to have exhausted itself. But the Church was no longer only a spiritual guide; it had become a political power. And it fought back for its physical and spiritual survival. It was strong enough to institute the Inquisition and put many to death as enemies of the Church. After the Reformation the Church staged a counter-revolution, the Counter-Reformation. But to no avail. The reactions of the Church produced counter-reactions. Theos as the organizing logos was dying. A new logos began to emerge. Needless to say, having been in power for so many centuries, and having spread to every corner of the Western world — there was a church in every poorest hamlet — the Church could put up considerable resistance, and the process of atrophy and dissolution was long drawn out.

It was not until the seventeenth and eighteenth centuries that a new civilization emerged, which was to change the entire spiral of understanding and indeed the very surface of the globe: the mechanistic civilization, which would give rise to the technological civilization. Before considering this cycle in detail, however, and its prelude the Renaissance, we shall briefly summarize the medieval cycle.

How should we look at medieval culture in toto? Every civilization is entitled to be judged by its greatest accomplishments. Chartres Cathedral is a great achievement not only with reference to medieval culture, but to all human cultures.

It contains a symbolic summation of all that medieval man stood for, longed for and aspired to; it displays the medieval logos superbly articulated. The cathedral is the vertical expression of the mystical longings of medieval man: its outside shapes reach upward to heaven to embrace God, while its exquisite internal geometry leads us back to the Pythagorean mysteries of Forms which cannot be fully comprehended by the rational mind. It is also wonderfully rooted in this world, a massive and palpable structure in which the physicalness of man is augmented. The interior is an unfolding of man's inner world, through its symbols, paintings, sculptures and other icons revealing and explaining the inner purpose of man and of the universe – all reassuringly united.

4. The Renaissance: the civilization that did not make it

Before we describe the mechanistic cycle, let us look at that important interlude, the Renaissance. The Renaissance is an intriguing and fascinating period in the history of the West, one of an extraordinary outburst and exuberance, a period of liberation which was, however, incomplete – it did not lead to a new path, a new civilization. For all its novelty, courage and exuberance, the Renaissance was an ephemeral flower. It did not create a new blueprint, a new logos around which a new cosmos could be woven, a new civilization developed. This was only to happen in the seventeenth century, when the Renaissance was spent.

Why did the Renaissance not make it? This may be considered an improper, even a silly question. The Renaissance did what it meant to do – it opened up new vistas on the physical world, and on the nature of man. In this respect its achievements are not to be questioned. The Renaissance was a profound awakening.

It was, first, the awakening of the senses. With Giotto we begin to *see* the world differently. Painters, and then ordinary people, rediscovered the lushness, beauty and exuberance of nature. Giotto was a revolutionary. To begin to perceive in a new way is a major accomplishment. Every new act of vision requires courage for its expression. For this expression invariably goes against the grain of established dogmas and canons.

After Giotto came Botticelli and Leonardo da Vinci. The period of the rediscovery of nature was intoxicating indeed. In an almost somnambulistic trance, Renaissance artists rendered nature in such compelling forms that these forms delight us five centuries later. The scenes of the mortification of the flesh, with their formal sterility and concentration on purely religious significance, are left behind. Clearly, a new spiral of understanding is guiding the new perception. This spiral is no longer God-centred, Theos-dominated. It is a man-centred spiral; often senses-centred, but not in a narrow, hedonistic way. The senses are the windows on the glory of nature and the world at large. Thus Leonardo da Vinci on 'learning from the objects of nature'.

The painter will produce pictures of little merit if he takes the works of others as his standard; but if he will apply himself to learn from the objects of nature he will produce good results. This we see was the case with the painters who came after the time of the Romans, for they continually imitated each other, and from age to age their art steadily declined.

After these came Giotto the Florentine, and he – reared in mountain solitudes, inhabited only by goats and such-like beasts – turning straight from nature to his art, began to draw on the rocks the movements of the goats which he was tending, and so began to draw the figures of all the animals which were to be found in the country, in such a way that after much study he not only surpassed the masters of his own time but all those of many preceding centuries. After him art again declined, because all were imitating paintings already done; and so for centuries it continued to decline until such time as Tommaso the Florentine, nicknamed Masaccio, showed by the perfection of his work how those who took as their standard anything other than nature, the supreme guide of all the masters, were wearying themselves in vain.[4]

The whole reads innocuously, almost as commonplace. Yet it contains its own mythology. 'Learning directly from the objects of nature' is a loaded phrase, a myth.

William Blake said: 'No man of Sense ever supposes that copying from Nature is the Art of Painting; if Art is no more than this, it is no better than any other Manual Labour; anybody may do it, and the fool often will do it best as it is a work of no mind.' And Cézanne: 'I have not tried to reproduce Nature: I have represented it.' And Degas: 'The ballet-girl is merely a pretext for the design.' And Picasso: 'I paint what I think, not what I see.' In each case there is a different understanding of what art is about, there is a different spiral of understanding in action which guides the perception and the whole artistic process. Blake and Picasso are splendidly aware that their perception is guided by their minds. Others are less aware. Leonardo and other Renaissance painters did not *just* discover nature and render it as it was. They *impregnated* nature with their dreams and visions. They brought sanctity to nature. Renaissance landscapes are alive precisely because they are infused with *spiritual energy*. Beneath the visible currents of the sensuous forms of life, a deep process of *re-sacralization* of nature is going on.

The Renaissance was pagan in many ways. But this neo-paganism was carefully concealed. Often the religious scenes, which the Church had to approve, were a pretext for worshipping nature. The deep spirituality pervades man's entire approach to nature. It is not the power to observe nature that is so important but *the power to worship nature*. When this power is gone, in subsequent centuries, the power of rendering nature through painting diminishes. For this reason we today could never match the beauty and mystery of the Renaissance landscapes – we are not 'heathen' enough to do so.

The Renaissance was a period of transition, belonging to three different periods. First, it nostalgically looked back to antiquity and wanted to resurrect it in its own shapes. Secondly, it was deeply steeped in the magma of medieval thought and practice, although on the surface it seemed to have transcended it. Thirdly, it was already anticipating the new shapes of man and of the world through which man would challenge his entire theocentric destiny and come to consider himself the master of his own destiny.

The *ethos* of the Renaissance was not continued into the next centuries. After a period of creative exuberance there comes a period of tedious plodding. After the elevation of man to demi-god (Renaissance man is *Homo Creator*), we witness the arrival of dwarfed conceptions of man: *Homo aggressivus* (Hobbes: '*homo homini lupus est*') and *Homo economicus* (Adam Smith). *Homo aggressivus* and *Homo economicus* combined spell out a shrunken vision of man. This shrunken vision is our inheritance from the seventeenth and eighteenth centuries, not from the Renaissance. The whole ethos of mechanistic and then of industrial civilization is so different from that of the Renaissance that it is more correct to talk about the denial of the Renaissance than its continuation.

In summary, the Renaissance did not produce its corresponding form of logos which could have given birth to a new civilizational cycle. The Renaissance was not cumulative. It expressed and exhausted itself in spectacular individual, usually artistic, achievements. You cannot build on Mona Lisa, you cannot continue it; it is perfect, finished, complete. Why did the Renaissance fail to produce a new civilizational cycle? Because it concentrated its energies entirely on the perfection of individual, discrete achievements? Or because its conception of 'man as the measure of all things' was too narrow? or because it did not have one unified vision, one over-arching metaphor (like the mechanistic metaphor of the seventeenth century), which would have allowed for a new, cumulative development?

With the exception of Athens in the fifth century BC, there was hardly any period in human history when so many spectacular individual achievements were created as in the Renaissance – to last and inspire, to shine as exemplars of what is possible and what our inner energies can accomplish. Were Renaissance philosophers not good enough, deep enough, original enough to weave their own cosmological tapestries? Or was it too early for them to do so? These are intriguing questions. Perhaps the significant point lies in the nature of Renaissance man as we now see him: his main energies were spent elsewhere – on building magnificent palaces, chiselling sculptures of unsurpassed perfection and power, and simply living and enjoying the realization that man is the measure of all things . . .

5. The engines of Mechanos are beginning to run a new civilization

The seventeenth century is only a continuation of the tumultuous sixteenth. Some major figures who shaped the modern consciousness, such as Francis Bacon and Galileo Galilei, belonged to both centuries. But as we proceed through the seventeenth century, there is a distinctly different flavour in the air. The titanic Renaissance figures disappear. A new sobriety and down-to-earth philosophy prevails.

The result is a new form of logos which I shall call *Mechanos*. Mechanos is a distinctively new way of organizing reality, a distinctively new way of understanding. The basic metaphor is that of a clock-like mechanism. The universe is considered a sort of mechanical clock, moving according to well-defined deterministic laws. To know these laws is to understand nature, and to have the capacity to control it. The system is simple, almost simplistic. With hindsight we know that such a simple schema could not have worked in the long run. Yet it is amazing that it has worked so well for so long – in spite of its naked simplicity. Indeed, the scheme has not only become successful but also terrifyingly powerful.

Is it because of its bloody-minded simplicity that the scheme has become so powerful? Or is Mechanos a malevolent god who gave us power as part of the Faustian bargain? – we enjoy it beyond our capacity to control it and the end will be inevitable doom.

But let us not contemplate images of doom. For the more we engage in imagining pictures of doom, the more surely (in a subtle and not quite explicable way) we bring about that doom – such is the power of the mind. What you most contemplate becomes real.

Francis Bacon (1561–1626) is of course claimed as one of the founders of the modern world-view. But he is as much a Renaissance man as he is the maker of the seventeenth century. He admired the Greeks. But he did not look nostalgically to the past. He looked forward towards the future, and with a great impatience. His utopia is expressed in *The New Atlantis* (1627). His view of knowledge was refreshingly novel; he called for knowledge that can generate. *The conception of knowledge as power was Bacon's distinctive contribution to our new picture of the cosmos.* He emphasized that the knowledge of the ancients was the knowledge of childhood, 'it can speak but it cannot generate,' and 'it is full of words but barren of works.' It can reflect but cannot transform. Bacon wanted and indeed demanded knowledge that generates and transforms (*The Great Instauration*, 1620).

Bacon was actually no builder of a new civilization but rather a visionary who opened up new vistas and in a compelling way made us want to follow those vistas. Galileo (1564–1642) was both a great scientist and a great philosopher. We have to honour his scientific genius, and especially his discovery of the law of falling bodies ($S = \frac{1}{2}gt^2$). But predominantly he was a visionary. He wrote inspiringly that the book of nature is forever open to our gaze, but in order to read it, we have to learn the alphabet in which it is written. It is written in the language of mathematics without which it is virtually impossible to understand a single word of it.

This compelling vision came to dominate the Western mind in times to come, and to such a degree that we finally desired to express everything mathematically, even the nature of love. It is not appreciated what a strange desire it was to be persuaded that the book of nature is written in the language of mathematics, and that we must try to express everything in mathematical terms. The single-minded attempt to express everything in the universe *and* in human life in mathematical terms was a fantasy bordering on phantasmagoria, if not an obsession.

Yet the combined visions of Bacon and Galileo – knowledge is power and it should be expressed in mathematical terms – became the kernel of our new understanding. The pursuit of this vision brought about an immense amount of power which in the end has terrified our wakeful hours.

In the scheme of the new understanding René Descartes (1599–1649) should not be forgotten. He was one of the chief architects of the Western mind. His *cogito ergo sum*, his separation of the body from the mind, and above all his invention of the reductionist method, are hallmarks of a new understanding. Descartes' *Discourse on Method*, a seemingly simple and innocuous little essay, has been immensely important in shaping our analytical and reductionist strategies; it laid the foundation for our atomistic-analytical approach to knowledge and the world. 'Divide and rule' was Descartes' motto: divide every problem into smaller problems, and smaller problems still. And then seek the solution to the big problem by the arithmetic addition of the solutions to the small problems. And *hope* that the meaning and scope of the big problem can be entirely exhausted by subdividing it into smaller problems.

It is worth emphasizing that the reductionist-analytical strategy is based on hope, namely that by going to more elementary levels and reducing large problems to their underpinnings – more elementary components – we can *adequately* understand big problems. Alas, we have discovered that in many cases this is not so. One cannot understand the nature of the cosmos by analysing cosmic dust; nor can analysis of the chemical structure of human bones reveal the nature of human beings.

When we look at historical development, we see that the new mechanistic logos developed at first slowly and rather tenuously. But it was a *cumulative* development. Once it acquired momentum, the unfolding of the mechanistic cosmology was relentless, compelling and fascinating in its inexorable rhythms.

Newton's *Philosophiae naturalis principia mathematica* (The Mathematical Principles of Natural Philosophy) of 1687 was the epitome of the new design of the universe. During the last three centuries we have been sitting at Newton's feet and licking his boots. What Aristotle did for formal logic in the fourth century BC Newton did for our understanding of the physical universe. Aristotle formulated the first outline of formal logic with such a compelling definiteness that for twenty-two centuries the field stagnated as everybody was convinced that Aristotle's was the last word in the field. Only at the end of the eighteenth century with John Venn and Augustin de Morgan did formal logic receive a new lease of life. So it was with Newton's mechanical conception of the universe: it has virtually imprisoned us in a deterministic straitjacket.

But let us not exaggerate. We wanted to be imprisoned. We wanted to share Newton's vision (which Blake called 'Newton's sleep'); and then, alongside Bacon, we wanted knowledge which is power. The rest of the story we know from our own lives. We are all aware that the mechanistic cosmology, via science and technology, has brought about enormous material benefits. But we are also aware of the dark side of the mechanistic cosmology – ecological devastation, human and social fragmentation, spiritual impoverishment.

After a reign of three centuries, the mechanistic cosmology is now collapsing; it has been doing so for the last seventy or eighty years. We have been slow and obtuse in acknowledging the fact, mainly because we have not yet worked out a new logos that would more satisfactorily explain the cosmos. We simply have not worked out a new spiral of understanding, which would be capable of creating a new cosmos for us.

Yet work on the construction of a new cosmology has been going on in many fields for at least a couple of decades. The various alternative movements have been converging around one central axis, *the axis of wholeness* which radically separates the new alternatives from the old mechanistic objectivist approach whose main premise was fragmentation and separation.

Our brisk journey through millennia has attempted to bring out at least three conclusions:

(1) That radical departures from past cosmologies are not only possible but inevitable.

(2) That changes in cosmology almost invariably go hand-in-hand with changes in the prevailing logos.

(3) That we are now in a period of epochal change in which the mechanistic cosmology is slowly giving way to a new evolutionary, holistic cosmology; and that mechanistic reason is giving way to a new logos which I shall call *Evolutionary Telos*.

The new methodology through which the Evolutionary Telos is slowly expressing itself I shall call the *Methodology of Participation*; its corollary is the *Yoga of Participation*, the subject of the next chapter.

Let me now summarize, by means of a picture, the four basic cycles (or cosmologies) of the Western mind, and the corresponding forms of logos that each cycle (cosmology) generated. Each cycle starts vigorously and lucidly, and then becomes more and more complex until its complexities become unmanageable. Instead of illumination we are ensnared in the web of incomprehension. The great knowledge paradox of each cosmology is that each form of logos aims at the ultimate comprehension of reality; instead it delivers us to a bewildering incomprehension. As each logos is pushed to its limits, in the process it destroys its own cosmos: the spiral of understanding (Fig. 1) bursts the walls of the cosmos it was supposed to serve. Such has been the story of the last four great cycles.

Each cycle has been organized, shaped and controlled by its specific form of logos. This logos, which represents the

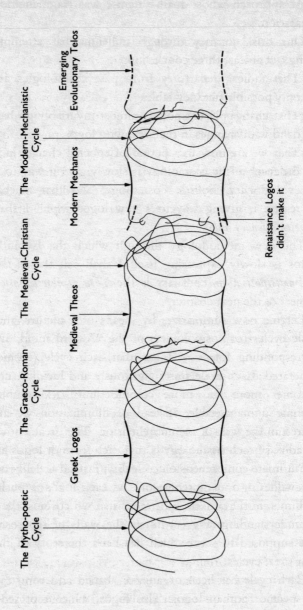

Fig. 1 *The major Western cosmologies*

essential simplification of the unmanageable reality of the previous cycle, is a stunning manifestation of the mind's limitations and of its powers: since it cannot dwell in complexities too intricate, the mind must impose its simplified patterns of understanding.

In brief, the history of Western civilization is the history of growing complexity, as represented by the ontological process of becoming, which, however, is punctuated by the infusion of simplicity, whereby the mind, by imposing a new order on reality, organizes it in a new and simplified way. The epistemological order is superimposed on the ontological order. Indeed, the ontological order simply mirrors the epistemological one.

6. Evolutionary Telos emerging as a new logos

We are now at the beginning of a new cycle. Is it the dawn of a new civilization? Of a new culture? Many would like to think so. Some desperately hope so. Beyond the despair and hope there is the inexorable rhythm of history. Human logos is unfolding, taking up new shapes as it encounters new problems and unprecedented dilemmas.

We should not look at our present situation as one of chaos and confusion, although partly it is. We should, rather, look at our present time from the depth of our spiral of understanding, and see how it is struggling to acquire a new shape in order to render the cosmos in a new shape. It is fascinating indeed to watch how the various pieces of the new cosmos are emerging. It is very likely that the pieces are already fitting together, forming one pattern. However, we are too close to it to discern the coherence of its structure. In the year 2050 or perhaps earlier people will be able to see and understand what is still a mist for us. It will be easy for them to do so with hindsight; the dust of historical events that clouds our present vision will then have settled.

What are the characteristics of the newly emerging spiral of understanding? What is the new shape of the universe we are about to inherit? To begin with, *there is a new sense of the depth of the universe*. Our universe is not only larger in dimensions but it is more exciting, more profound, than it was in the Newtonian era. Einstein was thrilled by the existence of mystery. Another term for this mystery is depth. The depth of the universe is also the depth of our mind. We cannot find new depths in the universe unless we find these new depths in ourselves.

Secondly, *there is a new sense of depth to the human person*. We have been mutilated by past history. We are aware of Auschwitz and Buchenwald. We are still haunted by the possibility of nuclear holocaust. Yet we have acquired a new sense of the beauty of the human condition, especially as we are aware how frail it is. A new sense of meaning and purpose is emerging; and a new sense of spirituality which is not tied to past religions. We are increasingly aware that we live in the participatory universe, which means that a sense of responsibility is thrust upon us, a responsibility so great and joyous as no generation before us has experienced – the responsibility for our own destiny and for the future of the planet.

Thirdly, *we are reclaiming meaning and spirituality as indispensable components of human life and the concept of person*. T. S. Eliot writes: 'Man is man because he can recognize supernatural realities such as truth, obligation, meaning, purpose and validity.' We no longer define the universe as a clock-like mechanism; and we are less inclined to define man as a machine. The attributes that Eliot attaches to the phenomenon of man – truth, purpose, validity, obligation and meaning –

are all aspects of the sphere of human life that can be called meaning at large. Yet another name for this sphere is spirituality. If we add to the sphere of meaning: culture, art, the search for a higher destiny, then we have arrived at spirituality. Indeed, the two spheres merge into each other. Meaning devoid of spirituality is an anaemic entity. Spirituality denotes an enhanced and fulfilled meaning. Within this form of logos, which I call Evolutionary Telos, the human being is defined as an unfolding field of sensitivities organized in patterns of meaning and spirituality.

Fourthly, *wholeness and connectedness are essential characteristics of Evolutionary Telos*. Almost each new paradigm that has emerged during the last thirty years has emphasized the importance of wholeness and connectedness.

Connectedness and wholeness are essential features for reading the book of nature in a new way. It is not the language of mathematics, as Galileo contended, but the language of wholeness in which the book of nature is written. Without understanding the language of wholeness we cannot understand the first thing about the beauty and coherence of nature. Thus wholeness is not only a descriptive term, showing how parts are united within a pattern, it is also an epistemological term. Wholeness and holistic thinking are modes of understanding. They pave the way to a new methodology which I call the *Methodology of Participation* (see chapter 6).

Because of the importance of wholeness and connectedness, many alternatives to the present mechanistic paradigm have been centred around these concepts. There are thus holistic medicine, holistic diet, holistic approaches to the body – by now well accepted and making their own way. On a deeper level, however, there is a holistic approach to life and knowledge which traditional cultures understood very well, but which is difficult to account for in the language of parts, which our language has become. On this issue Gregory Bateson is particularly illuminating.[5] Ecology conceived as the science of interconnected organic wholes has been of great importance in clarifying our understanding of the interconnectedness of all things, and in articulating the importance of holistic, connected thinking. In this sense ecological thinking is a forerunner of all holistic thinking, whatever the field of our endeavour.

Ecology and ecological thinking must be seen not as separate parts of a whole, not as another movement concerned mainly with the environment; but as an essential part of the process of the transformation of consciousness. Ecological thinking writ large becomes participatory integral thinking: thinking in accordance with the inherent laws of the cosmos — even if we do not wish to recognize these laws as absolute in kind. The forerunners of this kind of thinking were Bergson, Teilhard, Aurobindo and Bateson, and Heraclitus and Pythagoras in ancient times.

Fifthly, *we live in an open, non-deterministic universe.* Contrary to the Newtonian design, in which everything is governed by deterministic laws of the mechanistic kind, we now realize how subtle the universe is and how many different kinds of laws it contains. The very very small and the very very large in the universe are not subject to the mechanistic laws of classical science. Nor are the psychic phenomena that underlie the structure of human life. This is not to say that the universe is totally indeterministic and chaotic. The structure of our mind would not allow for that to happen. God does not play dice. True. But the depth of the universe requires a subtlety of the mind much deeper than Newtonian physics permits.

The five components of the new logos are: a new sense of the universe, a new conception of the human person, spirituality and meaning, holism and interconnectedness, openness and non-determinism. These should not be regarded as giving us a complete picture, but only as spelling out the bare bones. They should be considered as integral aspects of the same structure, of the same spiral of understanding which we call Evolutionary Telos.

In our analysis of the new emerging logos we have not mentioned many current endeavours, such as acupuncture and the discovery of non-Western medicine, the interest in and investigation of the paranormal and extrasensory phenomena. When a new culture is being born, all kinds of experiments take place. It is a part of the exuberance of the new. We should maintain a healthy, sceptical balance; not so much embrace the lunatic fringe as tolerate it – as a necessary part of the process of creation.

Our times are not unlike those of the Renaissance. Things are falling apart. But great creative energy is also released. There is a sense of doom. But out of desperation new visions are being born. The individual is liberated. We wonder, though, to what purpose. We must watch that our efforts and undertakings do not become too individualistic – as happened during the Renaissance. We have to conceive of projects that are cumulative in nature. Only in this way can we create a new structure that in the future will be called a new culture.

We are opening up, the cosmos is opening up, evolution is unfolding. Our new spiral of understanding must be par excellence evolutionary. We shall not forget about the past, since it nourishes us continually. The ancient spiritual traditions, Hinduism, Buddhism, Jainism, Sufism, were marvels of human invention. But we cannot solve our problems by attempting to use their spirals of understanding. Our path is *creative transcendence*. Such has been the story of the universe.

Such has been the story of human cultures. Such is our fate.

Summary

The Homeric heroes were rational. But their rationality was of a different sort from ours. Each cosmology engenders its own distinctive rationality. Rationality is derived from the backbone of a given cosmology and it serves it in its turn. There is a wonderful rationality underlying the whole ethos of the Greek culture of archaic times. This rationality is expressed through metaphors, myths and tales rather than in discursive ways. It is powerful and clear, nevertheless.

Around the sixth century BC the whole archaic formation slowly collapsed. The old tales of the universe and the old rationality were gradually replaced. The translucent Greek logos assumed its place in all its splendour. The achievements of this logos are supreme. Not only great temples were created, unsurpassed in their beauty and grandeur, such as the Parthenon and the Erectheion; new systems of thought emerged which were to nourish and inspire the Western mind for the millennia to come.

The lucid logos of classical Greece produced memorable and lasting achievements. It was light shining through everything the Greek mind touched. Yet around the fifth century AD came the exhaustion of the Graeco-Roman cycle, and the whole civilization collapsed. A different form of reason emerged, ultimately leading to a new cosmology. We enter medieval times. The predominant form of reason is one which we call Theos – reason inspired and guided by the monotheistic Judaeo-Christian God. The achievements of the new civilization are copious and splendid in their own right.

A great coherence exists in human and celestial realms, as both are guided and overseen by the benevolent, almighty deity. The Gothic cathedral is a visible symbol of hierarchy, and a central metaphor around which all earthly life is woven. Although medieval civilization was interested primarily in securing eternal salvation for its people, its earthly achievements were considerable. The first universities were established: the Sorbonne, Bologna, Oxford. The mechanical clock which measured time in the villages was a foretaste of great mechanical wonders to come. Medieval rationality differed from our own and that of the Greeks. It would be foolish to maintain that medieval people were irrational because they believed in God. Their God was the safeguard of their rationality. Given their assumptions, their civilization was a beautifully coherent one.

Botticelli's Venus emerging out of the foam of the sea marks the twilight of medieval civilization. The new motto of the Renaissance is: 'Man is the measure of all things.' Despite the creation of marvellous works of art, there is no unifying vision, no new logos which would serve as the foundation for the new cosmos. No new civilizational cycle emerges out of the Renaissance. The spiral of understanding of the Renaissance mind was not distinctive enough, not strong enough, not enduring enough to produce a new outline of the cosmos.

The Renaissance merely represented epicycles over past Greek philosophy.

With the seventeenth century we enter the new cycle of our mechanistic civilization. The organizing new logos I call Mechanos. Starting slowly and inconspicuously, this form of reason creates a new blueprint according to which knowledge is power, the power to transform nature to our advantage. This knowledge should be expressed in mathematical equations. Working out the details of this blueprint, we have

created a terrifying degree of power. The benevolent Mechanos is turning into a malevolent Moloch. The story of the
sorcerer's apprentice is re-emerging in a new context. We have
unleashed powers that we don't know how to turn back. In
enjoying the spectacle of physical powers, we have sadly
reduced ourselves in stature. In atomizing nature, we have
atomized ourselves. We have complete freedom and seeming
mastery over nature and our own lives, yet we are empty
inside and crave meaning, even if it comes from phoney gurus.
Our sterilized rationality has denuded our emotions and our
spiritual life. Amidst the sulphur of toxic dumps, amidst the
pollution of our rivers and our bodies, amidst the poison in
our food and in our minds – we courageously stare at a new
dawn.

The dawn of a new logos, Evolutionary Telos, can be seen
in various places. We are refusing to die with the dying
civilization. The new logos insists on the holistic nature of
life and on the interconnectedness of all there is in the
universe. The new logos is not afraid of mystery and asserts,
along with Einstein, that 'The most beautiful thing we can
experience is the mysterious. It is the source of all true art and
science.' Our new journey is just beginning. We shall need all
our courage, imagination and perseverance to make it a
success. We have no choice whether to continue this journey
or not. It is our evolutionary destiny.

CHAPTER 6

The Methodology of Participation and its Consequences

1. The objective mind and its problems

Ludwig Fleck, the Polish microbiologist and epistemologist, active before World War Two, studied in depth what would be called the making of the scientific mind in the field of microbiology.[1] Fleck noticed that when beginning students are given microscopic sections to observe, at first they are unable to do so. They cannot *see* what is there. On the other hand, they often see what is *not* there. How can this be so? The answer is simple – because all perception, particularly sophisticated forms of perception, requires rigorous training and development.

After a while, all students begin to see (under the microscope) what is there to be seen: specific forms and configurations *according to the patterns established by microbiology*. Students' perception has been sharpened and focused to perceive according to the rules of one specialized discipline; their minds have been sharpened to recognize and identify the phenomena that are important for their discipline.

In brief, microbiological observations require a trained perception, a cast of mind well acquainted with the universe of bacteria and other microbes. This cast of mind is inherently connected with the forms of observation specific to microbiology. At one point it makes sense to say that it is the mind that perceives, not the eye. The mind provides the framework, specific knowledge and specific assumptions for the eye to see. *The mind constitutes the universe which the eye then sees.* Put otherwise: our mind is built into our eyes.

The entire method of scientific objectivity is the training of the mind in a manner very similar to that we find in microbiology. The 'objective attitude' or 'scientific method' attempts to limit the perception of the world to what is assumed by science to be there; and attempts to deny what science's assumptions deny. Objectivity means clinical detachment and dispassionate forms of observation, the forms of perception that atomize phenomena that we investigate. Objectivity assumes that things exist in isolation, that every phenomenon we examine is the universe in itself, independent of larger wholes from which it has been cut out.

Now I want to argue that we have been conditioned by what I call the *Yoga of Objectivity*, which has been relentlessly practised in Western schools and academia. Although the term 'Yoga' may sound strange as applied to the process of imposing the attitude we call 'objectivity' on our minds, it is not ill-conceived.

The Yoga of Objectivity consists of a set of exercises specific to the scientific mind. These exercises are practised over a number of years, sometimes as many as fifteen – from the time pupils go to high schools to the time they complete their PhDs at university. The purpose of these exercises is to see nature and reality *in a selective way*. It takes many years of stringent training (just as it does in any other form of Yoga) before the mind *becomes* detached, objective, analytical, clinical, 'pure'. This frame of mind is seen as essential for dealing with scientific facts and scientific descriptions of reality. And so it is. Why? Because the scientific method has moulded the mind to be its servant. *The scientific view of the world and the objective cast of mind mirror each other*. In the scientific world-view the mind has become a hostage to a selective vision of reality. *The Yoga of Objectivity is a gentle form of lobotomy*.

Consider the mind of a child. It is the 'magical mind', as Joseph Chilton Pearce observes.[2] Children are magical creatures. Their worlds and minds are full of wonders, surprising things of great beauty. Consider the same magical child after fifteen years of schooling in *good* Western schools. What has happened to the magical mind? What has happened to the sparkling imagination? They have become amputated by the relentless training in the Yoga of Objectivity.

The ultimate result of the training of minds in the rigours of objectivity is not only the capacity to deal with facts in a detached and clinical way (we should really put the matter more precisely: it is not only the capacity of the mind to construct facts according to objective prescriptions) but something else. The mind trained in the Yoga of Objectivity over a number of years becomes cold, dry, uncaring; always atomizing, cutting, analysing. This kind of mind has lost the capacity for empathy, compassion, love.

The objective mind – when it begins to dominate the world – creates the atomic family, the atomistic society, the social and individual alienation; for alienation is a peculiar form of detachment. The atomized society and individual alienation (which are merely consequences of detachment) cause in the long run inner tension, frustration, anguish; which then give rise to extreme loneliness, anger and also violence. At least some causes of violence can be traced back to the Yoga of Objectivity, which creates desensitized people: cold, dry, uncaring, lost, anguished, deprived of values and emotions. This is the unwelcome result of the Yoga of Objectivity. The objective mind is so desensitized that it is oblivious of these consequences.

Many have pointed to the undesirable and, in fact, deadly consequences of the relentless pursuit of objectivity. We know the ills. We don't know how to cure them. Or rather we are afraid of throwing the baby out with the bath water. Objectivity is a part of the scientific method. Scientific method is a part of the enterprise of science. Science appears to be such a glorious, great and stupendous invention that we do not dare to question the necessity for its existence. Yet some people do. One of them is Paul Feyerabend, a distinguished philosopher and historian of science. He argues:

It is good to be constantly reminded of the fact that science as we know it today is not inescapable and that we may construct a world in which it plays no role whatever (such a world, I venture to suggest, would be more pleasant than the world we live in today). What better reminder is there than the realization that the choice between theories which are sufficiently general to provide us with a comprehensive world view and which are empirically disconnected may become a matter of taste? That the choice of our basic cosmology may become a matter of taste?[3]

Yet science persists, scientific method persists (although there is no such thing as Popper and his followers have shown[4]), and, above all, the Yoga of Objectivity persists. We have tried to *humanize* science, to blunt the sharp edges of objectivity. But to no avail. The Yoga of Objectivity has infiltrated the world. In the process, it has done great damage to human cultures and individual human lives. We are not ready to admit this for a subtle, if not a perverse reason. We want to be good disciples of objectivity. We want to be 'objective' in our judgement of objectivity. At a deeper level it is objectivity itself that manipulates us and prevents us from seeing it as the real villain.

Where is the solution? Obviously not in abolishing science, its rationality and its methodology – but in creatively transcending them. Science has been dramatically changing during the last fifty years. And so has the rationality of science. We need to be adroit and determined in drawing new epistemo-logical consequences following from these changes.

The science at the cutting edge of the last forty years has been based on a new epistemology – which has not been clearly articulated. This is the epistemology of the new cycle of Western civilization, which I call Evolutionary Telos, discussed in the previous chapter. The overall name of this epistemology is Methodology of Participation.

2. The methodology of participation as superseding the methodology of objectivity

Let us now unfold the hidden layers of the idea of wholeness. Wholeness means that all parts belong together, and that means that they partake in each other. Thus from the central idea that all is connected, that each is a part of the whole, comes the idea that each participates in the whole. *Thus participation is an implicit aspect of wholeness.* You cannot truly conceive the structure of wholeness unless you grant that the meaning of wholeness implies that all parts partake in it, or put otherwise – participate in it.

The idea of participation is among the most complex and beautiful in the history of the universe. Nothing could happen in the evolution of life and the universe without participation. Participation is at the core of our social life. Participation is the song of joy of our individual experience. The degree, depth and richness of our participation determine the richness and meaningfulness of our life. Those who for one reason or another refuse to participate impoverish their lives.

Alienation means estrangement and emptiness. One of the prime causes of alienation is our inability to participate, either through the designs of our institutions (which disengage us from life, and that means from participation) or through internal blocks. The capacity for participation means the capacity for reaching beyond. It is in this sense that the Upanishads maintain: 'He who thinks of God becomes God.' This is a figurative way of saying that he who deeply participates in God's being, in God's universe, becomes in the image of God.

All life is participation. The song of life is the song of participation. The sorrow of life is an estrangement from participation. When life has discovered the meaning of participation it has discovered its most important modus for growth. The process of participation is perhaps the most profound vehicle of the evolving universe. The participatory universe is merely another name for the unfolding of life in organized forms.

Deep participation means *empathy*, an almost complete identification with the subject of our attention. Empathy or identification is an aspect of the meaning of participation, thus an aspect of the meaning of wholeness.

Let us go one step further. A meaningful participation, when it involves empathy, implies responsibility. We cannot truly participate in the whole, of which we are a part, unless we take responsibility for it. Think of a good family. All that we have said about participation applies to good families as well as to all other wholes that work harmoniously. Participation is a responsibility. Shrugging off responsibility is often the prelude to estrangement and alienation; which means ultimately a disengagement from participation.

We can now easily see that the four concepts of wholeness, participation, empathy and responsibility co-define each other, partake in each other's meaning, feed on each other, form a circular mandala.

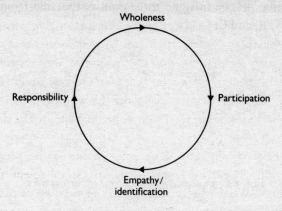

Fig. 1 *The mandala of participation*

The flow of meaning goes both clockwise and counter-clockwise. The meaning of each concept is not defined separately but in conjunction with other concepts. Each of the four concepts partakes in the meaning of each. The complete meaning is in the mandala of the four concepts, and not in any particular one.

Before we go into the analysis and development of specific aspects of the methodology of participation, let us reflect that there are different forms of participation; there is deep participation and shallow participation. The most tenuous form of the latter is what I call *linear* (or geometric) *participation*. Imagine two points, A and B:

A •   • B

They are separate and isolated entities. They are lonely in their isolated existence. Now we draw a line through them. They are now happy being conjoined. They participate in making a line; a low level of participation but participation nonetheless. If we imagine three points separated from each other: A, B, and C:

C
•

A •   • B

Fig. 2 *Context determines the form of participation*

Our first reaction is to assume that the three points form a triangle, or participate in making a triangle; while in fact they might be three points on a circle. It is the *context* that determines the form of participation.

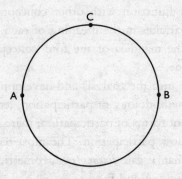

Context is a subtle phenomenon, invisible to the ordinary eye. Yet it binds things together, determines their nature, determines the nature of the relationships in which they are to each other, makes them belong to specific configurations (and not to any other kind of configuration), makes them perform their role according to the design of the whole.

Participation is a matter of context. Shallow context signifies shallow participation. Deep context signifies deep participation. Intriguing context spells out intriguing participation. Open context spells out open participation. Closed context signifies stultified participation.

Notice also the following. By engaging in deep participation, we create deep contexts. In brief, the depth and richness of the context depends on the depth and versatility of our participation. And vice versa.

Now the three points A, B and C in Fig. 2 represent a rather low level of participation. A more advanced level of participation occurs when elements or people participate in complex structures according to preprogrammed rules. Games are a good example of this form of participation; so is the computer. We participate when we sit in front of the computer, but on the computer's terms. When we create a new program – that is another matter.

Participatory democracy via the computer, and many similar forms of participation, when we are told that we have the freedom and power to participate and yet are constrained and bound by the internal rules (of the game in which we participate, be it participatory democracy via computers or games people play), are examples of this second form of participation, which I call *preprogrammed participation*.

Preprogrammed participation may be of two kinds: *genuine* participation and *pseudo*-participation. The former occurs when we play the rules of the game by being explicitly aware of them and accepting them in good faith. Such is the case when we participate in athletic games or when we play chess or checkers. The rules of the game are known and clear. Within these rules, we test our ingenuity and resourcefulness, and often stamina and endurance. In the process we fulfil ourselves. There is room for our creative intervention.

Pseudo-participation occurs when we are led to believe that there is ample room for our creative intervention, while in fact there is none, or very little. This happens when there are hidden internal rules within the game – which only the privileged know, and through which they manipulate the game to their advantage. We have an illusion of participation. We 'participate' by giving our silent consent to the power game of others. For this reason I call this form pseudo-participation.

This form of participation is very common in our world today. We are encouraged to participate yet severely restricted by the hidden rules of the game. In the end we are frustrated. We want to participate creatively. But we are muzzled and incapacitated by hidden rules.

We now move to another level of participation, which I call *co-creative participation* or *full participation*. Co-creative participation occurs when we are allowed the freedom of not only following the rules but also of making the rules, through which we can change the game as we go along. This form of participation, when we co-create with the universe, is the joy of our existence. It is here that our co-creative mind blossoms fully. It is here that our being receives fulfilment.

Yet there is still a deeper form of participation, which I call *creative participation* or *creation*. When great geniuses are involved in this sort of participation, great works of art bordering on miracles are created. Great artists are often linked with God in their power of creation, a power so impressive and awesome to ordinary mortals that they think it might come from God. At such moments those great artists are close to God. For God is indeed pure creation. We shall humbly submit that we never create *like* God. But the more creative we are the closer we come to God – whatever our definition of God. The participation that involves co-creation is a path leading to God.

We have thus distinguished four forms of participation:

(1) linear; (2) preprogrammed (genuine and pseudo); (3) co-creative; (4) creative.

Our status as human beings is enlarged by the degree to which we are allowed co-creative participation. Our status as human beings is degraded by the degree to which we are duped into participation which is a pseudo-participation, a form of preprogrammed participation in which somebody else holds the strings and attempts to make puppets of us.

While pretending that it offers us unlimited freedom, modern technology has really forced us into preprogrammed participation which is often pseudo-participation. Modern technology has often deprived us of our dignity and autonomy by increasingly coercing us into participation in essentially mechanical forms that deny our essence. Our autonomy, freedom and independence are diminished in proportion to the degree that our co-creative participation is replaced by a pseudo-participation. The more sophisticated the technology, the more it disengages us from life, and thus from participation. This consequence of technology is quite lethal, but usually overlooked.

A great danger in the coming age of computers is that our participation (in all walks of life) will become increasingly bound by programs which suit computers but which do precious little for humanity, which in fact subtly suppress our freedom, dignity and autonomy.

Whether our true participation is curtailed by a merciless king or a benign computer, the consequences are the same: frustration, anger, emptiness and alienation. True participation is joy and fulfilment. In the participatory universe, to be a full member of it, you must participate fully; the more fully the better. *We are sitting at the feast of life. Its name is participation.*

Now how do we translate those general insights into specific methodologies? How do we create a new rationality woven around the central concept of participation? How do we teach and learn the new methodology of participation? How do we teach and learn a new way of thinking? How do we evolve the Yoga of Participation? Some of these questions will be answered in the remaining part of this chapter. For more complete answers we shall have to wait for a while. We shall be providing these answers in depth as we develop and practise the methodology of participation on the scale of the whole civilization.

Let us summarize our discourse so far in a Hymn to Participation.

HYMN TO PARTICIPATION

Participation is the song of creation.
Participation is the whispering of life unfolding.
Participation is the common thread of all evolution.
Participation is the common prayer of amoebas and angels.
Participation is the oxygen fuelling the process of transcendence.
Participation is the song of our individual experience.

Whenever life emerges participation blossoms,
As the joy of life,
As the bond of solidarity,
As the pool from which all living beings drink,
As the yeast promoting growth and maturity.

When life discovered the meaning of participation
It had discovered its most important modus for growth.
Utterly simple and utterly profound is the meaning of participation.
Nothing happens in evolution without participation.
The language of solidarity is the language of participation.

To be aware is to participate.
To be asleep is to be estranged from participation.

To be alive is to sail on the wings of participation.
To be morose is to have one's wings of participation clipped.

Love is the deepest form of participation.
Where there is love there is participation.
Loveless participation is an anaemic involvement.
To participate is the first step to loving.

How deeply can you enter into the immensity of the universe?
As deeply as you can embrace it in the arms of your participation.
Everything else is a mere shadow. The real thing
Is our immense journey of becoming through participation.

3. Participatory research programmes

In the 1970s Imre Lakatos, who originally came from the Popperian school, and then became one of the most severe critics of Popper, introduced the idea of *research programmes*. The idea goes back to Popper, but it was Lakatos who made it the central point of his problematic and put the idea on the map. When the idea of the scientific method proved untenable, when the idea of the paradigm started to wane, research programmes became the rallying point for undertaking science, or at least philosophy of science, in a respectable and systematic way. Lakatos's research programmes are a scheme representing a mingling of three styles of thought: those of Popper (conjectures and refutations), of Kuhn (the march of science through successive paradigms) and of Feyerabend (the principle of cognitive fertility carried out by *whatever* method you apply – 'anything goes').

Research programmes as conceived by Lakatos are mainly, if not entirely, scientific research programmes: cognitive, objective, rational. They are designed to handle the accepted scientific-cognitive problems. In short, Lakatos's research programmes by and large accept the underlying *context of science*; and in fact consider this context as sacrosanct.[5]

We need to extend the *idea* of research programmes and make them an integral part of the methodology of participation. Or rather, we need to conceive of appropriate research programmes through which the methodology of participation would be reaffirmed, articulated and vindicated. We need to create research programmes appropriate to the context of the methodology of participation, and to the context of the universe in which this methodology is acted out and by which it is articulated. Thus the participatory universe requires new research programmes which would clearly spell out for us new intellectual strategies, new forms of perception, new forms of reasoning, new languages and new apparatus.

As we enquire into the nature of new phenomena, and new relationships that hold among recognized phenomena, we shall require new forms of perception, new ways of acknowledging and validating their existence. If we rely on present methodologies, we shall be sucked back into the context of objectivity. *Ascertaining a different universe requires a different methodology* – a different spiral of understanding, to take up a leading term used in earlier chapters.

Let us address some of the detail. How do we do the participatory research? What are some of its main characteristics?

The participatory research is the art of *empathy* –

is the art of *communion* with the object of enquiry –

is the art of learning to use *its* language –

is the art of *using* its language –

is the art of *talking* to the object of our enquiry (although this may at first sound strange, let us remember that stranger things are now happening in this life) –

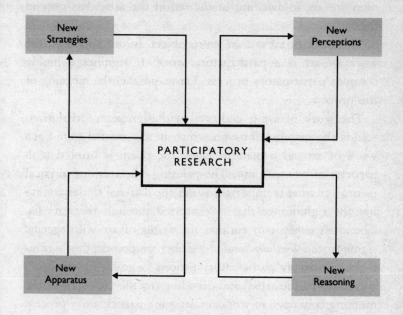

Fig. 3 *Participatory research programme*

is the art of penetrating from *within* —
is the art of *in-dwelling* in the other —
is the art of *imaginative hypothesis* which leads to the art of identification —
is the art of *transformation of one's consciousness* so that it becomes part of the consciousness of the other.
Some of these requirements seem to be almost too much for our minds trained in the rigours of objectivity. Yet surprisingly, most of these attributes of the participatory research are not alien to us. We know them from our own personal experience – from the experience of loving and being loved; from the experience of pain which enables us to understand the pain of others; from deep experience of great works of art, whereby through empathy and commu-

nion we are in-dwelling in the world the artist has created for us.

The work of art is a *sui generis* object. In our language: the work of art is a participatory work. It signifies a highly complex participatory process. Let us unravel the meaning of this process.

The work of art is endowed with significance that transcends the material through which it was carried out. Each work of art has a material layer: the poem is printed with particles of printer's ink. The painting has layers of physical paint. Yet what is important is not the material underpinning but the significance that is expressed through these media. The artist *intentionally* endows his works of art with specific significance. We *intentionally* decipher or decode this significance.[6] A deeply participatory process is going on. In brief, encoding (by the artist) and decoding (by the viewer) – of the meaning contained in works of art – is a participatory process par excellence.

The artist works within the layers of participatory consciousness of human culture. He endows his works with meanings that are significant within the context of a given culture. We (as receivers) tune into the context of this culture and pick up messages and symbolic significances which were laid out for us. We may do it sloppily, or beautifully, depending on the power, subtlety and range of our sensitivities. Participation in art, by making it and receiving it, is among the most significant of human endeavours.

Let us now try to articulate the idea of participatory research a little further. One of the crucial concepts is that of empathy. The aspects of empathy are: to *dwell*; *belong*; *share*; *give/take*. These are common sense concepts, colloquially used. Yet they also possess a deeper metaphysical meaning. We have to regain this deeper meaning in order to participate more deeply in the spectacle of the universe. The idea of 'dwelling in' is far-reaching, as Heidegger has shown us. We know its surface meaning through the idea of dwelling in a house. We know a deeper sense of dwelling because we all dwelled in the womb. This was a deep participation. Dwelling in the womb is a metaphor for the sense of positive identification.

Empathy, in brief, is a form of positive identification, a positive participation. To empathize is to become one with another, to beat the same rhythm with another (as the child did while in the womb), to understand through compassion and *from within*.

4. Participatory strategies

PREPARING THE GROUNDS FOR
PARTICIPATORY RESEARCH

We know the Yoga of Objectivity. We know what kind of preparation of the mind, of the laboratory, of the samples, of the apparatus, of the external circumstances it requires – the whole context is deliberately prepared.

In much the same way, we shall need to prepare the context for participatory research. The methodology of partici-pation is no sloppy messing around and hoping that results will come to us *deus ex machina*; or through mystic contem-plation. To prepare the grounds for participatory research will require various strategies, including what I call the Yoga of Participation. What are some of its aspects? What are the minimal terms for practising participatory research well?

They are:

Preparing one's consciousness.

Meditating upon the form of being of the other.

Reliving its past, its present, its existential dilemmas.

Supplicating to it for permission to enter it (just the opposite from cutting it with a surgical knife).

Praying to the other to let us in (prayer as a form of empathic energy).

In-dwelling in the other on compassionate terms.

Some of the above terms used, such as 'supplicating' and 'praying', may sound somewhat unsettling to the rational mind. They need not be – if the mind is open and generous. Praying denotes an attitude; it is a term expressing our reverential attitude towards the object of our enquiry. When we set up new intellectual strategies, we need to be open, experimental; not biased from the start. Our new strategies imply that we want to be on good terms with the cosmos, and understand things from within rather than crushing them. To meditate, to supplicate, to pray is to create new strategies. These are some of the aspects of a new kind of *dialogue* which we want to carry on *compassionately* with the whole cosmos.

What about the *results*? Before we jump too quickly and demand the results in traditional terms, we should reflect on some of these points:

What is revealed? And in what language?

How can I continue the dialogue?

What are the levels, forms and terms of this dialogue?

What kind of sensitivities does the other embody; operate through?

How does the range and power of my sensitivities help me?

Which of my sensitivities are most appropriate for the task at hand?

I somehow understand how it works in its own terms. . . .

how do I translate its terms into my terms, and then into intersubjective terms?

All these questions are part of our new intellectual strategies. And we must insist that these are meaningful, rational questions. There is no flight into fantasy or flight away from responsibility hidden in them. On the contrary, these questions require a release from within us of the new resources of intellectual energy, and, above all, new resources of imagination.

Simply, we have to make a transition from objective consciousness to *compassionate consciousness*. This transition will be one of momentous importance. I shall not go so far as to claim (as Thomas Berry does) that we shall need to reinvent the human being on the species level – although this idea may not be as far-fetched as it at first appears. Certainly, compassionate consciousness will be an integral part of the new human being if we do proceed with reinventing ourselves on the species level.

The participatory research programme here presented offers only the rudiments of new tactics and strategies. This outline alone is powerful enough to enable us to start a new research in any field *now*. The full articulation of the programme and a satisfactory validation of it will occur when we enact it collectively and create the compassionate consciousness as the vehicle of the new *participatory science*.

The question may be asked at this point whether the researchers, conditioned by the present mode of inquiry, would be inclined to switch over and start to pursue an altogether different mode of inquiry. My answer to this question is that genuine researchers never stand still and that researchers in science are increasingly aware of the limits of the methodology of objectivity. Moreover, I have a suspicion that many of them obtain their best results by secretly following the Yoga of Participation – by identifying with the object of their inquiry, by looking from within. They keep quiet about this part of their methodology for it is not officially accepted. Thus in my opinion the participatory methodology is already being practised – although usually in a rudimentary way. On rare occasions it is explicitly acknowledged, as was the case with Barbara McClintock, who received a Nobel Prize in 1983 for her work in biology done in the 1940s. She vividly describes the process of identification with the chromosomes she investigated. What she describes is the characteristic methodology of participation: 'I found the more I worked with them, the bigger and bigger the chromosomes got and when I was really working with them I wasn't outside. I was part of the [system] . . . it surprised me because I actually felt as if I was right down there and these were my friends . . . As you look at these things they become a part of you . . .'[7] Indeed, 'As you look at these things they become a part of you.' But you have to acquire the art of empathy first so that you become a part of them, so that they become a part of you.

Barbara McClintock's achievement has been a *cause célèbre* among feminist writers and particularly within the school of Eco-feminism, who hail in her the rise and articulation of the feminist epistemology.[8] Eco-feminists attempt to incorporate/ appropriate McClintock's methodology as a part of their overall philosophy. Much fresh and original thinking is coming from this as from other schools of feminism. I salute Evelyn Fox Keller who has written a comprehensive and in-depth biography of McClintock entitled *The Feeling of the Organism* (1983) in which she (Keller) celebrates the idea of the feeling for the organism and the feeling of the organism. I only wish to point out that what is termed 'the feminist epistemology' is in perfect accord with and indeed already articulated by the methodology of participation. It is my hope that Eco-feminists will recognize the merits of the methodology of participation, for that is what we all need to do.

The ideas expressed here are almost common-sensical. But we need to have an open mind to appreciate them for their far-reaching consequences. Above all, we need to apply these ideas at large – in science and in our own lives. Participatory methodology *will* be practised in the future because it is the methodology of the evolving universe.

I have my doubts, however, whether Barbara McClintock has chosen the right strategy by calling herself 'a mystic in science'. We are not yet ready for this kind of language, which is likely to put off working scientists rather than encourage them to emulate her example. In my opinion, McClintock's work and mind are an expression of a new rationality. The rational and the intuitive, the rational and the compassionate are not antithetical to each other but, on a deeper level of analysis, aspects of each other. This is what the methodology of participation wishes to postulate and justify; not mysticism in science but a new rationality and a new sense of the cosmos.

The entire discussion in this chapter may be regarded as a series of successive articulations of one concept, that of wholeness. We have unfolded the concept and shown what a powerful concept it is, and what it potentially contains. For wholeness implies participation. Participation implies empathy. Participation and empathy in action, while we do research, implies entering the territory of phenomena on their terms.

In this context, we must be aware of David Bohm's far-reaching book, *Wholeness and the Implicate Order* (1980). What is implicate order? What is explicate order? The two are inherently connected – the former becomes the latter. For Bohm all there is (ever was and ever will be) had been contained in the original Fire Ball, the state of the universe at the time of the Big Bang. This was the primordial implicate order – which contained all that was to emerge. As the universe has been unfolding, the implicate order (that which is there *in potentio*) becomes explicate order (the actualization of the potence). The story of the universe is, for Bohm, the transition from an implicate order to an explicate one.

Bohm's model is simple and staggering in its implications. For this reason it has found many followers. However, the model is *un*-specific, if not to say nebulous. We want to know *how* the implicate order becomes the explicate one; how the potential becomes the actual – through which powers, agencies, propensities, 'mechanisms'. The answer is not given. On the other hand, the model of the participatory mind provides some answers to these important questions. In the most abbreviated form the answer is: participation through the development of manifold sensitivities. The methodology of becoming is of course participation. For David Bohm wholeness is inherently connected with the implicate order. Wholeness conceals the implicate order. The implicate order conceals wholeness. Wholeness reveals itself as the implicate order become explicate. For the participatory mind, this wholeness reveals itself in the multifariousness of its participation. Participation is the flowering of wholeness: wholeness reveals itself through participation and does not make sense without it. Thus *participation is the essence of the universe in its unfolding*. The universe has become what it is because of specific forms of participation in which it has expressed its nature.

How can the two models – the implicate order and the participatory universe – be reconciled? Implicate order *needs* forms of participation to become the explicate order. The various forms of participation are the very vehicles through which the implicate order articulates itself. The implicate order as such is amorphous – the universe *in statu nascendi*. The universe acquires its distinctive shapes when specific forms of articulation, that is, specific forms of participation, arrive on the scene to transform the implicate into the explicate. In brief: *the patterns of unfolding are the forms of participation*. Undifferentiated unfolding is a precognitive chaos. Differentiated unfolding is the participatory mind in action bringing in its wake the manifold forms of participation. In short, Bohm's is a participatory model of the universe/mind. I have made explicate what is implicate in Bohm.

5. Participatory thinking

Thinking is a subject as old as mankind. The appearance of thinking may be considered as the threshold after which we welcome the emergence of human kind. We are so familiar with thinking, so well-trained in it. We think that we know what thinking is, and how to think well. All training in schools and academia is training in thinking. Yet we are still novices in the art of thinking. Great new discoveries in ourselves and in the cosmos at large will depend on the invention of new forms of thinking.

Albert Einstein said that with the explosion of the atom bomb everything was changed except our thinking. For mankind to survive we shall have to evolve a substantially new manner of thinking, he added. We have been slow in evolving this new manner of thinking. Some new types of thinking have, however, been proposed in recent years:

Systems thinking;
Cybernetic thinking;
Holistic thinking;
Reverential thinking.

Systems thinking, when it was first proposed in the 1960s, appeared to be of great promise. However, as time went on, it made itself a servant of scientific thinking. It has tried to be objective and assert only those phenomena that science recognizes and sanctions. It has accepted the context of science and its cosmology. It has been the tool of the scientific Weltanschauung. In no way has it challenged or attempted to transcend the objective modus of scientific thinking. For these reasons it has got stuck. It was not truly a new departure in human thinking.

Cybernetic thinking was the discovery of the 1950s. In truth it is much, much older. We have always intuitively known that there is a reciprocal relationship among living systems. We express the nature of this reciprocity by saying that we live in the give-and-take universe. However, to articulate this relationship in a precise language was an achievement. Cybernetic feedback loops are now a part of ordinary language. We have become accustomed to cybernetic thinking and no longer consider it to be a revelation or any form of salvation – partly because we have incorporated it into our own thinking, and partly because cybernetic thinking did not deliver what it seems to have promised, 'a substantially new manner of thinking'. A partial reason for this relative failure of cybernetic thinking is (again) the same as was the case with systems thinking. As time went on, cybernetic thinking was monopolized by and incorporated into the scientific universe; and in turn started to serve this universe. The potential for a new departure became used for the perpetuation of the old.

The power of the existing mechanistic paradigm is indeed great and devious. Its tentacles are so numerous and all-pervasive that a great many new departures have been 'sucked-in', reabsorbed by the mechanistic cosmology, and rendered impotent in the process.

In short, systems thinking and cybernetic thinking have been 'objectivized' and then coopted. In the process their potential novelty as *new* forms of thinking has been diminished. They have become status quo forms of thinking. Every big corporation and every big government uses systems thinking and cybernetic thinking. Are we better off as a species and as individuals for this reason?

Holistic thinking appeared as the aftermath of the ecology movement and the search for the holistic paradigm. Although widespread, holistic thinking cannot be expressed through one crisp definition. This is its drawback, and at the same time its forte. It is a drawback, because we cannot immediately pinpoint its basic characteristics; it is a strength, because it cannot be too easily coopted by mechanistic thinking.

We cannot provide a concise definition of holistic thinking because in fact there is a whole range of forms of holistic thinking – their nature and characteristics may vary from context to context. We have not yet worked out the topology of the various forms of holistic thinking.

Ecological thinking is one form of it. It represents thinking within the context of ecological habitats, and specifically in order to secure and safeguard the well-being of the habitats. Ecological thinking is at once *analytical* thinking – as it analyzes the nature of various relationships within large and complex habitats; and *normative* thinking – as our analyses are guided and inspired by the idea of integrity and well-being of the existing forms of life. As such, ecological thinking transcends the boundaries of objective thinking: its purpose is not only to acquire objective pieces of information, but to heal, to maintain well-being, and to enhance life.

Most forms of holistic thinking are normative in the sense mentioned above. Their purpose is not only to know, but to heal, to maintain life, and to make life more vibrant and radiant. Proponents of holistic thinking are often reluctant to give a precise definition of it. And for a good reason. There is a presumption within the scope of our present cognitive knowledge that *to give a precise definition is to sharpen the boundaries of the phenomenon* (in this case, of holistic thinking) *and make it intellectually respectable*. This tacit assumption serves the universe of objective knowledge.

Thinking assumes an enormous variety of forms of which objective thinking is just one. We are not born with the objective mind. Objective thinking is not an imperative of nature, of God; nor of the cosmos. But it is an imperative of objective science. Furthermore, objective thinking is not natural thinking. Most forms of natural thinking are normative in character – inspired by and pervaded with goals, desires, values. Objective thinking is imposed on us as the result of the practice of the Yoga of Objectivity.

Although so often claimed to be value-free, objective thinking is value-laden itself, as all forms of thinking are. The *value* of objectivity is the main value which objective thinking serves and perpetuates. This value cannot be justified objectively or rationally. There is no rational, value-free answer to the question: *why* should we think objectively? The demand for objective thinking is a desideratum of our axiological consciousness. We think that it is a *good* thing to think objectively and to arrive at objective descriptions of reality. Why? Because science tells us so.

But we must not oversimplify. There was a deeper reason why objectivity was hailed as a very good thing indeed. In the sixteenth and seventeenth centuries objectivity was an escape from the tyranny of religious orthodoxy. Thus objectivity was a vehicle of liberation and freedom. We can understand the desire for objectivity in this historical context. But this *desire* is certainly based on values – of wanting to escape from oppression, of wanting to live in freedom. Whichever way we look at it, either historically or epistemologically, objectivity is laden with values.[9]

Reverential thinking is exactly what it means to be – thinking infused with reverence. Its underlying assumption is reverence for life, reverence for all living beings, for all living systems. Reverential thinking is the foundation of right ecological thinking if and when the latter attempts to be truly life-enhancing – enhancing to all forms of life and not only some at the expense of others.

Thinking reverentially is not only using our grey cells in a new way. It is also embarking on a new set of values. When American Indians thought and maintained that there is a spirit behind every tree, they did not mean to say that there is a ghost-like apparition roaming around the tree. This was their way of expressing the fact that, for them, all living things have intrinsic value. This form of value and this form of reverence are acknowledged in the Orient in another way: there is a Buddha in every blade of grass.

To think reverentially is first of all to recognize human life as an intrinsic value; it is to recognize love as an essential and indispensable modality of human existence; it is to recognize creative thinking as an inherent part of human nature; it is to recognize joy as an integral part of our daily living; it is to recognize the brotherhood of all beings as the basis of our new epistemological paradigm. Reverential thinking is a vehicle for the restoration of intrinsic values, without which we cannot have a meaningful future of any sort.

Let us be aware that to think *about* reverence is one thing; to think *reverentially* is quite another. Thinking reverentially is not just ordinary or objective thinking about the desirability or necessity of reverential thinking; but it is the kind of thinking that compassionately embraces the other, that dwells in the other, that tries to understand the other from within. Reverential thinking creates a field of good energy; ultimately it is healing thinking. Reverential thinking is not a luxury, but is a condition of our sanity and grace. Those who do not think reverentially – at times at least – simply impoverish their existence. Thinking as a calculation is one thing. Thinking objectively, according to the requirements of science, is another thing. Thinking reverentially, when we behold the universe in its intimate aspects, and fuse it with our love, and feel unity with it, is yet another thing.

We have now arrived at the point when the stage is prepared for the introduction of *participatory thinking*. Participatory thinking is a culmination and synthesis of systems thinking, cybernetic thinking, holistic thinking and reverential thinking. Participatory thinking does not deny objective thinking but transcends it.

Participatory thinking can *become* objective thinking when the context of participation is limited to the mechanistic cosmology and when the terms of participation are strictly limited to the entities recognized and regulated by the laws of Newtonian dynamics. Yes indeed, objective thinking is a form of participatory thinking, but the terms of participation are severely constrained.

Participatory thinking is not only holistic. It moves to the heart of the subject we study and tries to penetrate it in accordance with its deepest nature; it moves in accordance with the deepest nature of persons we commune with. *Participatory thinking is a rational expression of the magic of in-dwelling.* Through it we can compassionately enter the other. Through it we can enter the immensity of the secrets of the universe, which reveal themselves to us if we possess enough courage, empathy and imagination.

Participatory thinking is co-creative. The co-creative élan of participatory thinking signifies a creative approach to our own life so that it is pervaded with reverential attitudes. This élan also signifies an attempt to heal the earth, and in general to help the universe in its process of becoming. There is no question but that participatory thinking is a crucial vehicle for mending the planet and maintaining its integrity, wholeness and beauty. In this context, Brian Swimee's words are very relevant. He writes:

. . . we must embrace and cherish our dreams for the Earth. We are creating with our imaginations a period of rebuilding, where the intercommunion of all species will guide our life activities. We must come to understand that these dreams of ours do not originate in our brains alone. We are the space where the Earth dreams. We are the imagination of the Earth, that precious realm where visions and organizing hopes can be spoken with a discriminating awareness not otherwise present in the Earth system. We are the mind and heart of Earth only in so far as we enable Earth to organize its activities through self-reflexive awareness. That is our larger destiny: to allow the Earth to organize itself in a new way, in a manner impossible through all the billions of years preceding humanity. Who knows what rich possibilities await a planet – and its heart and mind – that have achieved this vastly more rich and complex mode of life?[10]

This is participatory thinking at its best. Participatory thinking is akin to Buddhist thinking, based on compassion. Participatory thinking is also close to Christian thinking when it is based on love in its pure meaning. Participatory thinking is also close to Taoist thinking, for right participation means following the right path. There are many paths that are right. But there are also many that are wrong. Participatory thinking does not impose a straitjacket on anyone but gives us freedom and encouragement to participate in the glories of the universe to the fullest of our potential. Every culture must discover its own participatory thinking so that its people are not lost in empty abstractions or alienated from the vital pulses and rhythms of the universe.

To think well is to co-create with the universe. To think well is to participate constructively in the well-being of your organism. Plato says that 'Health is a consummation of a love affair with the organs of the body.' *Mutatis mutandis*: participatory thinking is a love relationship between yourself and the evolving universe.

Participatory thinking gives us the freedom of opening up, of creation, of in-dwelling in the immensity of the universe on a scale unprecedented in history. It invites us to enter where angels fear to tread. There is a beauty and a danger in this condition.

If mankind is to survive we shall need to evolve a substantially new manner of thinking – as Einstein proclaimed. Participatory thinking offers itself as the first step, indeed as the necessary step in the new design of the universe in which our individual liberation coincides with lasting peace on Earth.

6. Sensitivity of matter

The world is the creation of the human mind. Not the world as made of physical and non-physical elements, but the world as constituted in our knowledge.

The physical world has been made and remade many times in different cosmologies, each of which imposed on it its distinctive patterns, its distinctive sense of wholeness. Each cosmology is a triumph of the mind in moulding the diverse elements 'out there' into a clearly recognizable structure. Each cosmology is also a triumph of the richness of the inscrutable cosmos which, in spite of our numerous attempts to capture and describe it, still eludes us, as if saying: 'I am capable of assuming ever new astonishing forms if you dare to come to me with new powerful insights.' The cosmos is standing there, an enigmatic entity, still inscrutable, still open to new creative dances.

The cosmos invites the mind to ever new forms of dancing. The dance cannot be separated from the dancers. The human mind finds in the cosmos what it puts into it. The cosmos reveals only what the mind ingeniously assumes about it. The mind is the choreographer. The cosmos is the dancer. Deeper down, the mind is the dancer of which the cosmos is the choreographer.

Each culture and each system of knowledge finds the cosmos cooperative and obliging. The reason lies in the very essence of the participatory universe. The participatory cosmos takes delight in assuming as many forms and configurations as our imagination is capable of conceiving. The astonishing power of the mind brings out of the cosmos its astonishing characteristics. Yet upon reflection we should realize that these 'astonishing' characteristics are not in the cosmos *per se* but rather in the deep recesses of our mind – its power to elicit, to chisel out, to force out of the cosmos its new attributes. The cosmos is the original clay. The various world-views are specific pots made of this clay. Put in philosophical language, the cosmos or the universe is a primordial ontological datum, while the 'world' is an epistemological construct, a form of our understanding.

Matter behaves as the mind allows it. Let us put it more precisely. If mind is restricted, the behaviour of matter is restricted. If mind is liberated, the behaviour of matter is liberated.

Within the Newtonian frame of reference matter did not reveal more of itself than, so to say, the blind stuff, exemplified by billiard balls pushed against each other by some external force. And why was that so? Because the Newtonian matrix was a set of filters which selected only those aspects of the cosmos that fitted its preconceptions. The Newtonian matrix was an ingenious device which eliminated those phenomena that disagreed with its assumptions.

The Newtonian matter did not reveal more of itself because we did not want it to reveal more of itself. We deliberately assumed that 'matter' was that damn brute stuff out there. The Newtonian mind has constrained the behaviour and characteristics of matter to specific physical and deterministic structures. At the same time it inhibited any imaginative thinking about matter that could lead outside the deterministic-mechanistic framework. A frozen orthodoxy has prevailed which has represented a frozen view of matter and it has frozen our thinking on matter.

But all this has changed during the last decades. Minds have opened up. And 'crazy' theories about the behaviour of matter have been welcomed and cherished. An example. In October 1958, the physicist Wolfgang Pauli came to Columbia University to deliver a lecture. This was a great occasion, as he was to present his new unified theory of physics. A spirit of excitement and anticipation pervaded the lecture hall, which was crowded with past, present and future Nobel Laureates. Among them was Niels Bohr who was to comment on Pauli's lecture. Pauli indeed produced a single equation intended to unify all physical theories. When Bohr's turn came his essential point was that Pauli's theory was not 'crazy' enough.[11] A combat started between these two giants of contemporary physics during the course of which Pauli insisted that his theory was 'crazy enough' while Bohr maintained that 'no, oh no, it was not crazy enough.' After this meeting, Pauli abandoned his theory and died the next year.

Now physicists are not exactly known for being crazy or wanting to be crazy. Yet the spectacle at Columbia was revealing for a special reason. By the middle of the twentieth century it came to be recognized that a fundamental new theory of physics, which would be able to shed new light on reality, or at least on remaining parts of physics, would have to violate common sense in some fundamental way, and therefore would appear 'crazy' to begin with. The great new theories of physics in the twentieth century were the result of solitary geniuses who had the courage to think up inconceivable theories, thus 'crazy' theories. Some very strange characteristics were attributed to matter and then – quite unexpectedly – matter confirmed these characteristics, in a sense, agreeing to behave in a way that at first appeared totally strange. So strange have our new theories in physics been, and consequently so strange the behaviour of matter, that nothing is strange any more.

The mind has vindicated its creative prerogative, by making matter sensitive, exquisite and extraordinary. Obviously not *any* strange or bizarre attribute we want to see in matter can be found there. Matter cannot dance or sing. Yet in a strange way matter can sing. But it is a different music, and requires an ear different from one attuned to ordinary human music. What we have learned about the nature of subatomic particles, particularly when we look at them with the eye of a magical child, is nothing short of a strange cosmic dance; nothing short of a strange and wonderful (though not yet totally comprehensible) music of the universe. We shall hear this music and comprehend this dance only if we tune our minds, via participatory thinking, to melodies unheard before.

How does matter behave in these strange dances? As a

partner that obliges, and makes itself available to an extra-ordinary variety of figures and choreographies. Is there any other way of explaining the matter than that? Yes, through equations. But when we look more deeply into their context they become inscrutable. They conceal more than they reveal. For mathematical equations, particularly those of quantum physics, cannot be deemed *descriptions* of reality. Only a *very dim outline* of physical reality can be perceived through them. If there is any other picture or metaphor that emerges from the web of these equations, we do not yet possess the capacity to grasp it in a distinctly human way. To comprehend is to simplify; mathematical equations of quantum physics, for the time being, make the picture ever more complex, thus inscrutable.

But 'to the eye of the man of Imagination, Nature is Imagination itself' (Blake). What a wonderful anticipation! The future of evolution and of the human species belongs to the mind that can conceive the inconceivable, and then find it out there, in the universe, as the universe and imagination blend together.

Summary

We do not live in a senseless, stupid, selfish universe, but in a connected and participatory one. We have the power in our mind to make the universe stupid and disconnected. But the mind was not given to us for this purpose. The power of the mind should be exalted for it is both beautiful and terrifying.

> The mind is its own place, and in itself
> Can make a Heav'n of Hell, a Hell of Heav'n.[12]

The methodology of objectivity turned out to be a mixed

blessing. By pursuing it, we have been able to explore physical matter with a remarkable degree of thoroughness. Through it, we have also built immensely powerful technology. But the other side of the coin is menacing. We have created the atomized and decimated world – mainly as a result of the relentless pursuit of the Yoga of Objectivity which is imposed on us through the prevailing school system. The Yoga of Objectivity is a set of systematic exercises which the scientific method requires for the reification of its claims. The purpose of these exercises is to see reality in a selective way – according to the assumptions of science. The result of the Yoga of Objectivity is a gentle form of lobotomy – which we in the West all suffer; perhaps to the degree that we are not aware that we have been lobotomized.

We seek wholeness not for any capricious reason but because it is the foundation of our being. Wholeness is the matrix of meaning, and the basis for genuine understanding. The ancient Greeks knew these truths so well. For this reason they envisaged Harmony as an indispensable unifying principle bringing coherence to all. In the words of F. D. H. Kitto: 'A sense of the wholeness of things is perhaps the most typical feature of the Greek mind. The modern mind divides, specializes, thinks in categories; the Greek instinct was the opposite, to take the widest view, to see things as an organic whole.'[13]

The methodology of participation springs from one essential assumption: that the universe is one floating wholeness. Participation is embedded in wholeness. Participation is the oldest methodology that has ever existed. *Participation is the methodology of life as growing and evolving.* All life is participation. The song of life is the song of participation. Participation is the song of joy of our individual experience. The deeper and more multifarious the forms of our participation, the deeper and richer the universe in which we live. The real journey is our immense journey to becoming through participation.

There are at least four basic forms of participation: linear, preprogrammed, co-creative, and creative. It is within the co-creative form of participation that the human being expresses himself or herself most fully. If true participation is denied to us, we atrophy and wither. Our modern times are afflicted with all kinds of mental diseases and disorders because human beings have been denied the right to participation. An outburst of various forms of therapy in our times is a hidden response of life to reestablish the right to participation. *All therapy is an attempt to bring the person back to meaningful forms of participation.*

Life is engagement, a continuous dance of participation; while technology, particularly hi-tech, is disengagement, a dance of atrophy. Technology is damaging to our health primarily not because it pollutes our environments (including the mental one), but because it systematically disengages us from life, thus from participation, thus from meaning, thus from our essential nature. The prophets of technology triumphant are not even aware of the deep connection between healthy and meaningful life and deep forms of participation. Nor should we expect them to be so. They blindly serve the objective universe in which facile forms of linear participation prevail.

Participatory research is the art of dwelling in the other, is the art of penetrating from within, is the art of learning to use the language of the other; in short, is the art of empathy. When empathy is writ large and systematically explored and applied, it becomes a new methodology, a set of new intellectual strategies. What clinical detachment is for objective methodology, empathy is for the methodology of participation. Just as we need to create right conditions for conducting research within the objectivist methodology, so we need to create right conditions for doing participatory research. Among these conditions is meditating upon the form of being of the other; supplicating for the permission to enter the territory of the other – not in the spirit of mindless praying, but in the spirit of reverence for the other. Ultimately the contrast between objective research and participatory research is that the former is based on objective consciousness, while the latter is based on compassionate consciousness. The contrast between the two should never be lost from sight. He or she who never developed compassionate consciousness will never be able to undertake participatory research in earnest.

Participatory research includes and articulates what is nowadays called the feminist epistemology, and the feminist sensitivities – which are an integral aspect of the union: reason/ intuition. Although I have not said so in so many words, this entire chapter, and especially the last sections on participatory thinking and the idea of the sensitivity of matter, is an articulation of the new sensitivities and new epistemology that the feminist movements postulate and attempt to justify.

The imperative of holistic thinking, of holistic perception, of the integrated being, is today perceived by many to be of importance second to none. Eco-feminism is one of the new important voices but by no means the only voice. Although we are travelling by different roads, the destination is the same – the creation of a new mind, new sensitivities, new epistemologies which would be the cornerstone of genuine justice and equity in this world, and which would open for us a new chapter of our evolutionary journey.

An adjunct to participatory research, and indeed an integral part of it, is participatory thinking. Participatory thinking is a culmination of systems thinking, cybernetic thinking, holistic thinking and reverential thinking. Participatory thinking is the vehicle of the compassionate consciousness. Participatory thinking gives us the freedom of opening up, of in-dwelling in the immensity of the universe. Participatory thinking is the first step, and perhaps more than this, to what Albert Einstein admonished us to do – to evolve a substantially new manner of thinking if mankind is to survive.

As to the sensitivity of matter: the more sensitive the mind, the more sensitive becomes matter – and the universe – handled by it. The more intelligent the mind, the more intelligent the matter. The more obtuse the mind, the more obtuse the matter. Things reveal their nature in participatory interactions with the participatory mind. The magical child is always present in us.

CHAPTER 7

Structures, Symbols and Evolution

1. Structures and the ascent of evolution

> At the beginning God created the word.
> And the word become structure.
> And the structure became life.

In this chapter we shall consider how structures and symbols
contribute to the process of becoming of the universe. We
shall consider how mind expresses its prowess and genius by
inventing symbols which, on higher levels of the evolutionary
Odyssey, become the carriers of life. We shall consider various
types of symbols and how they express different cosmologies
and religions. We shall analyse what is unique in these symbols; and in what ways they create unique contexts of
participation.

Our criterion in assessing the validity of structures and
symbols will be their participatory prowess: how deeply and
significantly they contribute to our well-being. Our participatory mind is now extended into the realm of structures and
symbols.

The variety of structures is enormous, and so is the variety
of definitions of the term 'structure'. Some are more technical,
as in architecture and engineering sciences; some less technical,
as in biology; some less technical still, as in art and religion.
For our purpose I propose to use the following definition:
*Structure signifies an organized wholeness which enables us to distin-
guish orders through which the evolutionary ascent has been maintained,*

185

perpetuated and perfected. Wherever there is a discernible structure there is a principle of organization at work. Wherever there is a discernible structure there is a sense of identification of the whole to which the various parts belong. Wherever there is a structure there is some form of participation. Wherever there is a discernible structure there is a purpose. The purpose of all structures is to serve life. Thus structures must be life-enhancing. This last point requires a further elucidation.

In his classic work *The Science of the Artificial*, Herbert Simon discusses the architecture of complexity. He maintains that hierarchical structures are of great importance. For if structures were not arranged hierarchically, we might be unable to perceive their important features. Thus hierarchy helps us to perceive and navigate ourselves better in this complex world. Simon writes: 'If there are important systems in the world that are complex without being hierarchic, they may to a considerable extent escape our observation and our understanding. Analysis of their behavior would involve such detailed knowledge and calculation of the interactions of their elementary parts that it would be beyond our capacities of memory or computation.'[1]

What Simon says is informative, but it does not go to the heart of the matter. And the heart of the matter is the relationship between structures and the effervescence of life. Structures are recognized as organized wholes not only because they help our perception but because they help life. This point is of great importance. Life means evolution. Evolution means growing complexity. Complexity means appropriate structures through which life articulates itself. *The origin of all structures is the articulation of life.* Thus the purpose of structures is to create orders that are life-enhancing.

Now what about chemistry? It may be considered a *prima facie* science of structures but it merely analyses the place and configuration of chemical components within chemical structures. This is so only on the surface. When we reconstruct the context in some depth, we then find that these chemical components are building blocks of life. They are analysed and identified as structures because ultimately they are life-building blocks. To reiterate: the deeper reason for distinguishing chemical structures as structures (of a given kind) is that ultimately they are part of the order supporting life.

Neither nuclear bombs nor black holes create orders. They destroy orders. We thus obtain a clear distinction between structures and anti-structures. Structures help life and are life-enhancing. Anti-structures undermine life and are destructive of life. This distinction enables us immediately to see some of the problems of modern technology. In addition to its benevolent uses, modern technology has been quite prolific in devising anti-structures; that is to say, negative orders whose purpose it is to suppress the variety of life, to make it more and more homogeneous. Even if these negative orders were unintended, their consequences must not be ignored. We have arrived at an important ethical imperative: *in your work, in your behaviour, in your research do not engage in activities that result in anti-structures.* This alone could be the basis for a new, post-technological ethics.

It follows from our analysis that structures should not be confined to the products of scientific activities only, be it chemistry or biology. Nature itself is a stupendous form of structure.

Ecological habitats are distinctive structures. Evolution also can be seen as one enormous evolving structure. In truth, evolution is the greatest structure of all. It generates, articulates and nurses all life. This structure is so staggering in its complexity that we are often unable to see it in its totality. To see evolution for what it is: a life-supporting, life-giving and life-enhancing force, is a liberating experience.

On another level, religion and art create their own distinctive structures which are life-enhancing – not in the biological sense but in the social, cultural and spiritual sense. I shall argue later that religion (at least at its best) is a powerful originator of life-enhancing structures. So vital is religion that without it the ascent of man, as a human and compassionate being, would be inconceivable.

Before we proceed, one point should be clarified. It is claimed, in feminist and anarchist literature, that *all hierarchy is bad and should be abolished*. This view is mistaken; or at least so partially formulated that it makes a caricature of the issue.

For the feminists, hierarchies are identified with old patriarchal, exploitive social orders. In so far as these hierarchies are unjust, exploitive and poisonous to human and social relationships – in quite a variety of ways – they should be abolished. That part of the claim we do not question.

But this is only one type of hierarchy – exploitive and parasitic. Life, both biological and social, is pervaded with life-enhancing hierarchies without which the structure of human existence would collapse. Why is the brain more important than the arm? Why is the eye more important than the tooth? Our brain is encapsulated in a rather solid skull. Our eye is immediately (if intuitively) protected by the lid if an unexpected object is thrown at us. Nature has built these special defences around these organs because, in the hierarchy of life, they are more important than other organs. The mind (or the brain) is a supremely hierarchical organ; and so is the eye. They coordinate our voyage through life in a most subtle, cunning and beautiful way.

Our life is hierarchical through and through. We make these choices and not other choices in the name of our preferences; which are based on our values; which are based on our hierarchies – which are often based on the hierarchies of life itself.

It is therefore unwarranted and unjustified to claim that all hierarchies are bad and should be abolished. Such a proposition flies in the face of reason, and in the face of our experience; as well as in the face of the exquisite architecture of life itself. All architecture, whether man-made or nature-made, is based on some hierarchies.

In summary, the ascent of life goes hand in hand with the invention of structures. The pursuit and development of structures embodies and articulates new hierarchies. Hierarchies are vertical expressions of life-enhancing structures (see the works of Eigen, Prigogine, Jantsch). So the equation is simple: no hierarchies, no structures, no articulation of life.

Why is there so much resentment and animosity towards the very idea of hierarchy? For political and ideological reasons. For too long the dominant ideology of Western and non-Western cultures was that of Patriarchy. This particular hierarchy has brought about much grief and injustice. (It must be mentioned parenthetically that Matriarchy is a form of hierarchy as well.) Because of the accumulated injury stemming from one particular hierarchic structure the whole notion of 'hierarchy' is brought to grief. Political and ideological hierarchies are to be watched. They have a tendency to become malignant. It is for this reason that Democracy was invented – to rectify the degenerating shifts in political hierarchies, which are not based on participation.

2. *The origin of structures*

> The beginning of all architecture
> Is the waves
> Endlessly rolling on the sea.

How do structures originate and evolve? We are so prolific in designing and building new structures that we often lose

Fig. 1 *What do these shells have in common?*

sight of the origin of structures and their ultimate *raison d'être*. Let us take two shells (Fig. 1).[2] If we ask ourselves what these two shells have in common, the answer is easily forthcoming – it is that a mollusc lived in each. We can say that they are both forms of shelter. They are magnificent examples of structures that are life-enhancing. If we take a shell and a temple (Fig. 2) and we ask ourselves what they have in common, the first answer would probably be – nothing at all: the shell is small, frail, nature-made and designed to be a house for some organism. It is quite the opposite with the temple. However, on a deeper analysis we find that the shell is not so small, not so frail, and not so different from the temple. Upon reflection we shall find that each is a form of shelter, although sheltering different forms of existence. The shell shelters the mollusc's biological existence. The temple shelters important aspects of man's spiritual existence.

This is not the end of the story. We want to go deeper still. What is the ultimate thread that unites these forms? What do

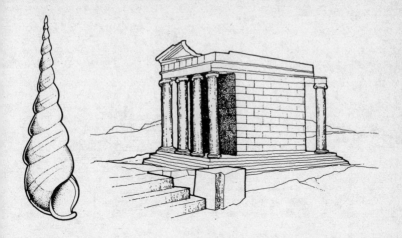

Fig. 2 *What does a shell have in common with a temple?*

they ultimately have in common, in addition to being forms of shelter? The answer is *evolution*. It is evolution that is their common thread. They are both forms of shelter but on a different level of evolutionary development. In its unfolding, evolution created various kinds of spaces in order to shelter different aspects of its being. On the level of the human being, evolution created new kinds of spaces to accommodate the increasing variety of human needs, including cultural and spiritual needs. Now, although they look so different, both the shell and the temple respond to the need for shelter; on different levels of evolutionary unfolding.

If we compare now three sacred buildings, Greek, Christian and Hindu (Fig. 3), then the answer to the question what do they have in common is again easily forthcoming: they attempt to provide a shelter for man's spiritual quests and qualities. They also make human beings feel at home in this large universe – by relating them to heaven and earth. This is at least what great temples do. They provide a special kind of space,

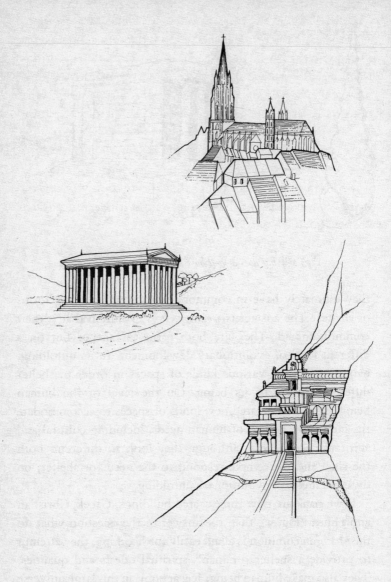

Fig. 3 *What do these sacred buildings have in common?*

a special kind of structure through which we are elevated.

The shell is the original shelter. It is the original geometry of the universe. In the beauty and exquisiteness of the shell – in its strength and symmetry – we witness the anticipation of our dwellings and of the symmetries of our temples. The more we learn about the magic of the shell the more able we shall be to design our dwellings and temples. For it is all a part of the same evolutionary rhythm: the continuous waves of the oceans created the shell; then our ribs; then the columns of the Parthenon. In creating the shell, evolution was already toying with the idea of the temple, and in between it created what we call the human shelter.

It is clear that the higher we go the more numerous are those subtle aspects of our shelter, which are not exhausted by the idea of physical shelter. When evolution made a transition from the physical to the cultural, and then to the spiritual, human beings, in response, started to build those new kinds of structures – temples and other monuments of art.

Temples are among the most significant structures evolved by human beings. They embody and express the great rhythms and symmetries of life. The secret of structures and their greatness lies in their *symmetry*. We find these symmetries fascinating and irresistible because deep down it is evolution in us that responds to its own evolutionary epic. Life was formed in the oceans through those millions upon millions of years of continuous waves, which are expressed in the shell, in the human ribs, in temples.

But even before the oceans became the cradle of amphibian and mammalian life-forms, evolution (in its early, pre-life stages) seems to have chosen symmetry as its underlying *modus operandi*. To every element there exists a contrasting element that holds the original element in balance. Balance and harmony are based on symmetry.

Thus the origin of all structures is symmetry. Primordial symmetry is expressed through life-enhancing rhythms, which form the basis of structures. Rhythm and symmetry may be altered, modified and imaginatively played with, as they are in great works of art and within cosmic structures themselves. What we ultimately consider as breath-taking beauty, of both man-made and cosmos-made structures, turns out to be refined symmetries woven into patterns of magnificent simplicity. The greatest temples ever created by man, the Taj Mahal and the Parthenon, are staggering in their simplicity – which is imposed on, and expressed through, the subtle and often dazzling variety of rhythms and symmetries.

Life, as conceived in this universe of ours, has been carried on through the structures based on rhythms and symmetries. From the rhythm of pulsating stars to the rhythm of sexual intercourse, we find rhythms and symmetries pleasing and enthralling because they are the stuff of life, the bearers of life, the underlying harmony and unity of life. All art, and much of our life (when lived significantly), is an epic struggle of the mind to weave the natural rhythms and symmetries into ever new structures.

3. Symbols and their role in the ascent of man

All this universe is in the Glory of God,
of Siva the God of love.
The heads and faces of men are his own
and he is in the hearts of all.

Svetasvatara Upanishad

Symbols are extraordinary entities. We use them so often. We use them daily. Yet they defy our rational grasp. They defy explicit definitions. Actually symbols define us as much as we are capable of defining them. Symbols use us in a variety of subtle ways. And so subtle are these ways that most of the time we are not fully aware of them. Symbols are frail creatures. But they can possess an explosive substance. After all, great revolutions were fought in the name of and inspired by symbols. You cannot break a symbol. But a symbol can break you; or can make you. Let us first see how symbols work in art, then in major religions; and then we shall move on to scientific symbols.

Works of art are, at best, examples of organized and orchestrated wholeness. More than that – through their symbols, they integrate us into those realms which they express. Works of art, particularly great ones, are holistic in a double sense. They represent a remarkable unity and completeness within themselves. But secondly, through their presence, through the relationships they establish with us, they draw us in – into their universe. The more significant the realm they symbolically represent, the more significant can become our integration. This integration, which is usually a journey upward, is really a journey of transcendence. Indeed, works of art are among the primary vehicles of transcendence.

Works of art are modalities of our existence. Their significance does not lie in their physical presence, although there is a physical substratum to every work of art, but in their spiritual, cultural and symbolic presence – and the consequences this presence generates. One of these consequences is that works of art make us feel that we belong, that we participate. What does it mean to say that we *belong* or that we participate? In the simplest sense – we feel at home.

Works of art, by giving us the sense of belonging, by making us feel at home, act as de-alienating forces. Alienation is the opposite of belonging. Wherever there is deep involvement in art, there is no room for alienation.

But the symbols of art and religion make us belong not only to earth but also to heaven. They extend and amplify man's existence into the sphere of the invisible. How do works of art make us belong to heaven? Through the power and meaning of their symbols. Symbols are the invisible vehicles which transport us into the realms they represent. Though they are mysterious, symbols should not be regarded as invisible ghosts. They are rather *intentional relationships*.

Whenever a given object of art or a given symbol works on us it is because the artist was able to endow a given physical configuration with a symbolic significance (be it in layers of paint on canvas or syllables within a poem). When our turn comes, we are able to decipher this significance and find it relevant to our existence.

There is then the initial act of *encoding*, and, at our end, an act of *decoding*.[3] Obviously there is a parallelism between the two. The intention of the artist and our capacity to decipher it must be somewhat congruent. In representational or naturalistic art, there is an unequivocal intention and an unequivocal reception – in representing what is there and in interpreting it. The encoding and the decoding (allowing for some variations) match each other rather well. We know exactly what the artist *meant* to convey and express.

In non-figurative art the initial intention is *not* unequivocal but deliberately multi-vocal, and sometimes indeed blurred. Thus the object of art becomes the basis for multivocal interpretations. But this is also true with regard to art with religious subjects. Its symbolism is multi-layered. Because of the complexity of what they convey, because of the complexity of the human psyche, and because the various parts of the human psyche may respond to different aspects of those multi-layered symbols at different times, religious symbols are open to many different interpretations. One of the reasons why religious symbols survive so well in art is that they touch the ineffable, express the deepest longings and aspirations of the human soul. In stretching us beyond what we can conceivably achieve, these symbols invite us to an infinite journey, always open, always offering new paths and possibilities.

The transcendent symbolism of religion cannot be overestimated in its importance for the ascent of *homo symbolicus*. Because man acquired the capacity to produce symbols much larger than his earth-bound existence, he could make something of himself. Our spiritual journey began when we started to project symbols and then attempted to live up to these symbols. Whether we take the restless, outward-directed Prometheus or the implacable Buddha, sitting serenely on the lotus flower, the symbolism emanating from each has inspired human beings to deeds and achievements that would have been inconceivable without these far-reaching symbols.

What are symbols in themselves? What is their ontological status? What form of existence can we attribute to them? These are very difficult questions indeed. How difficult they are can be testified by the case of Ernst Cassirer and his followers who wrote voluminously on symbols. In his philosophy of symbolic forms Cassirer gallantly struggles to provide a clear definition of the term 'symbolic form' and 'symbol' itself. However, instead of one clear conception, we have a fantastic proliferation of explanations, in which at least three different interpretations overlap, and sometimes vie for dominance with each other.

In some contexts it is the *ontological* interpretation that comes to the fore, whereby the symbolic form is related to (and not quite distinguishable from) Platonic ideas or Platonic forms.

In other contexts, the *phenomenological* interpretation prevails, which attempts to ground the meaning of symbolic form in the quality of human consciousness – in the particular mode of an animated totality of the experience of the phenomenon under investigation, and the symbolic form underlying it.

In other contexts still, the *mythic* interpretation is seen as most important, whereby symbolic form delineates the sacred from the profane; symbolic form stands then as a threshold to the realm of the sacred.

Now the philosophy of Ernst Cassirer is a universe in itself and no perfunctory summary or critique can do it justice. The work of Cassirer and other writers of the twentieth century is a living testimony of the importance of symbols on the one hand, and of their profoundly mysterious, non-discursive character on the other.[4]

Perhaps instead of asking what symbols are a more fruitful approach is to ask how we can ascertain the *validity* of symbols. How do they work? Obviously, there are some symbols that are very much alive, and some that are worn out. What does it mean to say that a given symbol, or a given set of symbols, is worn out? It probably means that a given set of symbols does not nourish our psychic structure any more, that its peculiar energy is exhausted, that we have outlived it, that we have evolved and that we now need different symbols to nourish us and to express our new directions, longings, aspirations.

Some religions survive better than other religions. Some works of art and some cultures are more enduring than others. What is the reason? The reason must be that their symbols are more universal and more sustaining than other symbols. For symbols do sustain, and often articulate, different aspects of our human condition – as can be clearly seen in the cases of Buddhism, Hinduism and Christianity, which I shall presently examine.

4. Dominant symbols in Buddhism, Hinduism and Christianity

Once upon a time Lord Buddha came to deliver a sermon.
He raised a lotus flower high above his head.
Then smiled and left without saying a word.

Buddhist text

Buddhism acquired the status of a universal religion when the great emperor Ashoka (273–237 BC), tired of wars, devoted himself to it. Ashoka is supposed to have built 84,000 stupas, in 84,000 villages.[5] Under his patronage an unprecedented spread of Buddhist art took place. It is at this time that the symbolism of Buddhist art was articulated, refined, and conveyed in thousands of statues. The symbolism is striking in its simplicity.

In comparison with other religions (especially Christianity), the repertoire of symbols within Buddhist art seems rather limited. The pervading symbol is that of the tranquil Buddha, sitting serenely on the lotus flower (Fig. 4). The lotus flower came to signify the quality of the Buddha – the inner peace of mind which is a precondition of real well-being and of happiness. The symbolism is simple. Yet it is powerful and universal. It is appealing to us all – for who does not desire happiness, inner peace and equanimity of mind? In this symbolism some of the noblest longings of the human race are expressed.

It would be hard to think about Buddhism, and what it signifies, without the symbolic significance of the serenely sitting Buddha; and also without the meaning attached to the lotus flower. To emphasize, the spread of Buddhism coincided with the flowering of Buddhist art, which meant precisely the flowering of its symbolism. During the past twenty-one centuries this symbolism has remained unchanged. It still has the power to inspire and guide.

There are many striking parallels between Buddhism and Hinduism: the same belief in reincarnation, in Nirvana, in Karma, in Dharma. Yet the symbolism of Hinduism is markedly different from that of Buddhism. The Buddhist symbolism emphasizes austerity. The symbolism of Hinduism, on the other hand, emphasizes the exuberance and sensuousness of life. This is especially striking in the erotic sculptures adorning the Khajuraho temple. To see explicitly erotic sculptures – of human couples copulating in a variety of imaginative positions – within the confines of a temple is too much for the Christian or the Muslim religious sensibility. To the Christian or the Hebrew these are not religious symbols, but rather an offence against religious feeling. Yet the Hindu mind looked at it all differently.

Even if the Khajuraho temple is considered to be an exception, the symbol of the Linga – which is the central symbol of Shiva temples, and which is a phallic symbol par excellence – only confirms the general élan of the culture. These lingas are an integral part of a religious faith. They are decorated with fresh flowers daily. They do not just symbolize the worship of the primitive sexual urge, but rather the sanctity of life, the miracle of life; they gloriously encapsulate the life abundant, the life that must be cherished and held sacred in all its aspects.

Hindu mythology is very colourful, very complex, and so are its symbols. The dancing Shiva is its most striking and perhaps the dominant symbol. It is the symbol of continuous metamorphosis, of the ceaseless becoming of life, also a symbol of the fluidity and essentially undefinable character of life.

Fig. 4 *The tranquil Buddha*

It is an enthralling metaphor to conceive of the universe (and of our life in it) as the dancing Shiva. With the rediscovery of the ancient Hindu traditions in recent years, the Western mind has been more and more excited and inspired by the Hindu conception of the dynamic and ever-changing nature of reality. This is the Heraclitean vision given a new lease of life. Actually, within the Hindu tradition this vision has never been abandoned as a living reality. Many Western thinkers of our time, particularly those with a background in post-Newtonian physics, have sought in the dancing Shiva a new metaphor, congruent with the New Physics, which would help us to transcend the immobile, static and petrified aspects of the Newtonian world-view. It is an open question whether we in the West, conditioned by different dominant symbols, can fully absorb and meaningfully integrate the immense consequences of the dancing Shiva (Fig. 5).

Let us now turn to Christian symbolism. One might see a parallel between the Hindu ideal of the abundance of life and Jesus's ideal of Life Abundant. However, it is not this ideal that dominates Christian consciousness and Christian symbolism, but rather the conception of life as transient, full of suffering, lived in the vale of tears.

The dominant symbol of Christianity is the cross: Jesus crucified on the Mount of Golgotha. It is this symbol that has been ingrained in our consciousness (Fig. 6). Through this symbol we are led to think of life on earth as misery. What a contrast to the Hindu conception of life! And also to the Buddhist, as symbolized by the serene Buddha.

Are we morbid as a culture because the dominant Christian symbol, the cross, when interiorized, has been devastating to our psyche, and made us morbid individually – never accepting joy as a fact of life, and always counting our sins and miseries? There was *no necessity* to elevate the cross as the

Fig. 5 *The dancing Shiva*

central symbol within Christianity. We may wonder why it was so elevated. This symbol has been haunting our imagination more than we are aware. It may be responsible for many of our neuroses. Our life is split in the middle by the growing awareness, emanating from the cross, that life is not for living.

The joyous élan of Graeco-Roman culture has been thwarted by the haunting metaphor of the cross which overshadows our daily existence. That this metaphor is not to our liking is indicated by the continuing popular desertion of Christian churches. Nietzsche's idea that God is dead was really only an acknowledgement of the fact that Christian symbols have burnt out their creative substance and become progressively empty.

Can Christianity renew itself? It has tried but without much success. It would seem that the best path for renewal would be to switch from the cross as the central symbol to the idea of Resurrection as the central symbol. The cross as the central symbol is very harsh. We need something more gentle, more life-enhancing, more positive. In the idea of Resurrection we have a powerful metaphor which can sustain us in our daily struggles, and can sustain us as a culture in the long run. For *life lived creatively is one continuous resurrection*. But there will be some problem in this switch-over. We shall need to invent an appropriate *image*, a striking visual representation, which in a simple and continuously nourishing way would remind us of the symbolic as well as the palpable meaning of Resurrection. Inventing such a new visual image would require an act of genius.

There is more respect for human life, and life in general, in both Hinduism and Buddhism than in Christianity. They both emphasize the precious and unique character of human life. After all, to be born human is the highest of all incarnations.

Fig. 6 *The symbol of Christianity ingrained in our consciousness*

Thus the Buddha on the preciousness and uniqueness of human life:

'O monks, suppose that the great earth were to become an ocean upon which a single yoke were being tossed about by the wind and thus being moved from here to there. If under the ocean there were a blind turtle, do you think it would be easy for it to insert its head into the yoke when it rises to the surface only once every hundred years?' 'No, Lord, it would not,' replied the monks. The Lord then said, 'In a similar fashion, O monks, it is extremely hard to obtain the human state.'[6]

If we compare the three dominant symbols of the three religions, the Buddha sitting on the lotus flower, the dancing Shiva and Jesus on the cross, we witness *three different spiritual odysseys of the human kind*. Only time will tell which of these three symbolisms is truly universal. One would be inclined to think, however, that Buddhism is, in spite of its seeming austerity. As a whole, Hindu symbolism is overwhelming to us in its exuberance – too many gods, deities and tangential stories. Christianity, with its morbid symbolism, has been at a low ebb for quite a while.

To invent new symbols, appropriate for a given age, is a very difficult task. Yet life has its ways. We continually invent symbols. These symbols are then tried out in real life. Some wither away quickly. Some show a remarkable vividness and capacity to inspire human imagination; these symbols stay on.

One of the new symbols recently invented, or should we say reinvented, is the idea/symbol/image of GAIA – the living earth. The Gaia hypothesis emerged rather recently.[7] But it has proved to be very inspiring to all sorts of people. Gaia, in the image of the planet earth photographed from a satellite, is a symbol of oneness, a symbol of unity, of interconnectedness of the planet earth – its oceans, continents, peoples.

Gaia is at present the best symbol we possess of the unity of the human race. Gaia is one of the new symbols of our time. Because of its far-reaching and profound consequences, Gaia has often been entertained as a theological proposition. There is a theology emerging around Gaia; sometimes it is called the theology of the earth.[8] There is a definite religious penumbra around Gaia, just as there has been around other significant and far-reaching symbols. The tenderness of Gaia and the tenacity of Gaia; the nourishing qualities of Gaia and the spiritual qualities of Gaia have been extolled by many. Thus a mythology is being created.

Religious symbols and, in general, cultural symbols are the creation of the human spirit, an outcome of our spiritual activities. Their role and function is to maintain and enrich man's spiritual domain. Religious symbols often try to provide consolation, uplift as well. Whatever the differences among religions, religious symbols were conceived as life-enhancing, as integrative. They attempt to integrate man with himself as well as to integrate the human being with the larger transcendent realm sometimes called God, sometimes the Eternal One, sometimes the Divine Cosmos, sometimes simply Nature.

Religion means wholeness. Disintegration of religious structures is often a prelude to individual and social destruction, whereby individuals are adrift, floating aimlessly without knowing why – there is no centre that holds, no structure that integrates and heals. *Religions and cultures are the very structures whose purpose it is to maintain the evolutionary ascent by articulating man's spiritual endowment*. The architecture of religious and cultural structures is no less exquisite and complex than the architecture of biological systems; and no less important for the maintenance of the well-being of the species.

5. Scientific knowledge and its enigmatic symbols

Equations do not explode.

Bertrand Russell

As religious symbols were considered all-important in the age of religion, so scientific symbols are considered most important in our time, the age of science. Is there any good reason to consider scientific symbols superior to religious and artistic symbols? Though considered more respectable, are they more valid? I shall attempt to demonstrate that the reasons for their alleged superiority are shaky at best; and question-begging most of the time. Indeed, the time has come to look more deeply into the nature of scientific symbols, their role in present culture, their validity, their participatory prowess.

Until recently science enjoyed a privileged status and its symbols did indeed have two sources of powerful justification.

The first justification of the validity of scientific symbols was related to the idea of progress. It was pragmatic in character.

The second justification was related to the idea of truth, and the idea that science had a privileged access to it. This justification was epistemic in character. Concepts of science and symbols of science were supposed to correspond uniquely to reality, which science was taken adequately to describe.

Let us examine both these justifications. We shall see that whatever validity they possessed once, they possess much less now. The pragmatic argument still holds a powerful sway over the minds of most people. According to this argument, science is good because it delivers the goods. It has helped the human condition. It has enormously increased our material standard of living. It has uplifted the human race. In this sense science, and its symbols, have met the evolutionary criterion for all structures and symbols, namely, their life-enhancing quality.

Yet the legacy of progress is now a very mixed blessing. Progress is no longer treated as sacrosanct, a sacred cow, and is indeed viewed by thinking people with grave misgivings. We have all learned by now the meaning of the dreadful fall-out of progress: a sense of frustration and stress, and of the meaningless of life; the destruction of the environment and of many species; the loss of the sacred. This fall-out has been one of the consequences of scientific symbols in action.

Thus progress has turned out to be a double-edged sword. Whoever wishes to take credit for all the blessings that science has brought to us must also take the responsibility for the negative consequences of science and technology. Thus the argument seeking justification of the validity of scientific symbols in terms of progress is crippled nowadays.

The pragmatic argument is further weakened by the fact that in the twentieth century, by splitting the atom, science has unleashed enormous destructive powers. The symbol of the atomic mushroom is now part of our mental landscape. The possible horror of nuclear war is still haunting our dreams and making us uneasy in our daily living.

Bertrand Russell has written that 'equations do not explode.' Yet they do. In the popular imagination scientific symbols are of first importance because scientific knowledge can unleash so much power. The problem of evil now takes on a new dimension. The demonic powers that were once attributed to evil forces are now attributed to science, its symbols, its equations. It does not help to protest that this is not how scientific symbols should be viewed. In the minds of many people the end of the world will come not through the intervention of God or some evil forces, but simply as the result of scientific inventions, and those dreadful equations that explode.

The protagonist of science would want to insist that this is the secondary ground for the justification of scientific symbols. The primary ground is related to science's role as the guardian of truth. Let us therefore consider the second, epistemic justification.

How well are scientific symbols justified as bearers of truth? What do they actually represent? Put otherwise, what do they symbolize? The answers to these questions were relatively easy when the physical universe was considered as given and describable by the deterministic laws of Newtonian mechanics. Within the framework of classical science, the laws of science simply represent and describe the objective order out there. Our symbols are then faithful and ultimate descriptions of reality. Scientific symbols, in short, symbolize the physical reality existing independently of us. We witness here a straightforward application of the correspondence theory of truth: our symbols correspond to the reality out there.

This was the basis of *realism* (or metaphysical realism), the doctrine that claims reality to be knowable, faithfully describable in terms of our knowledge, especially scientific theories. Empiricism is a version of this (metaphysical) realism. It claims that science is the kind of knowledge that faithfully describes reality. Within the doctrine of empiricism, scientific, or more generally, cognitive and physicalist symbols are most important because *they give us a supreme access to reality*, which is physical in character. This is the basic argument for considering scientific symbols superior.

Yet this position is now part of the story of the past. The simple-minded realism that holds that the world exists as we describe it in our scientific theories can no longer be seriously upheld. The strange thing is, however, that although most scientists know this truth, they behave as if nothing had happened in physics in the twentieth century, as if their symbols directly corresponded to reality. This is certainly not a minor oversight but a fundamental conceptual myopia, a form of blindness, or a form of *ir*rationality.

We now recognize that 'objectivity' has been a myth; at best a first approximation. To imagine that our theories and concepts (thus our scientific symbols) objectively grasp and depict reality out there was a noble dream, but a dream nevertheless. We now know that our mind is built into our theories. Our instruments are built into our theories. Our specific human faculties and their limitations are built into the structure of our theories. Our sensitivities are built into our instruments and our theories. We simply realize that we cannot 'photograph' reality objectively in our theories. If all this is so, then the old model based on the correspondence between our symbols (concepts and theories) and reality collapses.

The outcome of these arguments is that the epistemic justification of scientific symbols also collapses. We have naïvely believed that scientific symbols correspond to reality because we *assumed* so from the seventeenth century onwards. After three centuries of scientific experience, we now know better.

It is time to return to our basic question. What is the status of scientific symbols?

Their status is dubious, to say the least. Scientific symbols are still treated as sacred dogmas while the justification of their validity, both pragmatic and epistemic, is undermined. The whole architecture of scientific symbolism is now in shambles.

We might seek refuge in the coherence theory of truth and the coherence conception of knowledge by claiming that some symbolisms are better than other symbolisms because they cohere better with the body of accepted knowledge. The coherence theory is always difficult to justify rationally. There is always the difficult question: how do we assess the *fit* or the coherence? By what impartial criteria? More important still is the fact that nowadays our knowledge is so *incoherent*. We do not have a coherent system of knowledge any more. This again is so often overlooked.

How is the validity of scientific symbols, therefore, to be judged? Ultimately all symbols are to be judged by their contributions to the well-being of life, to the well-being of the human species and the well-being of other beings. This assessment can sometimes be done directly – when, for instance, we assess a knowledge of carpet-weaving when looking at a beautiful carpet. Sometimes it can be done only indirectly since our symbols are several steps removed from palpable life. Then the assessment can be very difficult indeed.

Now, although quantum physics has done more than any other discipline to persuade us that the old realism (and its objectivity criterion) does not hold, it is itself in deep conceptual trouble. For what is the status of mathematical symbols used in quantum theory? We entertain within the field many strange notions which are in need of a deeper ontological examination. Henry P. Stapp writes: 'Quantum theory does not resolve the problem of mind and matter. It circumvents the problem by declining to give any picture at all of the physical world, except the vague one that dimly emerges from the set of statistical rules it provides.'[9] Might it not be the case that statistical theories that are used for the 'description of reality' (the phrase must now be used in inverted commas) were born out of an ontological cul-de-sac rather than out of genuinely new thinking?

The growing esotericism of modern science, its remoteness from life and from culture, has been a cause of alarm among scientists themselves. So writes Erwin Schrödinger, one of the most distinguished of them all:

... there is a tendency to forget that all science is bound up with human culture in general, and that scientific findings, even those which at the moment appear the most advanced and esoteric and difficult to grasp, are meaningless outside their cultural context. A theoretical science unaware that those of its constructs considered relevant and momentous are destined eventually to be framed in concepts and words that have a grip on the educated community and become part and parcel of the general world picture – a theoretical science, I say, where this is forgotten, and where the initiated continue musing to each other in terms that are, at best, understood by a small group of close fellow travellers, will necessarily be cut off from the rest of cultural mankind; in the long run it is bound to atrophy and ossify ...

The argument is well stated. Science cannot survive as an esoteric branch of learning. Its roots are in the soil of human culture; it must nourish culture at large. Science indeed is one of the glories of the human mind. Its spectacular successes in penetrating what was once beyond the human power of perception inspire us with awe.

At present, however, science is in a double crisis. One is a crisis of identity. Science no longer knows what it is, and what it wants to be. The other crisis is that of the relationship between science and culture in general. The onus is at the moment on the shoulders of science to show that its enterprise, and specifically its symbols, truly serve culture in the broad sense.

Classical science developed not only symbols, but a whole liturgy. Part of this liturgy was the conquest of nature. Now this liturgy is dead. And no new liturgy has arisen – if only because, as Stapp and others tell us, science no longer knows how to conceive of reality, how to describe it, how to conceive of symbols that no longer directly correspond to reality but that nevertheless are not empty formulae signifying nothing.

When we compare scientific symbols with religious symbols or the symbols of art, what are the most significant differences? Scientific symbols do not touch us. They leave us cold. They do not excite us. They leave us indifferent with regard to what they symbolize.

For what is the participatory content of scientific symbols? In what way do they make us participate? What is the result of this participation – for our total universe, and specifically for human meaning?

How deeply can you enter into the immensity of the universe? As deeply as you can embrace it in the arms of your participation; as deeply as your symbols engage you in the spectacle of the intentional universe.

The symbols of God in various religions were not conceived as the result of the vanity of man or as a consequence of the irrationality of man. They were conceived as essential actors in the cosmic drama of becoming. What can a scientific equation do for us vis-à-vis an image of God? Scientific symbols are pale shadows of the extraordinary richness of the realities that religious symbols unveil to us and in which they allow us to participate.

Yet some symbols of science do exert a great fascination over our minds. The equation $E = mc^2$ is a marvel of human invention. And what a terrific potency it contains! Yes, precisely. It is a Faustian delight that we experience when we contemplate this symbol – for it is a symbol of a great power, the power that can explode and destroy. If it is the most significant equation that has ever been formulated by the human mind, it is also the most ominous – its visible symbol is the mushroom cloud over Hiroshima. Need we say more?

6. The mind as the creator of symbols

> Seen and unseen, heard and unheard
> Felt and not felt, the mind sees all
> Since the mind is all.
> Prasna Upanishad

Thus we come back to the phenomenon of the mind, which is the maker of symbols, the interpreter of symbols, and the coordinating agency of all symbolic activities.

The cunning of reason is endless, Hegel insisted. Yet it is not the cunning of reason that is of paramount importance in the ascent of man but the endless inventiveness of the human mind. The history of various cultures is a compelling testimony of how versatile, inventive, powerful and creative the mind is. Each culture is a different *symbolic skeleton* for deciphering the world in an ever new way. Cultural anthropologists, astonished by this versatility, began to treat each culture as separate, as a monad. Thus cultural relativism was born. Instead they should have seen in the variety of cultures a supreme manifestation of the great potency of the *universal human mind*. It is this potency that makes our mind a *participatory mind*.

The theatre of the mind is endlessly inventive. It writes the script in which the actors are people as well as objects of the outside world. Scientific theories are part of the theatre of the mind; they choreograph 'facts' and other aspects of the physical world so that they dance according to the tune of physical theories. At the very least we can say that our theories make physical phenomena behave according to the script of the play called 'Science'. Those phenomena that refuse to behave are chased out of the cast of the play. They are outcasts . . . Until a new play comes around, a new script is written in which they are given a legitimate part.

There is nothing that is excluded from the theatre of the mind. If anything is excluded from the mind, it is 'outside reality'. The theatre of the mind sets the boundaries to reality, defines and redefines these boundaries. 'Reality' does not have fixed boundaries. Whatever boundaries we find in it, they are imposed by the mind. In the very notion of boundaries there resides the phenomenon of mind, its peculiarly creative, transforming and defining powers. Whenever we handle the boundaries of reality, we handle the mind that delineates these boundaries.

The creation of symbols is one of the peculiar powers of the mind. In the making of symbols we have found another way of augmenting ourselves. For symbols have facilitated a new, important stage of our evolutionary articulation. By developing symbolic codes we have brought art, religion and philosophy to fruition. In the process we have articulated ourselves as social, cultural and spiritual beings.

The creation and perception of symbols is one of the uniquely human sensitivities. Take away this sensitivity, or this power of the human mind, and you deprive Homo Symbolicus of that which differentiates him from monkeys and other primates. It is our symbolic activity, the power to conceive symbols, and to use them extensively in an extraordinary variety of ways, that separates us from our brothers down the evolutionary ladder. Even if there is some symbolic activity going on among the primates, it is of such a low level of intensity that to all intents and purposes we can say that they have not developed the sensitivity for making symbols that are then integrated into their life-styles.

The deeper the mind, the deeper the symbols. The deeper the symbols, the richer the world we live in. Thus the richness of our life can be defined by the depth and richness of the symbols (and other forms of sensitivity) through which we can receive, decipher and transform the abundance of life.

Symbols do not exist in isolation. As long as we are within a culture (any culture for that matter), we are constantly under the influence of symbols. And this influence is subtle and often subterranean. For so often, symbols act on us through our subconscious and through our unconscious. Our psyche is structured by the symbols of our culture. The

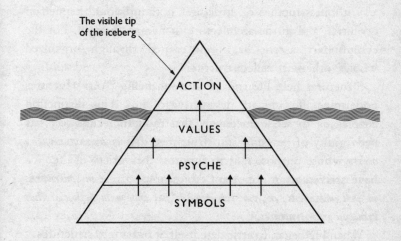

Fig. 7 *The pyramid of culture*

structure of our psyche shapes our values. Our values shape our action. Only on the level of action can we clearly describe what is happening. Action is the visible tip of the iceberg of which the hidden parts are our values, our psyche, our symbols (see Fig. 7).

The dominant symbols, as interiorized in our psyche, are three steps removed from our action. Moreover, at various points of the process leading from symbols to action, there are other forces that affect the outcome. Symbols are stronger than logic. Logic is often at their mercy.

Summary

The origin of all structures is the articulation of life. Structure is an open-ended scaffolding on which life can climb and flourish. All structure is a dwelling for life. The joy of structure is the blossoming of life woven around it.

Without structure or structures nothing would happen in evolution and in the architecture of human thought. For the evolutionary ascent has been carried through organized wholes, otherwise called structures.

Structures help life and are life-enhancing. Anti-structures undermine life and are destructive of life. This distinction enables us to see immediately that modern technology has been guilty of devising anti-structures, that is to say, *negative orders* whose purpose it is to suppress the variety of life. We have arrived at an important ethical imperative: *in your work, in your behaviour, in your research, do not engage in activities that result in anti-structures.*

When life began to articulate itself, it burst into structures.

When human life began to articulate itself, it burst into symbols.

Symbols continue the odyssey of structures on the level of culture. They make life enhancing on the spiritual level. Symbols share with structures the importance of rhythm and symmetry, particularly symbols of art. Yet the ultimate religious symbols seem to address themselves to a sphere of their own − as they attempt to reach out in order to symbolize man's oneness with the Ultimate Wholeness. The ultimate religious symbols do not articulate. They integrate.

Religion integrates.

Art articulates.

Science describes.

We devour symbols, and our lives are shaped by them. Tell me what your dominant symbols are and I shall tell you how you envisage the meaning of your life. If symbols were to be removed from us, we should spiral downwards to the level of monkeys. The greatness of our being is in proportion to the greatness of the symbols we contemplate, identify with, live by. Symbols are among the most profound inventions evolution has ever conceived.

The dominant symbol of Buddhism is the Buddha serenely sitting on the lotus flower − the symbol of eternal peace. The dominant symbol of Hinduism is the dancing Shiva − the symbol of the universe in perpetual transformation. The dominant symbol of Christianity is Jesus dying on the cross − symbol of the impermanence and suffering of life. Are we morbid as a culture because the dominant symbol, the cross, has acted on our psyche so as to *make* us morbid, preventing us from accepting the joy of life as a natural phenomenon?

When we compare scientific symbols with religious symbols, the striking difference is that scientific symbols are non-intentional; they are only descriptive or denotative. We as human beings live in an intentional universe − this is where values reside, this is where our emotional life resides. Because scientific symbols are not intentional, they leave us cold, they do not partake in our intentional life.

The symbols of God in various religions were conceived as dynamic actors in the cosmic drama of becoming. Scientific symbols are pale shadows of the rich complexities that religious symbols unfold to us and enable us to participate in.

We do not know what symbols are. They are mysterious entities which relate us to the world, to each other, and above all to the life of the spirit. In the existence of symbols there is contained part of the mystery of being human.

Of all the mysteries of the human existence, the mind is the most intriguing. It is both transparent and inscrutably opaque. It is the maker of symbols. It is the interpreter of symbols. It is the ruler that decides what relates to what and why. Two billiard balls, hitting each other, do not know that they are related by cause and effect. Our mind does.

We cannot unravel the complexity of the universe by looking at objects only. We can do it by looking most deeply into the mind. The universe does not hold secrets; only the mind does. All new *insights* are the flashes within. The contours of the outside world reflect the topography of our mind.

The deeper the mind, the deeper its symbols. The deeper the symbols, the richer the universe.

The glory of the universe is the unfolding epic of ever more penetrating symbols through which the destiny of the World is being realized.

CHAPTER 8

The Individual Spiral of Understanding

1. Our individuality and our universality

We are all individuals. We are all a part of the human family. Between these two truisms there lies a profound truth that in spite of being highly individual, we are universal beings; and in spite of being universal, we are highly individual. And the problem is to explain satisfactorily how our universality can be justified while our individuality is emphasized, and vice versa.

The epistemology of participation, based on the idea of the spiral of understanding discussed in previous chapters, attempts to explain how our individuality and our universality coexist with each other. It attempts to explain the vicissitudes of our individual lives and what happens when we grow mentally and spiritually; what happens when, in meditation, our horizons and our being are immensely enlarged – in short, how the phenomena of individual growth can be integrated into the fabric of culture and seen as congruent with the growth and manifestation of the universal mind.

Let us anticipate some of the argument and broadly sketch the canvas. Why do the Amazonian Indians appear to us to be such a different people from ourselves? Because their spiral of understanding makes them understand the cosmos in quite a different way from ours. Why do remote cultures seem to be so 'weird' in comparison with our culture? Because their spirals of understanding and their cosmoses are often so different from ours. Why does the world and thinking of Greeks of the fifth century BC appear so familiar to us? Because their spiral of understanding has become (via Rome, Christianity and the Renaissance) incorporated into our thinking and our perception of the world.

Why can two people of the same culture come to a violent disagreement over familiar things? Because their respective spirals of understanding may be so different that they interpret the phenomena in thoroughly different ways.

Why, in spite of all the examples cited, is understanding possible among people, even belonging to different cultures? Because we are one species, with common ancestry, and one mind that unites us all; and this is in spite of, and in addition to, the endless variations and manifestations of this mind.

2. The pain of becoming

When we grow physically, our body grows. When we grow mentally (intellectually, culturally, spiritually), our spiral of understanding grows.

How did the infant become Krishnamurti, the man of light and wisdom? Not merely by growing more grey cells. Actually, from the age of twenty-five we are continually losing grey cells – by millions every year. Krishnamurti and others who represent light and understanding grow spiritually by developing the spiral of understanding to the point that their mind is seen as light.

What happens when each of us grows in understanding, compassion, wisdom? Our spiral of understanding enlarges. And the way it does so is very subtle, mysterious and complex. Take some specific instances. We are suddenly struck with a new insight; or a new revelation dawns on us so that we see the world differently; or we see our relationship with another person completely differently. What does it all mean? It means that our existing spiral of understanding, by acquiring a new dimension, has pierced the walls of our hitherto existing individual cosmos. Our individual spiral of understanding is no longer what it was; it is now changed; significantly.

A radically new knowledge, as compared with that which the cone of our cosmos contains and is built upon, may shatter our world, and it may be a traumatic and agonizing experience. Such an experience may even be tragic – if we are unable to reassemble the pieces. On the other hand, piercing through the walls of the cosmos may be a liberating and exhilarating experience, after which we are elevated and start to live in new dimensions. This happens when new insights and new understanding enable us to transcend the old shell which is felt as a confinement and a prison. Each of these transformative experiences has a similar nature but dramatically different existential consequences: on the one hand, the shattering of the cone whereby we are shattered; on the other hand the loosening of the confining walls of the old cone, enabling a transition to a larger cosmos, within which we are liberated and enhanced.

How our individual growth takes place has been explained by many theories. Yet none of them explains this growth satisfactorily, and none probably ever will. One of the most significant theories of personal growth is that of the Polish psychologist K. Dabrowski, who postulated the idea of 'positive disintegration', according to which we do not grow mentally in a smooth, homogeneous, uninterrupted way. The process is discontinuous, at various times. There are some specific junctures at which a disintegration of the old personality (or of the old being) takes place. After a partial disintegration, we reintegrate on a new level, within a new spiral of understanding. When the process is completed, we call it 'positive disintegration'.

But sometimes we do not make it, the disintegration of the old is not followed by the reintegration of the new, like Kaspar in *The Tin Drum* we remain in a continuous state of disintegration, refuse to grow up, perhaps mentally ill for the rest of our life. It is a fascinating and awesome process, our journey through a partial disintegration, until, if we are lucky, we emerge out of the tunnel in a renewed shape.

This process of positive disintegration happens more than once in our life cycle. The first occasion is the transition from babyhood to childhood. A three-year-old child doesn't want to be treated as a baby any longer. It wants to be treated almost like an adult, it wants to sit on a normal chair, eat with a normal spoon. The baby is moving to another stage of personhood.

Another transition of this kind happens when the teenager is in the process of becoming an adult. The whole personality changes. The whole being changes, often accompanied by all kinds of ridiculous tantrums. There is no rational or logical explanation for the erratic and inexplicable behaviour. Deep down the spiral of understanding is reconstructing itself.

In our mature life too – if we are lucky – radical transitions occur when the old spiral is dismantled, and a new one is painstakingly reconstructed, and we become a new person. Why are these transitions so painful? Because literally, *we have to rebuild our cosmos*. Our identity is modified in the process. The old psychic niches are upset and uprooted. This is a disquieting and painful process.

Our idea of the spiral of understanding explains not only those big, traumatic, epochal changes, but also smaller and subtle ones. We do not change overnight. There are usually small, subtle changes going on all the time. In our daily lives there are moments of 'small revelations' as a result of which the whole cone of understanding is subtly though imperceptibly changed. It is then that our spiral of understanding pierces the cone – here and there . . . through new cracks new light slips in. These new 'cracks' may become our new sensitivities. For new sensitivities are new windows chiselled out in the blank walls of the cosmos.

In brief, in our development we do not grow smoothly and continuously. The discontinuities lead to tensions and sometimes to crises. These crises can sometimes be resolved within the existing psychic structure. Sometimes, however, they presage a transition to another structure. The crucial transitions are never easy and always painful. For what we experience is *the pain of becoming* – which cannot be alleviated, if we are to grow and mature.

Becoming is not a logical process. It is an emergent process; and a creative one. The creative process of any kind means giving birth to something new. Like giving birth to a baby, it is full of pain. Such is the nature of our contingent universe: *to create is to experience the pain of becoming. To be in the process of becoming is to experience creative pain.*

If pain is a precondition of real growth and real becoming, then we should not attempt to avoid it or try to escape it. For if we succeed in this escape, we may very well escape the process of growth itself. 'No pain, no gain.' To freeze one's development in order not to suffer is tantamount to psychic death.

Now the nature of the spiral of understanding helps us to comprehend why pain is an inseparable part of becoming. This comprehension may even provide some solace. In periods of real growth and becoming, the foundations of our psychic structure are impinged upon. Our stability and identity are challenged and unsettled. We feel insecure. This insecurity, extended over a period of time, particularly when it is acute, resolves itself in pain. Our being is in pain because it wants to stay where it is, while our becoming unanchors it and says: Come on, we must keep moving, we must fly. *The tension between being and becoming is a fundamental one in all evolution*, and in our individual lives as well. The result of this tension is always pain.

We may say, in brief, that the suffering of becoming is an inseparable part of our maturity and our spiritual growth. It is not the suffering that crushes and destroys, but the *suffering of becoming* that is part of the unfolding structure of the evolving universe.

As we evolve we change.

As we change we shed old skins and old shells.

As we reconstruct within we suffer the temporary disloca-tion of our identity.

As we suffer the inner dislocation, we are in pain.

All this is natural and inevitable.

The conclusion therefore is that pain is part of natural growth. We must not try to avoid it. But we must not court it either. It will come, as a part of real growth. That is the way to look at suffering from a larger evolutionary perspective.

3. Personal truth

Let us return to our consideration of the nature and growth of the individual spiral of understanding. First we should notice that it is not uniquely our own. Our mind is made of the mind of evolution, of the mind of the species, of the mind of the culture, of the mind of our family. Each of these larger minds is grafted on to our own, and so deep and pervading is the influence of these minds that it is astonishing that as individuals we still have a mind of our own.

We are so distinctly shaped by our culture – its assumptions, perceptions, prejudices and myths. Can you escape the influence of your culture, while it has shaped your spiral of understanding and your sensitivities from the cradle? (Sensitivities should never be forgotten, as they are the outreach tentacles of our mind!) We are profoundly influenced by our families. What is left that is our own?

Yet regardless how deeply we are steeped in past history and larger minds, and how profoundly we have been influenced by our culture, society and system of education, ultimately the spiral of our understanding is uniquely our own; just as our face, so similar to many other faces, is yet unique. It is therefore possible and justifiable to speak of the unique forms of perception of an individual; and also of his/her unique world-view which, although it is shared with many other individuals, yet may possess some features that are utterly singular.

If we go as far as that, then we can go a step further and ask: is it possible and justifiable to talk of personal truth? This last question is an extremely delicate one, particularly from the standpoint of established epistemologies. The problem is: how can we adhere to universal truths which are valid in virtue of the shared world-view (within a culture or a group of people) and at the same time recognize personal truths?

Let us see how the situation looks from the standpoint of the spiral of understanding. When we recognize universal truths (the truths of a given culture), we acknowledge that our spiral of understanding coincides with that of the culture. The reasons for that are many. We have been formed by the same biological, social and cultural circumstances as other members of our culture. We then sing in unison with that culture. Sharing universal (trans-subjective) truths is a precondition of our existence as social beings, capable of communion and communication with others.

The situation is different when we wish to defend our personal truths. Let us note, to begin with, that we then do not deny universal truths (which we share with others), but we rather insist that in addition to an enormous area of overlap of our individual spiral with the universal spiral of understanding, there are *some* aspects of our own spiral which are *unique and not reducible* to the universal spiral.

Why do we, each of us, have a different and unique spiral of understanding? Why is the cosmos so diverse? Why is it so that each snowflake is different? Perhaps the simple answer is: the cosmos delights in variety. Life needs variety for its exuberance and resilience. The human body, and the body of every animal, is a miracle of complexity. The human brain is one of the most complex creations of nature and of the cosmos. This complexity, when translated into individual minds, resolves itself in a myriad of different spirals of understanding. Those aspects of our individual spirals that are outside the universal spiral are the ones that make our world-view a little different, our perceptions a little different, and finally our truths a little different – not in all aspects but in some aspects of our perceptions of the world. Those idiosyncrasies of the individual spiral are usually small. They are most of the time suppressed and sacrificed for the sake of the common good. We don't want to make fools of ourselves by appearing different. Social and psychological pressures urge us to conform.

But there are times when the idiosyncrasies of our individual spirals of understanding (expressed as personal truths) become especially important for the individual. There are times when the individual does not wish to or is unable to suppress his/her truth. As a consequence a clash follows.

Religious heresies and new religious visions (so often suppressed in the name of universal truths) are an eloquent example of these unique perceptions that are expressed as new truths. At first they are personal truths. Only after a time, when others can 'see' these truths, do they become sharable and possibly universal. What do we mean by saying that others can 'see' these new truths and finally accept them? Simply that others have been able to change their spiral of understanding and so have become able to recognize that what was once deemed to be an individual heresy, or an individual idiosyncrasy, is now a *sharable* insight. Such is the story of every major and minor religion. After a new religious movement is established, many people share a new vision. Many spirals of understanding are now tuned to the same melody.

This transition from an individual, idiosyncratic truth to a collective sharable truth happens not only with regard to new religious visions. It also happens with regard to *scientific visions*.

The unrecorded history of science is the history of pains, dashed hopes, discarded visions which were not accepted by others. If no one had wanted to believe Galileo, if no one had paid any attention to his experiments with falling bodies, preferring to repeat established orthodoxies (as many did); if, in the process, no one had restructured any individual spiral of understanding so as to tune it to empirical science, the scientific world-view and science itself, as we know it today, *might never have arisen*. There was no necessity for science to emerge. When Einstein was asked why science did not originate in the East, he replied that the fact that science did not originate in the East does not need any explanation. What needs an explanation is that science emerged at all.

New scientific insights are similar to religious ones. In order to recognize their novelty, we need to restructure the spiral of our understanding. The law is universal: in order to see and understand new phenomena or new aspects of phenomena, we have to restructure the old spiral of our understanding. The acknowledged history of science is a repository of those insights that *made it*, by becoming accepted by others. Many scientific insights (as well as many new religious insights) never made it. For one reason or another, other individuals were unable or unwilling to switch over, to restructure their spirals of understanding to the requirements of a new insight, vision, perspective. In those circumstances, the new insight remains forever a personal truth of the inventor.

If we now reflect on our personal lives, we can clearly remember the instances when other people were telling us: 'This is how I see it; this is my truth.' This kind of perception and this kind of truth may have been at variance with the accepted norms. By and large, we are not very tolerant of personal truths and perceptions. Sometimes they are a manifestation of a sick mind. This has to be acknowledged. However, we also have to acknowledge that each individual mind is different. This opens the door to the recognition of personal truths which are a manifestation of the uniqueness and idiosyncrasy of the individual spiral of understanding.

Yet we have a problem here vis-à-vis established epistemologies. Existentially and psychologically, we have no difficulty in recognizing how different and unique we are as individuals. We celebrate and cherish this uniqueness. We are prepared to admit that our world-views are somehow different – because of the unrepeatability of our respective spirals of understanding. But even if this is granted, we still have difficulties in *justifying* the notion of personal truths. We are told that whatever our subjective make-up, including the structure of our mind, truth is a different category. Truth is supposed to be sacrosanct, immune from our existential individuation.

Let us address this point. Why is personal truth deemed so inferior and, in a sense, unfit to be recognized as truth – although in our hearts we often recognize and cherish it? The reason lies in our established philosophies, and particularly the ruling epistemologies, which can be very dictatorial and overpowering masters.

As a young man I read and discussed with my students Michael Polanyi's book *Personal Knowledge*, which anticipated some of my ideas. I read Polanyi's book with a sort of understanding, yet could not really accept the arguments he advanced. I was too much under Popper's influence. My spiral of understanding – in epistemological matters – was Popperian. So I had to reject the notion of personal knowledge. Agreeing with Popper, and other luminaries of the Western tradition, I had to assume, almost a priori, that there is no such thing as *personal* knowledge. If it is knowledge, then it must be *universal*. I regret now that I did not read Polanyi's book more deeply and with more understanding. Yet I know that at the time I could not have done so. My spiral of understanding was fixed. Moreover, I was formed and shaped in the best schools. I had my doctorate in philosophy from Oxford. I participated in Popper's seminars in London. What else could you wish for?

Actually, the most determined watchdogs of orthodoxy are not the mediocre minds from mediocre schools, but the brilliant ones from the best schools, for they think that they know best, being the brightest. They have the arrogance to perpetuate orthodoxy, in spite of all its weaknesses. Their brilliance is the licence for their arrogance. Even if they are given lucid, rational arguments in favour of different positions, they are unable to listen (as I was unable to read Polanyi's book properly). Their minds are in a cage. It is not easy to get out of this cage, particularly when you think that it is a palace. As far as philosophy is concerned, some of these cages have been constructed and maintained through centuries and millennia!

Let us remind ourselves that in most Western philosophical systems reality is assumed to be 'out there', independent of us. It is assumed furthermore that reality is knowable and that we can most adequately grasp and comprehend this reality out there through the categories of intersubjective knowledge.[1]

A very important role in this scheme of things is played by the correspondence theory of truth, or the classical theory of truth which underlies most Western philosophical systems. Truth is here conceived as the correspondence between reality and its descriptions. Both descriptions and reality are deemed to be trans-subjective. Thus it is implicitly assumed that what matters in the acquisition of genuine knowledge is the universal mind – as embodied in each of us singularly. The individual mind is screened out of the equation. To emphasize: the universal mind or the mind of the culture is the reigning monarch which outlines the boundaries of reality. It is this mind that establishes the correspondence between reality and its descriptions.

The whole scheme which Western philosophy (particularly science-oriented) so cherishes is on the one hand boldly optimistic, and on the other hand surprisingly crude.

(1) It assumes that we are all possessors of the universal mind, which is somehow embodied in each of us in the same

form and apparently in the same degree; because of this, it allows us to operate as the same universal beings.

(2) It assumes, moreover, that reality is knowable or accessible to us and can be *adequately* described in our theories; it assumes that we can *equally* well comprehend these theories – because of the first assumption.

(3) It assumes furthermore that our mind does not change historically and individually. We are supposed to have the same structure of mind – unchanging and fixed, yielding the same kind of knowledge through the eons of time.

All these assumptions are optimistic and curiously enough, democratic. They make us cognitive equals. Yet when examined in depth these assumptions strike us as rather crude. To begin with, it *cannot* be legitimately claimed that we all have the same universal mind embodied in us in the same form and degree. We are not just simple carbon copies of the same mind. Moreover, it is *naïve* to assume now, after the revelations of quantum mechanics, that reality is independent of the way we explore it and independent of the nature of the mind. Further still, it is *a gross oversimplification* to assume that the mind has not changed evolutionarily, historically, culturally. In consequence: as the knowing mind has changed, so have our descriptions of reality changed, so has our truth changed. That much must be clearly admitted. However, after two and a half millennia of a specific philosophical tradition, we have become blind to what lies outside this tradition. Inadvertently, we have all become the guardians of this tradition. And to such a degree that the culture almost automatically singles us out as *ir*rational if we seriously question the tradition.

To be coherent, to be rational, to make sense is to uphold the basic assumptions of our metaphysics. Because this metaphysics is so prevalent, in spite of its obvious defects, we have great difficulties in acknowledging personal truth. For the same reason we have great difficulties in questioning the notion of the firm, unalterable reality out there. What we are up against is the legacy of the Platonic/Aristotelian metaphysics reinforced and legitimized by the metaphysics of Thomas Aquinas. The way out of this pitiful cognitive predicament (as we have argued in earlier chapters) is to stop talking about reality and instead use the term reality-making. The change of language implies innumerable and far-reaching consequences.

In the twentieth century we have already had at least three significant departures from the legacy of Aristotelian rationalism: those represented by the attempts of Whitehead, Heidegger and Teilhard de Chardin. Although they markedly differ in their respective idioms, each is a clear departure from the metaphysical legacy of Aristotle, with its atomism and its correspondence theory of truth that lies at the heart of Western metaphysical realism: here is reality made of easily discernible, unchangeable fragments, each of which we can adequately describe in our language by establishing the relationship between it and our discrete descriptions of it.

In Heidegger, Whitehead and Teilhard, truth and thus reality are conceived in a manner different from that of metaphysical realism of the Aristotelian variety. Without bracketing these three thinkers closely together, we should recognize an essential difference between them and the entire body of classical doctrines of Plato, Aristotle, Aquinas, Descartes and Newton whose views loom very large over our intellectual horizons. These classical doctrines have monopolized our spirals of understanding. Indeed, our spirals of understanding are hostage to these noble yet now insidiously damaging traditions which imprison us in a box of stultifying 'reality'.

I have argued for the legitimacy of personal truth, but I do not wish to enshrine personal truth as all-important. Nor do I wish to eulogize the individual spiral of understanding as all-important. We are evolutionary creatures, social creatures, cultural creatures. To that degree our truths are common. Yet the individual mind and its truth – as reflected in the unique aspects of its spiral of understanding – must not be ignored. Therefore, a distinction must be made between shared (universal) truths and personal truths. In chapter 10 I outline participatory truth, which attempts to reconcile individual and intersubjective forms of truth. In the same chapter the notion of ultimate truth is outlined – which is the nexus of all truths.

4. The meaning of transformation

Transformation is a beautiful term. It embodies a multitude of virtues. Whatever aspect of evolution or of our lives we take, transformation has been at work. In recent times the term has become too popular, and therefore cheapened.

In our shattered world we all desire transformation, if only in order to heal ourselves, and become whole again. Since so many people desire transformation and wholeness, this demand must somehow be met. It is indeed often met in a superficial way. Weekend workshops are offered which promise to lead us to a complete transformation. Instant solutions are still in vogue in our culture. We are narcissistic people with spiritual pretensions. We have attempted to combine two incompatible things: the easy, painless process and the idea of a thorough transformation. Alas, these things cannot be combined.

A meaningful transformation, which brings about a new structure of our being, can be no easy, weekend affair. The Illustrious Ones knew better when they exhorted us, sometimes gently, sometimes not so gently, on the necessity of discipline – which often includes the path of austerity.

In 1985 I paid my second visit to Dharamsala, in northern India, to see the Dalai Lama. The little mountain village in the foothills of the Himalayas is almost entirely occupied by Tibetan refugees, with the Dalai Lama's palace perched on a nearby hill. During my first visit some three years earlier, I had been moved by his simplicity and his genuine concern for all sentient beings. I was also impressed by the way Tibetan monks are trained, or should we say, train themselves: endless memorizations of classical texts ... and at the end of the process – the mind breathing universal compassion, which they call the Great Compassion.

I stayed at a little state-run hotel – extremely clean and efficient, with the meals brought to my room whenever I so desired – with no extra charge. One afternoon I heard a knock on my door. I went to the door. I saw a Tibetan monk with a European face; or shall I say, I saw a European man in the garb of a Tibetan monk. My first fleeting reaction was ... 'Oh, no! I didn't come here to suffer Western man in Tibetan garb.' However, *habitus non facit monachum*, I thought to myself. He introduced himself as Songye Samdrup. And we started to talk.

He came from a good bourgeois Swiss family of the name of Dreyfus. His father had wanted him to be a doctor – rather predictably. But that was not to his son's liking. Indeed, the whole lifestyle of the Swiss bourgeoisie was not to his liking. He said to me: 'I took life rather seriously and did not want to waste it on trivia.'

After having tried various alternative paths, one day he went to a lecture by a Tibetan lama. He liked what he heard. Soon he found himself in Dharamsala – much to the alarm of his father. He liked the Tibetan way of life, of thinking, of training the mind. He decided to stay. He was sent to one of the large Tibetan monasteries in southern India. He stayed there many years absorbing the learning, the language, the culture.

He finally reemerged, after some fifteen years, to become a *geshe* (not to be confused with Japanese *geisha*), which is a Tibetan name for a learned man; the term 'doctor' approximates the idea. But the title *geshe* is much more difficult to obtain. Dreyfus became the first-ever European geshe. One has to know something of the ordeal to appreciate the achievement.

The learning in Tibetan monasteries is scholastic in high degree. One learns by heart all the classic texts; and then major commentaries; as well as major arguments pro and con. The tradition is still verbal, as it was at Oxford and at the Sorbonne in the fourteenth century. It usually takes some twenty to twenty-five years to master the texts and dialectical skills (for this learning is a continuous battle of arguments) before one is ready for the Big Examination for the title of geshe. One is in one's forties, sometimes touching fifty, before becoming a learned man in the Tibetan tradition.

The Big Examination is, rather, an intellectual battle that takes several weeks. In the presence of several hundred monks of a given monastery, the candidate is grilled, each monk asking whatever subtle and devious question he chooses.

Mr Dreyfus, now known by his Tibetan name Songye Samdrup, had gone through all this not long before I met him. He became a geshe in his late thirties, a rather early age. He was one of the protégés of the Dalai Lama. In the process of absorbing Tibetan learning this Westerner became 'one of them' – a complete Tibetan monk, speaking perfect Tibetan and thinking as they do.

On the afternoon when I met him, Mr Dreyfus not only

knew about my proposed visit to the Dalai Lama, but also of the proposed dialogue (conceived by the Director of the Tibetan Library) between local lamas and myself on the nature of mind. When I had talked to the Director two days earlier, he asked me what I was working on. I said the participatory mind; and then explained what it was all about. He said: 'Your theory reminds me of one of our theories called "Mind Only". Will you talk to some of our lamas on the subject?' And so a symposium was organized, the first of its kind. We debated in a setting which had a touch of the Byzantine and also of how I imagined Oxford debates of the fourteenth century. On my left were two incarnated lamas, on my right two geshes; further down two interpreters. We sat on cushions on a raised platform, while the audience sat below on the floor. It was one of the most memorable debates I have ever attended.

The main question which I raised was: 'To what degree are Buddhist techniques of moulding the mind artful and ingenious impositions (on the mind of something that is not at first there); and to what degree do they simply *elicit* the nature, the endowment and the attributes of the human mind?' Put in a simplified way: 'To what degree do Buddhist methodologies and techniques of the mind correspond to the architecture and ontology of mind?'

During the debate I simplified the question further: 'Is the mind inherently compassionate or is compassion acquired?' When I put the question in this sharp and succinct manner they were rather surprised by it, as if they had not thought about the question before. Which was rather surprising to me, for compassion and the compassionate mind is the subject of their daily discourses. Towards the end of the discussion a tentative answer emerged. Yes, the mind is inherently compassionate. But it was not a very firm answer. During the rest of the debate (and indeed through the bulk of their studies) the Tibetan lamas seemed to be saying: even if the mind is not compassionate, we can make it compassionate. The endless Tibetan techniques of controlling the mind are created for this purpose.

Compassion and the compassionate mind are so much taken for granted in the cultures inspired by Mahayana Buddhism that the question is never raised whether it is possible to attain compassion, but only: what is the best way of arriving at it, and of cultivating it? In the Buddhist framework human nature is assumed to be noble. Compassion is an aspect of this inherent nobility – even if it has to be elicited through arduous work.

All of this is in contrast to the Western tradition, particularly the present nihilistic outlook on human nature. In the Western scheme of understanding compassion does not even enter the picture. Bombarded by shallow theories of human nature, as well as by the crass ideology of profit-making, we take the selfish-aggressive nature of man to be self-evident truth. When I talk to my students at American universities about my encounters with other cultures, when I tell them about Tibetan Buddhists, they listen to these stories as if they were Sinbad the Sailor tales. When I look deeper into their minds, I realize how thoroughly their spiral of understanding has been formed and conditioned by the ideology of the crass, materialist, consuming West.

Now let us draw some conclusions. The fact that a young middle-class Swiss could become a Tibetan geshe strikingly demonstrates that our mind has an almost infinite capacity. But the development of this capacity is an arduous process, and so is the process of the transformation of the spiral of understanding that accompanies it. No shortcuts to glory. No superficial ego-massage as a substitute for a meaningful reconstruction. No stroking as a substitute for working on one's soul.

Needless to say, I am not recommending the route of the Tibetan geshe for those who seek to attain deeper meaning and spiritual fulfilment. There are all kinds of yogas and procedures leading to transformation. All spiritual work based on systematic exercises is a Yoga of Transformation.

However, we are bound to ask: are there some underlying rules and principles which can help one in embarking on the path of a genuine transformation – as contrasted with a mere ego-massage? I shall attempt to provide some of these principles. As in previous chapters, we are using the term 'yoga' in a broad sense, as a set of strategies and principles which lead to a new mind set, to a new spiral of understanding. There are at least ten principles of the Yoga of Transformation.

(1) Become aware of your *conditioning*.

(2) Become aware of *deep assumptions* which you are subconsciously upholding.

(3) Become aware of the most important *values* that underlie the basic structure of your being, and of your thinking.

(4) Become aware of *how these assumptions and values guide and manipulate your behaviour, action, thinking*.

(5) Become aware *which of these assumptions and values are undesirable* because they dwarf your horizons or arrest your growth in one way or another. (Example: 'I am an inferior person'; example: 'The world is a machine and human beings are a kind of machine'; example: 'There is no compassion in the world, all is greed and competition – I must do as others do.') Each of these assumptions may be held at a deep subconscious level, and from there may be controlling you.

(6) *Watch and observe the instances of your actions and behaviour* while they are manipulated by the undesirable

assumptions/values. Identify clearly the causes and the effects.

(7) *Articulate alternative assumptions and values* by which you would like to be guided and inspired.

(8) *Imagine the forms of behaviour, actions and thinking* that would follow from the alternative assumptions/values.

(9) *Deliberately try to bring about the forms of behaviour, thinking and action* expressing the new assumptions. Implement your new assumptions in your daily life. Watch the process. *Repeat the process.* Practice is important.

(10) *Restructure your being* in the image of these assumptions; which is to say, restructure your spiral of understanding. Point ten merely recapitulates and summarizes previous points.

The perceptive reader will notice that the methodology of participation (discussed in chapter 6) and the yoga of transformation overlap with each other. The methodology of participation is formulated for the universal mind, which wants a rational justification for a set of alternative strategies that will spell out an antidote to the perils of objectivity.

The yoga of transformation, on the other hand, is a set of strategies for the individual mind that is on the path of self-transformation. Each of these sets of strategies could be translated into the language of the other set, so that the yoga of transformation becomes an adjunct of the methodology of participation, and the methodology of participation becomes a part of the strategies of the yoga of transformation.

The gift of transformation is not one given to you from heaven, but one that you give yourself at the end of the long, arduous but exciting journey.

5. The spiral of understanding and meditation

Let us now consider the spiral of individual understanding during the process of meditation. We need not worry at this point what meditation is. Suffice it to say that it is a process of deep relaxation combined with a process of deep reflection – a process of going into the depths of ourselves that enables us not only to rest deeply but somehow detach ourselves from the busy ticking of our mind – according to its usual routines. The form of meditation does not matter for the moment. It may be just observing your breath, as is the case in the Teravada schools of meditation. It may be a guided imaginary tour, or any kind of meditation in between.

If meditation is successful we gain during the course of it a capacity to look at ourselves; and more importantly at our own mind – from a distance. During such moments we can really see how conditioned our minds are and how conditioned are the forms of our thinking. We are looking then, as it were, at our own spiral of understanding from a vantage-point outside the spiral – which does not often happen in our busy lives.

Now during prolonged periods of meditation we can not only step out of our spiral but actually enlarge it. This happens when we are able to find in what way it constrains us; more specifically which assumptions our spiral holds and how these assumptions affect us. Reasoning with assumptions is a most difficult task. They invariably control our thinking from a hidden layer below. Now during the process of meditation, when the discursive and coldly rational functions of the mind are suspended, it is easier to 'talk to our assumptions', to question and examine them, than during normal periods when we simply act these assumptions out.

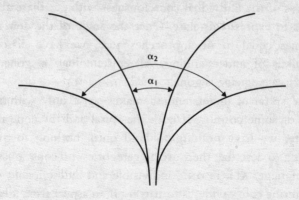

Fig. 1 *As our spiral of understanding is enlarged from α_1 to α_2, so is our cosmos*

Meditation can thus be used as an aspect of the yoga of transformation.

When we enlarge our spiral of understanding, our cosmos is also enlarged. Returning to our picture of the cone of the cosmos in chapter 3, we can say that the angle of the cone of the cosmos grows, which signifies an enlarged cosmos. In Fig. 1 α_2 represents the enlarged cone of the cosmos α_1 (the original cone, the original cosmos of the individual).

Now suppose that we enlarge the cone of understanding further and further. The angle of our cone increases. Our cosmos enlarges and enlarges. What happens if we keep enlarging this angle? Extraordinary things happen! If during meditation, or through some other means, we succeed in transcending all assumptions, liberating ourselves from all spirals of understanding, then we become infinite, our understanding is infinite, our cosmos is infinite. There are no constraining walls to our cosmos then; there are no walls of any kind.

This is the state in which the Atman meets the Brahman, when one is united with the One, the state of ultimate oneness of the individual consciousness with . . . there are no words to express this state. Once the angle of the new cone becomes equal to or approaches 360°, we have dissolved all spirals of understanding. All epistemology is gone. All discursive language is gone.

The spiral of understanding makes sense only within the walls of some cosmos. If both the spiral and the cone reach infinity, we have nothing to hold onto, nothing to grasp, nothing to describe; there are no categories, no consciousness, no language. ALL IS ONE, indivisible and indescribable – for to describe is to divide, is to parcel off an aspect from a larger whole.

Although this state is clearly beyond words (and we should be foolish to try to describe it), yet playing with the idea is a rational act, like many mathematical exercises in which we play with infinity. The use of our spiral now becomes a means of expressing in words what otherwise is unsayable, namely the oneness of all things – seamless and indivisible – when the angle of the spiral of understanding reaches 360°.

Can we ever reach this state in any form of meditation? Even if we do (in however brief moments), there is no way of conveying it in words. Mystic poetry and great religious teaching on the nature of God attempt to convey this seamless infinity. But truly, this is to no avail. For what they convey are *fragments*. However, these fragments seem to give us a glimpse of this infinity – of which we cannot speak. Meditation is still lamentably neglected in the West as a strategy of understanding.

6. The fable of the brain's two hemispheres

Once upon a time we recognized a single brain. Then came neurophysiologists poking into various functions of our grey cells. They soon discovered that different parts of the brain were responsible for various functions of our thinking and behaviour. Then, in the 1970s, they generalized their findings and asserted that the left side of the brain is *predominantly* responsible for abstract, discursive and analytical thinking and action, while the right side of the brain is *predominantly* intuitive, emotional, artistic, integrative. The word 'predominantly' must be stressed in both cases for no claims were made that we know with absolute certainty how these hemispheres work precisely. Nor was it claimed that all forms of thinking and action must be generated either by this or that hemisphere, and that none can be generated by the two hemispheres working in unison. For example, when we compose music, it is obvious that the two hemispheres are simultaneously involved. For composing music is a highly intuitive and artistic activity and, at the same time, highly structured, and, let us say it – analytical. And so it is with many activities we perform *daily*.

Yet the appeal of the splitting of the brain into two distinctive hemispheres was enormous. We like neat divisions. This is part of the heritage of Cartesian dualism and also of Cartesian crispness. Now we decry Descartes' separation of the mind from the body. We also decry Descartes' analytical method, which neatly and clinically separates all things into isolated compartments, for this method is responsible for much of the process of atomization, and following it the process of alienation. Yet deep down we seem to love this Cartesian-clinical sorting out! The separation of the brain into two *distinctive* hemispheres is essentially a Cartesian exercise, a split that divides what we know as working in a unitary way in our own lives.

When one looks deeper into the causes of this general enthusiasm for the brain's two hemispheres, one cannot escape the conclusion that the reason why the public and the scientists are so eager to accept the two hemispheres is that the workings of the brain are explained in *physical* terms. Thus the situation is very revealing: it is physical science *again* that asserts its dominant position and we bow to it. We are so conditioned to accept as genuine only *physical* explanations. It boggles the mind how absurdly reductionist we have become – even when we attempt to explain the highest mysteries, such as the mind.

In one sense splitting the brain into two hemispheres is an easy way out. We have finally found the scapegoat: it is the left hemisphere that is the culprit. It is the monster in our midst that paralyzes.

The 'discovery' of the two hemispheres, as working according to two different patterns and functions, may have been important for identifying *some* of our problems. However, the adulation of the split as explaining them *all* has created a conceptual myopia in the wake of which some real and deeper problems are explained away. Our two hemispheres are out of balance. The left hemisphere is an ogre intimidating and suppressing our right hemisphere. We are the innocent victims.

Perhaps the two hemispheres of the brain are always out of balance. Perhaps the balance between the two, if there is one, is a dynamic one, collapsing from moment to moment, and reestablished from moment to moment. Perhaps we don't even know what the balance of the two hemispheres is. For how can we? Can we imagine a person or a method that can decide for you and me the right balance of the two hemispheres – while analysing the functions of the respective hemispheres in terms of their neurophysiological underpinnings? I submit that there isn't such a person or a method if only because what we call *balance* is not a neurophysiological category (or a scientific one) but an existential state of being which is assessed on the scales of our soul as we experience life in its more subtle and meaning-impregnated moments. Thus ultimately it is not a matter of neurophysiology but a matter of metaphysics.

I am not denying that the left hemisphere of the brain is the focus of more analytical and abstract functions. I am not denying either that in our scientific-technological culture the left hemisphere is favoured and (because of our education and training as well as the demands of the technological society) developed much more vigorously than, and often at the expense of, the right hemisphere. But I am weary of the hasty conclusions that are drawn from these facts. The hasty conclusions prompt some to seek liberation by abolishing the tyranny of the left hemisphere and by wanting to live by the right hemisphere alone. The Nobel Laureate Sir John Eccles has repeatedly stressed that we know very little at present of how the neurophysiological functions of the brain can satisfactorily explain the workings of the mind; perhaps in a hundred years, he suggests, we might know something more on the subject.

There is indeed a grave imbalance in our life if we allow abstract analytical modes of our minds to dominate our being to the point that we become dry sticks, devoid of emotional life and withering in the straitjacket of objectivity, logic and functional rationality.

But another form of imbalance is possible and often occurs, namely when we try to live by the right hemisphere of the brain alone. We then end up in emotional messes. Our emotional life runs rampant and we become a slave to it. The reasoning by pure brain is a mistake in the long run. But reasoning by blood alone is equally dangerous. Emotions running loose may be as dangerous to our balance as excessive rationality freezing it.

The sense of order within our being is a subtle thing. All cultures and most religions have tried, often in a most subtle way, to impose emotional control on us. These controls are called ethical codes, codes of honour, duty, obligation. They often include the process of sublimation of our sexual urges, and other manifestations of our imperial ego.

Thus the right balance of our being does not mean going overboard to worship the brain's right hemisphere and allow it to run loose. *The right balance is a proper articulation and the right orchestration of our sensitivities.* The heart and the emotions have to be cultivated in the form of appropriate sensitivities. Only then do we become masters of our own life – by mastering multifarious sensitivities that make our life abundant. Through the articulateness of our sensitivities we weave patterns of meaning. Unarticulated emotions can become a torrent that messes up our being. Articulated emotions, when crystallized in enduring works of art, are things of beauty, the joy of human life, and the pride of evolution.

Thus the right path to wholeness is not a superficial synthesis of the brain's right and the left hemispheres but the cultivation and articulation of human sensitivities, including wisdom and compassion, which in a subtle and uncanny way shape and delineate the uniqueness of the human person.

7. A model of the integrated self

The models of the self are as numerous as the various conceptions of man. We shall here look at three basic ones, and then propose a fourth, on the canvas of which I shall attempt to develop a model of the integrated self for our time. Since this is not a systematic historical examination of the various theories of the self, only essential backbones of the various concepts of the self will be sketched here.

Each model of the self not only reveals what it considers to be the essential meaning of human life but is in fact *a disguised form of religion*. The first is the Hindu. In this model the individual self receives its meaning by participating in the Absolute Self. When the Atman (the individual self) completely merges with the Brahman (the Absolute Self) and dissolves in it, the individual self is completely redeemed, fulfilled and at peace. The strife is ended, and the Nirvana achieved. In this model the individual self acquires its significance by the presence in it of the Absolute Self. The individual self is sustained by the Absolute Self, and finally dissolved in it.

This model has many variants. It is quite evident in many monotheistic religions, including Christianity, Judaism and Islam, within which the individual receives the greatest fulfilment when he/she is united with God and dissolved in God. I have chosen the Hindu model as the exemplar because within it the relationship between the individual self (the Atman) and the cosmic self (the Brahman) is very clearly spelled out; while this relationship is often confusedly spelled out in Abrahamical religions.

The second model of the self is that of Plato. The individual self (the soul) is imprisoned in the prison of the body; or at least limited and constrained by the body. The process of liberation and of self-actualization is one of overcoming the coarseness of the body. This occurs through the process of Enlightenment. The individual self then merges with the Form of the self. Plato's programme of liberation consists of the realization of the god-within, which is identified with the absolute Form. The meaning of life and the meaning of the self are related to the essence of man – the Form underlying our existence. In the Hindu model the self (Atman) is liberated by *dissolving* in the Brahman (the Cosmic Self). In Plato's model (as well as in the Buddhist one), the self is liberated through its own effort, until the self reaches the very core of its being – the god-within.

The third model of the self is the *existentialist* model of Sartre and his followers. There is no absolute; there are no essences in this model. The self is conceived as a drifting monad without a higher aim or purpose. Since the individual existence is wretched and meaningless, the best we can do is to enjoy it perversely. Though overtly atheistic, the existential model possesses its curious ideology. It is one in which God is dead. The universe has no purpose or meaning; nor do we. Existential despair is a natural state. There is no abode for our hopes and higher aspirations. There is only brute matter out there. And *us* – freaks from the standpoint of the vast, mute and cold universe. Viewed historically, the existentialist model of the self is a derivation of other models representing the philosophy of resignation such as Epicureanism, cynicism, hedonism – all born at the time of the shrinking of man.

The fourth model of the self that I wish to propose is the *participatory* model. The individual self and the cosmic self are in the process of continuous evolution, each contributing to the other as evolution goes on. The individual self does not merge with the absolute self or the form of the self that is ready, out there, and waiting for us. The self is *projected* into Omega, which is the cosmic self at the end of time, and which is also our individual self at the end of time. In continually upgrading itself, the individual self contributes to the cosmic self.

Meaningful life, in the evolutionary model, is the life of continuous becoming. Continuous becoming signifies continu-

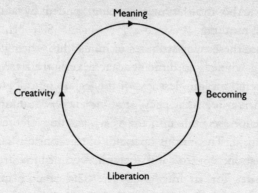

Fig. 2 *The mandala of the life of continuous becoming*

ous creativity; it also signifies continuous liberation from the shackles of old being, which wants to hold us back. Thus meaning = becoming = liberation = creativity. And conversely, creativity signifies liberation; and also signifies becoming and ultimately the attainment of meaning. The four concepts co-define each other; they form a mandala pattern (Fig. 2).

These four concepts outline a new theology. The name of this theology is: 'We are God in the making', through our creative potential, through the process of continuous becoming.

How does the evolutionary model of the self help us to become integrated selves in our time? What are its practical consequences? Taking these questions a step further: what are the most important aspects of the integrated self?

Being at peace, which means attaining the optimal state of being; not grumbling, not being torn by ever new desires, ambitions, envy, jealousies.

Being whole, which means not being fragmented, decimated,

scattered. Above all it means being guided by a coherent pattern of meaning.

Why are these two attributes of human life – being at peace and being whole – so difficult to achieve nowadays? Because of the overall meaninglessness of the technological world – its frantic drive for efficiency, its violence. Meaninglessness and violence are built into the very structure of the techno-logical world. The modus operandi of this world is efficiency, fragmentation, control and manipulation, which are hardly prerequisites for an integrated life. The other major cause of the meaninglessness of our present world is the shatter-ing of old myths and symbols, with which we could identify, and around which we could weave the tapestry of our meanings.

The key to meaningful reconstruction lies in the idea of participation. How deeply can you enter into the immensity of the universe? As deeply as you can embrace it in the arms of your participation. Everything else is mere shadow. The real thing is the immense journey of participation. Therefore, choose the modes of your participation well. For those modes spell out the shape of the meanings of your life.

If you choose to participate in the rat-race and cut-throat competition, only strife will follow; and the shattering of peace within. If you think that you cannot avoid the rat-race and competition, it simply means that you are not ready to choose a way of life that leads to the integrated self. The integrated self is not a gift of heaven. It is a gift from yourself – if you are determined to work on yourself with the single-mindedness that the highest human attainments require. The integrated self is one of the high attainments of the human species. In comparison, most high-tech achievements are low attainments.

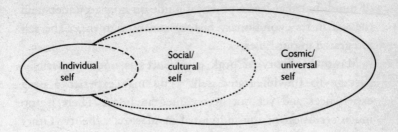

Fig. 3 *Positive image of the self*

The integrated self cannot be arrived at by merely avoiding the rat-race, cut-throat competition and other stress-laden pursuits. Let us not confuse the quest for excellence and perfection with ruthless competition. The integrated self is accomplished by the positive construction of the self. What kind of positive image of the self should we maintain while we strive for the integrated self? It is the image of the individual self that is harmoniously merging with and meaningfully participating in the social self, and then the universal self.

Fig. 3 suggests neither the submerging nor dissolving of individual self in the social and the cosmic selves, but a meaningful and deep participation in each.[2]

The integrated self is not a static entity. In different periods of our life, in different stages of our becoming, we sculpt ourselves in different shapes, we strike a different form of balance between the universe and ourselves.

What are the right strategies for attaining the integrated self? Among these strategies are the yoga of transformation, the methodology of participation, and an in-depth understanding of the spiral of understanding. The reader who has read thus far will have realized long ago that this book is not only a theoretical treatise on the new epistemology and a new theory of mind, but that it is a practical guide on how to understand the self in its evolutionary history and how to make the self integrated in our times.

Maslow's theory of peak experiences is not necessarily a passage to the integrated self.[3] You may experience peak experiences and yet not be an integrated self. There is too much seclusion of the individual in Maslow's theory. Other psychological theories of self-satisfaction and self-contentment are of a similar sort: they seclude the individual and hardly ever offer a passage to the integrated self. Any theory that caters to the selfish interests of the individual is suspect as a vehicle of the integrated self, regardless of how eloquently it is expressed and how well it is justified. Self-integration and self-interest are two different things.

To be truly integrated, you must participate in the interests of the human family and of the cosmos at large. If you only cultivate your own garden, if you don't participate in some kind of heaven which is above you and beyond you, you cannot be genuinely whole and integrated. We do not need to invoke Hindu terminology according to which the Atman is part of the Brahman, or Christian terminology according to which we are children of God, in order to realize that there is more to the individual self than this self itself.

The key to our selfhood, the key to our self-realization and to self-integration, lies in the appropriate forms of participation. The universe of participation is immensely powerful, if we make participation an inherent part of our universe.

8. The participatory mind and the space of grace

Unwrapping the sense of human meaning leads us directly to the idea of the universe that is endowed with a purpose. But more than just any purpose – a deeper purpose, a transcendent purpose, a purpose touching on the sacred. In brief, sacredness, of the universe and of human life, is inherent in the idea of life that is permeated with deeper meaning.

The meaning of the sacred cannot be understood unless the meaning of life is understood. The 'meaningful' and the 'sacred' are inherently connected. They present two facets of the same phenomenon. 'Sacred' is a religious term for expressing the ultimate depths of human meaning. On the other hand, 'deeply meaningful' is an existential expression for those special reverential moments of our life that we hold as sacred – although we do not use the term.

In the last chapter of *Mind and Nature: A Necessary Unity* Gregory Bateson relates the sacred to the beautiful. He writes: 'The *sacred* (whatever that means) is surely related (somehow) to the *beautiful* (whatever that means). And if we could say how they are related, we could perhaps say what the words mean. Or perhaps that would never be necessary.'[4]

This last chapter of Bateson's book is enigmatic. It is a sort of postscript. It is written in the form of a dialogue (with his daughter). Bateson had difficulties in openly discussing the sacred – as we all do, after having been conditioned by a secular and narrowly rational education. In a conversation with me, a year before his death, Bateson confided that his next book was to be about the sacred, its place in human life, its necessity for human existence. The title of the book was decided, *The Angels' Fear*, an abbreviation of the phrase 'where angels fear to tread'.

When faced with inexorable difficulties we may want to restate Pascal's wager argument. What is more rational to assume: that you are a divine being and live in a divine universe? Or that you are a biological-chemical machine which subsists in the purposeless physical universe? What do you gain by believing the former? The deep meaning of your life, the beautiful, the sacred. What do you lose? Nothing. Therefore you must bet on the divinity of your existence. Pascal might have argued: to conceive of the divine cosmos in which we are divine agents is a necessity of life in which meaning is to prevail. And Bateson might have added: and in which the beautiful is at home.

What is the meaning of sacred space? Does it exist of itself, independently of the mind, by its 'objective' characteristics, so to speak? Or is it created by the human mind? We often hear about sacred geometries, of Chartres Cathedral for example. It would appear that these spaces are sacred *as they are* and *because of what they are*.

But can it be so? Can sacred spaces be declared as such *without* the participation of the participatory mind? Is it not the participatory mind that makes spaces and geometries sacred because of its dispositions and powers?

We become God when we experience some spaces as sacred, at whatever brief moments of time. Or more precisely, we assume the characteristics of God when we enjoy a spiritual experience. Alternatively, we experience the world as sacred because God dwells in us at the moment of these experiences.

'He who thinks becomes God' (Upanishads).

He who participates in God becomes God.

He who participates in the context of God becomes God.

He who is capable of creating the context of God becomes God.

Being at one with God is participating in God's plan. (God's plan when spelled out means: he/she who has the power of empathy and of deep identification (on the emotional, spiritual and intellectual levels) with those attributes through which we conceive of God – becomes God.)

He/she who lives in Grace inhabits sacred spaces.

He/she who lives in Grace possesses the reverential frame of mind and is guided by reverential perception.

Let us try to articulate these rhapsodic insights through the categories of participatory mind. The reverential frame of mind and reverential perception create the space of grace. The space of grace, on the other hand, transforms the mind into a reverential one. *When the participatory mind enters the space of grace, it becomes the reverential mind.* The reverential mind is the form of attunement of the mind that allows us to enter the space of grace.

The space of grace, or God's space, is always there, always around us. In order to enter it, we must possess an appropriate vehicle to deliver us there. The reverential frame of mind is one such vehicle. The state of mystic contemplation is another. The Christian conception of revelation is another. 'The state of mystic contemplation' or 'the Christian conception of revelation', when analysed in depth, reveal themselves to be forms of *the reverential state of mind – forms of the participatory mind after it has entered the space of grace.*

Do we enter the space of grace through some kind of divine gate or is this space created by ourselves? According to the traditional view, especially the Christian view, grace is considered a gift, God's gift. It is bestowed on us whether we deserve it or not. Within the Hindu framework the state of our individual grace is a gift of the Brahman, is bestowed on us by the Brahman – conceived as the absolute everlasting ground of being from which everything springs and by which everything exists and moves.

In both the traditional Christian framework and the

traditional Hindu framework, grace is explained as *deus ex machina* – by the intervention of divine powers residing outside ourselves. Participation in God is then an act of divine mercy bestowed upon us from outside. (Admittedly there is a considerable difference between the Christian and Hindu interpretations of grace, since in the Hindu framework Karma plays an important role.) Now according to Plato's conception of God-within, and also according to the Buddhist idea of self-realization, it is a different story. You clear away the rubble from the path of your life to reach God-head which resides within (Plato); you work on yourself to release the Buddha which resides within you (Buddhism).

Within the framework of the participatory mind, (as with Plato and Buddha) it is our mind which creates the attributes and structures that enable the mind to become reverential. Through this act we create the space of grace.[5] When the mind is in a permanent condition of reverence, we have created within ourselves the state of grace. The space of grace, or sacred space, is created by the condition of the mind that experiences 'ordinary' spaces in an extraordinary way.

The divine mind is part of evolution divinizing itself. The experience of divinity is part of the natural process. There are no occult forces, no supernatural interventions, no magic – except the magic of becoming. Thus magic is part of the natural process. The point is that the natural (at certain pivotal junctures) manifests itself as magical.

Let us note however that creating a reverential mind out of 'ordinary' mind is not a matter of chance, or playing some form of cosmic roulette. It is a matter of discipline, exercise, practice, attuning yourself to the highest light. The Buddha has taught: Be forever awake. Be forever watchful. Keep your mind clear. A well controlled mind is a source of great joy.

In the Eastern traditions we possess an enormous array of

exercises, of yogas which enable us to so train our mind that it becomes reverential. The state of the ultimate enlightenment of which the yogas and the Buddhas speak signifies experiencing reverentially all reality around oneself. One lives then in a sacred space – because one has made all space around oneself sacred. When the mind is totally liberated and enlightened one lives in the space of grace because one has created the structure of experience within oneself that receives everything as sacred.

Through its natural magic, evolution has created mind. Through its natural magic, the mind co-creates with reality. A part of the process of co-creation is the creation of reverential space. When one lives permanently in reverential spaces one lives in grace. Participatory mind is a vehicle of divinity. For there is no other vehicle to deliver us to divinity.

Summary

Our individuality and our universality are engaged in a continuous eternal dance. We are not monads. We are not carbon copies of the same universal mind. We share vast realms of our experience with others, including language, symbols and the appreciation of art. Our individual spiral of understanding merges with the universal spiral, but not completely. It is shaped and determined by the universal spiral, but not entirely. We are the guardians of our own spiral. It alone determines the meaning and the shape of our life.

The individual spiral of understanding evolves continuously. In its evolution there are discontinuous jumps. When they occur our cosmos is in disarray. The recomposition of the spiral of understanding in our own life is always a painful process. These are the pains of becoming. We must not avoid them. For in avoiding them, we would avoid our greater destiny.

Becoming is not a logical process. It is an emergent process, and a creative one. To create is to experience the pains of becoming. To be in the process of becoming is to experience creative pains. As we evolve, we change. As we change, we leave behind the old shells. As we reconstruct within, we suffer a temporary dislocation of our identity. As we suffer the inner dislocation, we are in pain. All this is natural and inevitable. Pain is a part of individual growth and of evolutionary growth. We must not try to avoid it. But we must not court it either.

Truth is a sublime subject and a difficult one. When we talk about truth, we often imagine it to be something given from above, something so mighty and universal that we simply must bow to it. Yet truth is a matter of understanding. Truth is indeed a form of understanding. All understanding is a function of our spiral of understanding. When we recognize universal truths it simply means that our individual spiral sings in unison with other spirals. At such a time universal truths prevail.

However, our individual spiral of understanding cannot be entirely expressed through the universal spiral. There are aspects of it that are unique, idiosyncratic, singular. These aspects are usually suppressed, since we are encouraged to conform. Yet there are times when the idiosyncratic aspects of the individual spiral surface and assert themselves – against the prevailing opinion. At such times the individual expresses his/her personal truth.

Personal truth is not a contradiction in terms. It is as justifiable an epistemological product as universal truth – if we comprehend the meaning of the spiral of understanding (individual and universal) in any depth.

There are instances when personal truths become universal ones. It happens when other individuals 'begin to see our way.' Those individuals have reconstructed their spiral of understanding which now enables them to comprehend the new truth/vision. This happens in religion and in science. Every new insight, whether religious or scientific, begins with a personal truth. Every new great philosophy starts as a personal truth. Every new religion starts as a personal truth. Every new social design starts as a personal truth.

We all desire transformation – even if we are Buddhas. To seek transformation is to seek an entrance to heaven, however small this heaven may be. From genuine transformation, which changes our being and our spiral of understanding, we must separate out a variety of superficial ego-massages which abound in our times and which are but weekend-long transformations. A cosmetic massage is better than nothing, one might maintain. But the other side of the coin must not be overlooked. In opting for a superficial massage we may be actually preventing ourselves from attaining a genuine transformation.

Whether our mind is inherently compassionate or whether compassion is an acquired trait is an open issue. What is clear however is that the existence of the compassionate mind is as much a part of human nature as is the existence of the aggressive mind.

Universal compassion is not limited geographically among the world's peoples. Tibetan monks are not unique in being able to tune to it: Western Europeans can accomplish this feat as well. That the young Mr Dreyfus could become a Tibetan *geshe* eloquently testifies to the fact that the human mind is almost infinite and that almost anything is possible for it. The potency of the mind does not actualize itself without an effort. Transformation is work. Sometimes it is a Herculean task.

Whatever route to transformation you choose, be aware of the power of the assumptions of the system in which you grew up. Deliberately try to bring about the forms of behaviour, thought and action embodying the desirable assumptions. Try to implement the new assumptions in your daily practice. *To become a Buddha, you must behave like one.* This also applies to the model of the integrated self. To be a part of the process of God in becoming, to be at peace and whole, you must hold strong images of your wholeness in your mind – your wholeness as part of the overall harmony with yourself and with the larger cosmos. The integrated self is one of the highest attainments of the human race. The art of living is second to none. The art of sculpting yourself is as difficult as the art of carving *David* out of raw marble.

Basic models of the individual self are not numerous.

(1) The Hindu/Christian model. God exists outside; He infuses meaning into our lives.

(2) The Plato/Buddha model. Godhead exists within; the realization of meaning is the actualization of our divine potential.

(3) The existential/hedonistic model. No God; alternatively – we are gods unto ourselves; meaning is limited to our ego-based, self-contained journey.

(4) The participatory/evolutionary model. Evolution is God-in-the-making; meaning emerges in the process of our evolutionary becoming.

Meaningful life, in the evolutionary model, is the life of continuous becoming. Continuous becoming signifies continuous creativity; it also signifies continuous liberation from the shackles of the old being. Thus meaning = becoming = liberation = creativity. We should become used to thinking in concepts that organically feed into each other. Holistic thinking and participatory thinking transcend atom-by-atom arrangements. *Mandala thinking* is another name for holistic thinking.

To participate in the highest realms of human experience is to participate in the sacred. This form of experience is a form of magic. But it is natural magic. We create this magic, or the space of grace, by cultivating the reverential mind. When one lives permanently in reverential space, one lives in grace.

We were born in difficult times. We can feel sorry for ourselves. And justifiably so. But being sorry for ourselves will not help us to take our evolutionary destiny into our own hands. Critical times such as ours break many lesser souls. Yet such times are a challenge to our ultimate substance. Those who have it will prevail – to give testimony to the indestructible fibre of the human condition; to the qualities of endurance, perseverance, courage and hope upon which will be built a new spirituality – a positive residue of the anguish of the century.

Hope will be very important in this endeavour. Hope is the spring eternal. Hope is part of our ontological structure. Hope is the scaffolding of our existence. Hope is the nourishment that sustains us daily. Hope is a precondition of our mental health. Hope is the oxygen for our hearts and souls. Hope is the ray of light that separates life from death. Hope is the eternal flower that blossoms against the snow.

Hope is a reassertion of our belief in the meaning of life; and in the sense of the universe. Hope is a precondition of all meaning, of all strivings, of all actions. To embrace hope is a form of wisdom.

We should not forget meditation either, for it is an invaluable mirror in which the spiral of our individual understanding can be beautifully reflected upon. The rational man does not shun meditation, for it can be a powerful tool of self-transformation.

CHAPTER 9

The Universal Spiral of Understanding

1. Different cultures – different spirals – different perspectives

Our culture is our bondage. Our culture is also our liberator. Our culture is our nourisher. Our culture is also the mesmerizer – keeping us transfixed in the mould it has established, and hardly allowing for alternative perspectives.[1]

We are returning to our discussion of the spiral of understanding. The participatory model of the mind assumes that there is a close fit between the cosmology of a given people (or a given society, or a given culture) and the knowledge this culture has produced for the understanding of the world. To return to our image of the cosmology (or world-view) as being delineated by a cone opening upward, and within this cone the spiral of understanding very closely matching the shapes and dimensions of the cone (Chapter 3, Fig. 2): at one point the two are indistinguishable – the cone of our cosmos determines the spiral of our understanding, and vice versa, as we established in Chapter 3.

We consider our world-view superior because we were so taught by our culture. We consider our world-view as the only true one because our culture has conditioned us to think so. We are happy victims of our culture's perspectives because we acquired them with our mother's milk. It can be disquieting and unsettling when people from completely different cultures look at phenomena familiar to us in a completely different way. We want to ask: how can they?

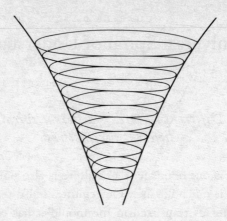

Fig. 1 *The spiral of understanding*

Until the twentieth-century most Western anthropologists, both European and American, while trying to understand other cultures, did so in their own terms. They tried to translate the various other cultures into the language, categories and stereotypes of their own. They imposed their matrix, their spiral of understanding on different matrices and different spirals of understanding. This often led to all kinds of misinterpretations. As the result of Western ethnocentricity these anthropologists declared, when the other matrices did not fit their own, that these other cultures were irrational and primitive.

Only in the twentieth century, and particularly the second half of the twentieth century, have anthropologists begun to understand other people in their own terms: by submerging themselves within these other spirals of understanding, by seeing from within. And then things started to appear differently. Many of these 'primitive cultures', when we try to understand them from within, exhibit an extraordinary degree of unity and connectedness.

When two radically different cultures meet each other,

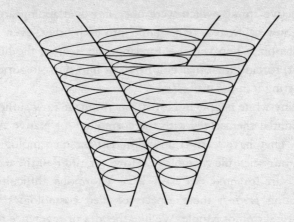

Fig. 2 *Spirals of understanding of two different cultures*

their universes and consequently their spirals of understanding do not match each other. They usually partly overlap. But there are areas in which there is no overlap. Fig. 2 represents two different cosmoses and their respective spirals of understanding.

The areas that do not overlap are usually difficult for each culture to comprehend. These are the phenomena that are 'beyond the cosmos' of a given culture, beyond the categories of its understanding. If two spirals of understanding do not overlap at all, then we are in real trouble – there is no communication possible. We have so far been unable to establish a communication with extra-terrestrial intelligences. Perhaps they are willing to communicate with us. But our respective spirals of understanding may be so different that there is no point of overlap. Therefore we have nothing in common, we cannot communicate; we cannot enter into each other's cosmos.

When the gap between two incompatible cultures is somehow bridged, it simply means that those parts of their respective spirals which were once not overlapping are now somehow calibrated, translatable into each other, even if this translation is non-verbal – for language is often the limiting factor, forcing the other culture to fit into our categories and distorting it in the process.

Many white people in North America have now sufficiently acquainted themselves with the cosmology of Native Americans. They have learned how different these cosmologies are from our scientific cosmology. However, after all these differences are granted, we still have enormous difficulties in accepting *precisely* those aspects of their cosmologies which our spiral cannot handle. We like the idea of reverence for life – for all life – postulated in many of these cosmologies. We like the idea that the fox is my brother and the birds are my sisters. After all, Saint Francis proclaimed similar ideas. But when we go deeper, the trouble begins, particularly with such pronouncements as 'There is a sacred spirit behind every bush and every tree. It is a living force.' We have great difficulty in accepting such statements. The first reaction of our scientific mind is that they *really do not mean it*. When we are assured that they do, we try to get around it by saying to ourselves: they must mean it in some figurative way – not in a concrete, palpable sense, as when *we* say that something exists out there.

Our spiral of understanding attempts to manipulate the situation and convey it in its own distinctive terms. To accept the meaning of the statement uttered by Native Americans that there is a spirit behind every tree and it is a continuous living force requires much more than the understanding of particular words and of the whole statement made of them. After we have understood the statement linguistically, we still do not accept it. It doesn't square with our spiral of understanding, with the reality this spiral represents. So to accept this statement concerning the presence of invisible spirits behind every tree and every living form requires a reconstruction of our spiral of understanding. And this is a difficult task indeed.

We Western people often defend ourselves (sometimes surreptitiously, or in our subconscious mind) by maintaining that after all these other people are talking about something *invisible*. We do not want to be taken for a ride. We do not want to populate the universe with unnecessary entities. There is a presumption at the back of our minds, if dimly held, that our world is not populated by unnecessary entities and that we entertain as existent only the things that are palpable, concrete, touchable, visible. We think that in our universe there is no place for invisible phenomena, for ghosts behind the scenes. This is our presumption. But it is far from the truth. For we *do* populate our universe with invisible entities, just as much as Native Americans do. The electrons, the protons, the quarks, the whole legion of other invisible entities through which we explain the visible are all part of the Western legacy, and part of Western rationality.

In every culture there are invisible forces and presences which interact and interfere with the visible realities. They make the deep underlying matrix. They are a part of our mythology which nourishes and controls. We all live by the invisible. *It is the invisible that controls the visible.* And it is so in all known cultures. The nature and the quality of the invisible determines the nature and the quality of our lives. Whether you are an Amazonian tribesman or a nuclear scientist the invisible is there behind the scenes, manipulating your existence.

Let us now consider the phenomenon of Qi (Chi), which is the Chinese term for vital energy, which pervades not only our entire body but the whole universe – that is, according to the Chinese system of belief. The phenomenon of Qi is celebrated in China, Korea and Japan alike and completely woven into the culture. Acupuncture is a manifestation of it. For a long time the Western mind would not even consider that there is any true validity to the phenomenon of acupuncture. On empirical grounds we have been forced to admit that acupuncture works, and therefore that there must be *something* to this flow of energy on which it is based. We cannot make sense of acupuncture in Western terms yet. Even less can we make sense of the nature of energy called Qi.

Within Chinese culture, as well as in the Korean and Japanese cultures, Qi is taken as much for granted as the existence of electrons in Western culture. Certainly you cannot see or touch electrons, but they manifest their presence everywhere – in the visible reality. Equally certainly (to the Chinese, Korean or Japanese mind) you cannot touch Qi, but it manifests its presence everywhere. If you were to remove the concept of Qi and its derivatives from the Chinese dictionary, you would have made a complete havoc of the Chinese language.

Who is rational? In what terms is this rationality to be assessed? By what kind of transrational and yet rational criteria do we determine the rationality of other cultures and of our own?

Almost from the beginning of recorded history, Chinese culture, the Chinese medical system, the Chinese concept of health and healing have been connected with Qi and woven around Qi. What shall we say, from the standpoint of the Western mind-set – that it is another mythology? If so, it is a very powerful mythology, which is actually capable of creating a palpable reality; just as our scientific mythology has done; and as other prescientific mythologies have done. Each has created a reality corresponding to its myths.

This cannot be right, we want to protest. Reality is not a figment of our imagination, and is not at the mercy of our mythologies. The first part of this statement is correct. Reality is not a figment of our imagination. But it is at the mercy of our mythology, and especially of our spiral of understanding.

We have to liberate ourselves from the straitjacket of Western cosmology (read: mythology) which maintains that it is the only true one. Each cosmology has made such a claim; and none can *prove* its superiority over other cosmologies; for each structures, composes the universe in a different way.

We should then look at the phenomenon of Qi in such a way that we do not mystify it on the one hand, and do not lose our rational faculties on the way to apprehending it on the other. Incidentally, we may be a shade too touchy about our rational faculties. We have to release ourselves from the continuing constraints of our assumptions, of our spiral of understanding, of the rigid clutches of our rationality – that is all.

We have to realize that what we witness in the phenomenon of Qi is that part of the Eastern spiral of understanding which our spiral does not convey and has so far found no means of conveying. What can we do? Obliterate the Eastern spiral of understanding and declare it non-existent because it doesn't correspond to ours? Or enlarge our spiral of understanding so that it incorporates Qi? Certainly, the latter course is the one we want to follow. We do not yet have the instruments and concepts within our Western spiral of understanding to *validate* the phenomenon of Qi, but intuitively we often understand it quite well.

The history of science is nothing if not a continuous process of validation of insights and hunches that at first appeared to be 'crazy' and beyond this world. What is reality if not the web of imaginative conjectures? The more imaginative the mind, the more interesting the conjectures. The more interesting the conjectures, the richer the reality around us. *The ascent of mind is making the unbelievable the believable*.

The phenomenon of Qi will be comprehended when we in the West develop much subtler and deeper concepts which will be capable of grasping the variety of non-visible phenomena. This will happen when our mind becomes more attuned to these phenomena, more sensitive to them. We may in fact have to develop an altogether new sensitivity (we are back to the issue of the mind as a repository of sensitivities). When we do develop this sensitivity (some people already possess and use it for healing purposes), then we may even invent the apparatus that will enable us to register Qi, and perhaps even measure it. We all know intuitively the difference between life and death. The Chinese term for 'death' is 'broken Qi'. There is much to be said for the culture that connects the two phenomena in such a subtle and illuminating way.

Let us draw some conclusions. The spiral of understanding, and the cosmos corresponding to it, determine what is visible and what is invisible within a given culture and how the two realms are related to each other. The spiral also relates the visible and the invisible to what is considered the meaning of life within a given culture. Thus the spiral of understanding not only provides the cognitive grid for our intellectual understanding, but also provides a normative matrix within which things are valued and evaluated. Taken in total, the spiral is a normative agency. It never just sits there objectively and delivers merely cognitive commands. The spiral is inherently normative, even if its normative judgements are subtly concealed under the veneer of objectivity. *The spiral continuously pulsates with life, for it is an embodiment of life itself*. Its overall purpose is understanding. But understanding is an exquisitely complex process, of which cognitive or intellectual understanding is only part. Objective/cognitive/intellectual understanding is an end of the *normative* spectrum.

This leads us to the conclusion that all knowledge is normative. Its purpose is to help men to live and to promote harmony between human kind and the rest of creation. Understanding for the sake of understanding is really based on the desire to comprehend the cosmos at large, is to satisfy man's sense of wonder, is to provide him with a sense of psychological security. In the ultimate analysis, these are normative quests. In every act of human understanding, human values are concealed.

Let us return to the spirals of understanding of different cultures. Let us see how particular facts and particular perceptions are at the mercy of the spiral. During one of my seminars, an intelligent student from the College of Engineering of the University of Michigan said 'I would like to see levitation, and be convinced by it.' When his statement was unravelled, it transpired that he didn't believe in levitation and was not prepared to believe it because it did not fit the system – the spiral of understanding of Western science by which he was rigorously trained, and of which he already considered himself a guardian. When I asked him whether he would be prepared to do special exercises, to practise yoga, which might help him to understand levitation and make levitation possible, he was bewildered and inadvertently said 'No, why should I?' Levitation, he thought, could not be believed under any circumstances.

A more dramatic case occurred at Kyoto in the spring of 1986. During an international conference on the meaning of Qi, a scholar from mainland China brought with him a young man from Tokyo, who possessed special psychic powers. The young man from Tokyo, wearing a sleeveless shirt, performed an 'experiment' for us. He held a metal tablespoon in his hand

and gazed steadily at it with great intensity for about eight minutes. Then the stem of the spoon appeared to start to quiver – the metal clearly showed malleability, as if the stem of the spoon was made of wax . . . and in a moment the bowl of the spoon fell while he was still holding the handle. That was breathtaking! You didn't want to believe it. But you couldn't disbelieve it either.

The scholars from Asian countries seemed to have less problem with the acceptance of the phenomenon than we from the West. We Westerners by and large didn't know what to do with this gift. In particular, the chairman of the conference, a distinguished scientist, was very agitated. He just didn't want to believe what he saw. Afterwards he tried to minimize the whole thing, while most of us were pondering deeply about its significance. He said, 'So many of these things are frauds.' I asked him, 'Do you think that this one was a fraud? Did you not see it with your own eyes?' He responded, 'Well, he may have hypnotized us.' I asked him, 'Do you think that he did?' 'I don't know,' he responded, perplexed and bewildered, and impatient with my questioning.

This was clearly one of the instances when the Western mind was prepared to use any excuse, however flimsy, to defend its own spiral of understanding. What was really at stake was not this particular occurrence of metal spoon-breaking by some invisible energy. What was at stake was something much larger. It was the cherished spiral of understanding that was challenged at its core. In a sense, Western rational knowledge was challenged. What was also at stake was the individual spiral of understanding of a distinguished scientist who had worked for some forty years within the scope of certain assumptions and then these assumptions had been shaken at their roots during a ten-minute session.

We have to be very sensitive to the fact that when two different spirals of understanding meet each other, what is at stake is not just a different interpretation of certain facts (we don't really care about these minor facts). What is at stake is the validity of the cultures that these respective spirals represent. What is at stake, on another level, is the validity of our own cherished mind. *We never think little of our mind*. And when some of its assumptions are questioned, its structure is threatened. We have already analysed the problem – how difficult it is for the individual when his/her spiral is threatened.

For this reason the dialogue between the old guard (the defendants of the Newtonian world-view) and the proponents of the new paradigms (based on the New Physics, spirituality and wholeness) is so very difficult. The difficulties, as a matter of fact, are not intellectual or merely cognitive. Every individual proposition could be agreed upon with enough patience. *The difficulties are existential and cosmological* – since they have to do with the nature and the consequences of our spiral of understanding. The spiral often represents our entire past life. To threaten it is to threaten our identity.

The proponents of the new, those brave souls who work on the articulation of the new logos, which we have called Evolutionary Telos, may be well advised not to pit themselves against the established authorities, or to try to convince them. In a sense they are not convinceable. *They do not want to believe that which threatens their spiral of understanding* – which is so much cherished, so much appreciated; and which has often brought so many dividends to them, including recognition and sometimes fame. There is no evidence that is conclusive or persuasive enough *if* a person does not wish to believe in 'strange' phenomena which are outside his structure of understanding.

Perhaps the road to renewal leads through convincing the young, who are not entirely conditioned by their culture's existing spiral of understanding. The road to renewal particularly leads through addressing ourselves to children. For children, anything is possible. The world is magic. The more magic the better. Magic is for children part of the natural order of things. Children are truly divine beings. They co-create with the universe effortlessly. Their fall starts when one rigid orthodoxy is imposed on them. Their magic world then wanes. They are brought to the earth. They become dull. As we adults are. Their imagination dries up and infinite options are reduced to a few pedestrian choices. This is what we call 'realism'.

2. Brains, minds and computers

The relationship between the brain and the mind is fascinatingly complex and problematical. On the one hand we insist that the study of the brain belongs to the realm of neurophysiology. We then want to explain the workings of the brain in terms of its underlying chemistry – what the various cells do in chemical terms. On the other hand, we want to use the results of this study for understanding the nature of the mind – its subtle cognitive, emotional, volitional and spiritual functions. At this point we want to use the chemical nomenclature for explaining the higher intellectual functions of the mind.

And it does not work. For a simple and fundamental reason: chemical terms (or neurophysiological terms) *do not contain the capacity for explaining human meaning*. You may give me all the chemical reactions that happen in my brain, you may map all the neurophysiological relationships that occur when I say to another person, 'I love you,' and you will never, if you stick to your scientific terms only, be able to explain the true meaning of 'love'; of 'justice'; of 'goodness'; or of 'truth'.

The fundamental conceptual point to be borne in mind is that within the present scientific endeavour there is nothing in the universe of, and in the language of, chemistry that can begin to give us the meaning of such concepts as 'justice', 'truth' or 'love'. So the very idea of *explaining* higher intellectual and cultural attainments of the human mind by reducing them to their underpinning neurochemical components is, quite simply, nonsense.

Yet there is an obsession in the present Western culture to do just that, to explain the mind through the brain.[2] The cognitive imperialism of Western physical science has so pervaded our minds (yes, our minds) that almost instinctively, we demand explanations for nearly everything in physical terms. This can be seen not only among scientists but among ordinary people, who distrust trans-physical explanations; or should we say who have been conditioned to expect some kind of physical explanation at the end of any chain of explanations. So when we talk about the nature of the mind, they somehow expect to learn how it all works through the machinery and the chemistry of the brain, what neurophysiological interactions are responsible for what. Ordinary people inadvertently want to close the reductionist loop and see simple physical-chemical patterns: because neuron gamma-223 hit the neuron alpha 26-k a love relationship occurred. Many reductionist explanations such as we see aplenty in current specialist literature are *au fond* just as much of a parody as this.

No one denies that there is a material basis for the activities of our mind. No one denies the existence of chemical and neurobiological processes in the brain that are connected with the activities of the mind – in the same way in which no one would deny the existence of billions of electrons built into the chips of my computer on which I am typing these words. But the electrons and the electric circuits explain *nothing* of the program or the software that enables my computer to be a word processor. The electrons, the chips, the circuits and the whole machinery of the hardware are the necessary pieces, a precondition, but they do not explain the function of the word processor. Even if I could *describe* the function of the software through the behaviour of the billions of electrons, I could not *explain* it. The necessary material basis of the brain is not sufficient explanation for the higher functions of our mind. Descriptions and explanations are different things altogether.[3]

The fact that I am not discussing any findings concerning the mechanisms of the brain at any length in no way invalidates my findings about the nature of the mind. It is a (reductionist) mistake to assume that it is only by understanding the brain that we shall understand the mind. *We shall understand the mind by understanding the mind*. Yet the lure of science is great and almost irresistible. Somehow we want to believe that there should be a simple scientific explanation of everything, including the mystery of the mind. We have to remember, however, that if the mind were so simple that we could explain it, we should have been so simple that we couldn't. Still the incurable curiosity of the human mind demands: I want to know! This is a very wholesome impulse indeed. But it is a conceit of science to promise, if only implicitly, to explain it all.

There are at least three strategies being employed while science attempts to reduce the mind to the brain, and in general attempts to explain very complex phenomena through the underlying simple physical-chemical structures. One strategy is what Karl Popper calls 'promissory materialism' (which should be properly called 'promissory reductionism'): give us more time and we'll explain it all; it is all a matter of time; physical science has the universal key to all doors – earthly and heavenly.

This promissory reductionism has worked very well in explaining the structure of matter. But it has not worked well at all in explaining the structure of the human psyche. Actually, promissory reductionism has not worked so well in explaining the structure of matter. For when we thought we had finally arrived at rock-bottom, and explained matter in terms of atoms and subatomic particles, the bottom fell out of physics, and we are now increasingly bewildered as to how it all works and what it all means in terms of ultimate subatomic particles; if there are such things as *ultimate* and *particles*. The physical can no longer explain the trans-physical through the physical if only because (on the level of subatomic particles) it requires the trans-physical (quarks, etc.) for the understanding of the physical.

The second strategy is to plead relative ignorance. Sir John Eccles and others insist that we are only in the early days of understanding the brain itself. We understand very little of it, they maintain. Perhaps in one hundred or two hundred years, when we know much more about the brain, we shall be able to explain through it the phenomenon of mind. This is a cautious and enlightened version of promissory reductionism. Yet even in this enlightened approach there is a tendency to think that somehow the brain will explain the mind.

The third strategy is more far-reaching. It maintains that we have *to create a new science* to understand the brain and the mind together. Among others, Ilya Prigogine has maintained, in his book *Order out of Chaos* (1984), that we have to create a much more encompassing science which will be able to explain not only the physical but also the historical – living systems in their evolution as bound by time which is irreversible. The notion of the irreversibility of time requires the creation of a new science. The laws of present physical sciences are based on a conception of the universe in which time does not matter; or should we say postulate the theories that assume that time is reversible – while in living systems time is of the essence: to understand these systems is to understand how they change in time, through time, because of time.

The participatory mind does not deny that the time will come when we shall understand the brain and the mind together. But this understanding will come about *when increasingly we shall comprehend more and more of the behaviour of the brain through the categories of the mind and not conversely* – by attempting to reduce the mind to the stuff and the categories of the brain.

Thus instead of the process of reduction there will occur the process of *upduction*, or *transduction* (if I can coin the term), whereby the content specific to the knowledge of the mind will illumine the understanding of the behaviour of neurons and chemical cells comprising the hardware of the brain. And what do I mean by this process of *transduction*? The meaning of the term follows directly from the methodology of participation and its specific strategies. To understand the behaviour of the brain cells through transduction is to recognize the intelligent, participatory character of their interaction with each other. By understanding how they cooperate, how they participate in the larger projects of which they are a part, we shall be able to understand their chemical behaviour. In the process we shall come to distinguish various new forms of sensitivity (specific forms of seeing) of brain structures. We shall come to distinguish subtle patterns of cooperation and participation among the chains of neurons. All these terms, 'intelligent' 'participatory', 'sensitive', 'seeing', 'cooperative', are terms that belong to the universe of the mind. *Transduction* means endowing neurophysiological underpinnings with the attributes and properties so far reserved for man's higher intellectual functions.

This process of *transduction* will contribute to a profound transformation of all sciences. Actually this process is already occurring – in a groping kind of way. It has been occurring in the work of individual imaginative scientists such as Barbara McClintock, whom we have already discussed. I would imagine that the number of such scientists is actually legion. But they hide their participatory methodology because it is not officially approved.

One of the recurring problems of our time is whether the computer is not really an analogue for the brain and ultimately for the mind. Let us examine this claim. In passing let us notice that computer ideologists have continually made outlandish claims as to what computers can do and *will* do. In the past their claims have been proven to be quite often hollow. But this does not seem to deter them from making outlandish new claims. The Nobel Laureate for Economics Herbert Simon claimed in 1957 that in ten years' time the computer would become the world champion in chess, if it were allowed to enter the world championship. This prediction turned out to be an empty claim. As far as I know, Simon did not apologize for his mistake. Instead he went on to make new claims.

The announcement was made in the 1960s, with great fanfares and gusto, that computers would soon master language sufficiently to be able to 'read' and 'write' themselves. The pattern recognition in natural languages has proven to be far more subtle and complex than was anticipated by computer specialists. Every normal six-year-old child is quite a master of language. The most sophisticated computers are dumb in comparison. So ten years after the announcement (that computers will soon match us in language skill) this claim was also quietly abandoned.

But this game is still going on – with a great gusto. Exaggerated claims are made. Then forgotten. Then new claims are made – again promising 'phenomenal' breakthroughs. Then again quietly forgotten. Even after Roger Penrose's book *The Emperor's New Mind* was published (1989), in which he shows (actually *proving* it mathematically) that the computer can never become an adequate analogue for our brain/mind, the young computer Turks have kept going undaunted. The reason? *They want to believe in their brave new world.*

3. Interactionism and the participatory mind – the historical record

At an international conference on 'Biology, History and Natural Philosophy' held in Denver in 1966 I presented a paper in which I argued (in a final section entitled. 'The Interaction Between Knowledge and the Mind') that 'the conceptual structure of the mind changes with shifts and developments in the structure of knowledge.'[4] I further argued that we must assume that there is a parallel conceptual development of our knowledge and of the mind. Knowledge forms the mind. The mind formed by knowledge develops and extends knowledge still further, which in turn continues to develop the mind. Thus there is a continuous process of interaction between the two. Although they are independent categories as far as their meaning is concerned, viewed in overall cognitive development, knowledge and mind are functionally dependent on each other, and indeed inseparable from each other. They are two sides of the same coin; two representations of the same cognitive order. The concept of mind must include the knowledge that has formed it and that it possesses.

This was an early formulation of my idea of the participatory mind. I did not then have the idea of the participatory universe as the background. For this idea, to my knowledge, was proposed for the first time by John Archibald Wheeler in 1974.[5] However, the outline of the whole participatory model is in my paper of 1966, as I argued explicitly that the *conceptual development of science is paralleled by the conceptual development of the mind*. The conceptual arrangement of the mind with its specific patterns of thought thus mirrors the development of the conceptual net of science with its complicated mesh of concepts. The continuous interactions between the mind of a scientist and the science he engages in are actually interactions between the mind of an individual scientist and a particular science. But the result of these individual interactions constitutes a new stage in the development of science and a new stage in the conceptual development of the mind.

In the conclusion of my essay I stated explicitly:

The model of the mind outlined in this essay is a dynamic matrix which allows for the study of this interaction, and thus for the study of conceptual change. Latent in this model is the idea of evolutionary epistemology. Evolutionary epistemology is the discipline which provides a new perspective on the nature of our problems concerned with the growth of science and of conceptual change. This discipline when worked out in detail will be an alternative to the logico-empiricist epistemology that has been for too long dominant in twentieth-century philosophy.

Eight years after writing my Denver conference paper, in 1974 I contributed an essay entitled 'Karl Popper and the

Objectivity of Scientific Knowledge' to a volume on the philosophy of Popper,[6] in which I commented on his philosophy of the Three Worlds, especially World 3. (In this system, World 1 is the world of physical objects, World 2 is that of mental constructs or mental acts – psychological reality, and World 3 is the world of ideal objects, including the meaning of scientific concepts and theories – the cognitive reality, existing independently of our mind.) I said that Popper's difficulties stemmed from one source, namely from his insistence that 'there is no similarity *whatsoever* on any level of problems between contents [i.e. results expressed in cognitive (intersubjective) terms] and corresponding processes [i.e. mental processes leading to these results].'

In the conclusion of my paper I said explicitly that there must be a relationship between Popper's third world and his second world (the world of mental processes):

. . . there must be a parallelism between the structural units of the third world (the intelligibles) and the entities of the second world through which we grasp and comprehend the content of scientific statements and theories. *We comprehend them because the cognitive order is as it were grafted onto the mind. It is only by recognizing the mind as a part of the growth of knowledge that we can arrive at a consistent idea of objective knowledge and thereby a consistent justification of the objectivity of knowledge.*[7]

I emphasize the last two sentences in order to indicate that the concept of the participatory mind is here in my text of 1974. This parallelism between the order of the mind and the order of our 'objective' knowledge was obvious to me. I was surprised that others – including Popper – did not see it equally clearly: '*as knowledge grows so does the mind; one reflects the growth of the other.*'

Popper, while responding positively to some of the things

I said in my essay, disagreed with the most important topic; he denied any parallelism between Worlds 2 and 3.[8] But three years later, in 1977, in a volume written jointly with John Eccles, *The Self and Its Brain*[9] (in setting out these details I have no wish to overwhelm the reader with minutiae, but simply to sketch out the historical record concerning the development of the theory of the participatory mind as briefly as possible), Popper *unambiguously* came to recognize the interaction between World 2 and World 3 (indeed, the subtitle of the book is *An Argument for Interactionism*): 'The levels can *interact* with each other. (This is important for the mind-brain interactionism).'[10] And further: 'If we admit the interaction of the three worlds, and thus their reality, then the interaction between Worlds 2 and 3, which we can to some extent understand, can help us a little towards a better understanding of the interaction between Worlds 1 and 2, a problem that is part of the mind-body problem.'[11]

Eccles further reinforces the idea of the interaction between Worlds 2 and 3, by actually maintaining that the interaction between World 2 and World 3 'is happening independently of the brain and then gets coded back on the brain. I think it is first the self-conscious mind exploring into its own resources, the immense potentialities that are available to it.'[12] And together Popper and Eccles eulogize interactionism between Worlds 2 and 3 in dialogue IX.[13]

The Zeitgeist works on us all. We articulate what is 'hanging in the air' – I in my way, Popper in his way. It is strange to me, however, that only three years after we had clashed fundamentally on the question of the relationship of mind to knowledge, Popper came round to my position without, as far as I know, mentioning our debate at all. Had he forgotten it? Or did he choose to forget it?

In spite of my many disagreements with him, I owe Popper

much. His philosophy enabled me (in the early 1960s) to liberate myself from the straitjacket of many dogmas of analytical philosophy. Some of the insights expressed in *The Self and Its Brain* are penetrating indeed. One of them Popper puts as follows:

From an evolutionary point of view, I regard the self-conscious mind as an emergent product of the brain; emergent in the way similar to that in which World 3 is an emergent product of the mind. World 3 emerges together with the mind, but nevertheless emerges as a product of the mind, by mutual interaction with it. Now I want to emphasize how little is said by saying that the mind is an emergent product of the brain. It has practically no explanatory value, and it hardly amounts to more than putting a question mark at a certain place in human evolution. [So far I can subscribe to everything that Popper says. But I can hardly agree with the last statement of the paragraph that follows – H. S.] Nevertheless, I think that this is all which, from a Darwinian point of view, we can say about it.'[14]

This identification of evolution with Darwinism is a serious mistake – conceptual and evolutionary, to say nothing about its moral implications. Darwinism and especially social Darwinism can so easily lend itself as a tool of exploitation and oppression. Evolution is cooperation par excellence, not vicious competition as the Darwinian model would have it. The models we choose determine the nature of the world around us. Let us therefore choose well so that the models we have created do not limit us and do not oppress other people.

As far as the notion of evolutionary knowledge or evolutionary epistemology is concerned, my disagreement with Popper is as follows. His concept of evolutionary knowledge is too narrow and almost exclusively limited to scientific knowledge, and it is marred by an unexamined adherence to Darwinism. My evolutionary model of knowledge has been one claiming that the three: mind, knowledge and reality are intimately connected with each other. We cannot do justice (in any truly evolutionary model) to any of these three concepts without simultaneously examining the other two, and by seeing how they really are aspects of each other.

4. Some forerunners of the participatory mind

At best we can only retouch what has been given to us. We have a voice of our own – the individual spiral of understanding. But at the same time, another voice is speaking through us; in fact, many voices – the universal spiral of understanding. Evolution speaks through us. Genes speak through us. The voices of the great ones speak through us. To recognize this is both chastizing and exhilarating. It is humbling to know that one's voice is so small. It is exhilarating to know that one's voice contains so many other voices. Amidst the symphony of other voices, we add a little melody of our own. This is as much as we can expect.

As I have mentioned in earlier chapters, the philosophy of the participatory mind has been inspired by many, beginning with Plato. In the twentieth century I would consider myself a continuation of Bergson, of Teilhard and of Popper (despite the narrowness of his scientific rationalism). To these another name must be added, that of Jean Gebser.

Jean Gebser (1905–73) is one of those solitary thinkers who are important for the twentieth century, and at the same time almost completely neglected. He was a poet, a man of letters, a philosopher. Above all, he was the creator of a new synthesis. His magnum opus is entitled *The Ever Present Origin* (1985).[15] But this is a difficult, tortuous book to read. A concise rendering of Gebser's philosophy can be found in

Georg Feuerstein's *Structures of Consciousness: the Genius of Jean Gebser: An Introduction and Critique* (1987).[16]

Why is Gebser important? Because he has the courage to think large. He has the imagination to pose great questions. We are at a juncture of human history when understanding the nature of consciousness is very important – for the awareness of who we are and, perhaps even more important, where we can go in the next stage of our evolutionary journey. The twentieth century has been called by many names. One of them is the age of analysis. But equally importantly it has been the age of the rediscovery of consciousness. From Carl Gustav Jung, via Mircea Eliade and Joseph Campbell, we have been rediscovering the nature of myths, we have been awakening to the beauty and the magic of consciousness. Gebser is an important part of this process of repossessing ourselves by understanding rationally the prerational stages of our consciousness.

Gebser's scheme is ambitious, vast, panoramic, as he attempts to reconstruct the *structures* of human consciousness from the time around one million years BC to our time. I find his discussion of the early stages of this period, speculative as it is, very illuminating. His reconstruction of the structure of consciousness in historic times I find less illuminating. Gebser is right that the immense burst of creative energy in the Neolithic period needs to be duly appreciated. This is for him the mythical structure of consciousness. He writes: 'The essential characteristic of the mythical structure is the emergent awareness of soul. Magic man's sleep-like consciousness of natural time is the precondition for mythical man's coming to awareness of soul.'[17]

Some of Gebser's conjectures are enticing to contemplate. Because the world may be considered 'a mirror of inner silence', he suggests that Neolithic technology may be seen as a reflection of the creativity of imagination – in contrast to modern technology which is based on the egotistical opposition to nature.

Gebser's reconstruction of the stages of structures of consciousness in recent history I find confusing and unsatisfactory. I argued in chapter 5, while discussing Christianity, the Renaissance and the mechanistic age, that we can and should distinguish three different structures of consciousness in those times. Gebser, however, lumps the three periods together under the label of 'objectivized consciousness'. In my opinion, much more discernment is needed than Gebser allows. The Christian consciousness (as based on the idea of Theos) and the mechanistic form of consciousness (as based on Mechanos) are so different that subsuming them under the same label does great injustice to each.

The strength of Gebser's model is that it allows for the future development of consciousness. I share Gebser's view that our mind and our consciousness are far from completed. The evolutionary journey is going on. What new structures of consciousness or new forms of mind the future will bring as evolution unfolds, not even God may know at present.

5. On the dangers of subjectivism

When I was a student of engineering in the 1950s, we still believed in the hard palpable universe 'out there'. When I started teaching in the 1960s, the scientific world-view was still considered the only rationally justified one. This world-view proclaimed that science adequately describes reality existing objectively and independently of us 'out there'. However, the confidence of science as the arbiter of all that exists started to wane in the 1970s.

The waning of this confidence had many causes. Among the important ones were the conclusions of quantum physics, which fundamentally challenged the principle of objectivity; and the revelations of astrophysics, which conveyed to us that we do not know much about the nature of the universe, including the nature of the laws of science.

In the 1980s, very quietly but definitely, science started to retreat from its claims that its theories are about reality and that we really know what reality is. Instead science moved into a rather modest position as it started to proclaim that scientific theories are really *models* which may or may not have to do with reality. Reality as such has been left behind as 'this elusive thing' of which we do not know much and which may be beyond our grasp anyway. Gradually reality has been relegated to the domain of the subjective experience of individuals.

The most telling test of this overall transition came for me in the spring of 1990. I was teaching at the time a class on 'Technology and Man', at the University of Michigan, to a group of graduating seniors in engineering. A bright group it was. We finally broached the subject: what is reality? Much to my amazement *none* of them opted for an objective or even a semi-objective concept of reality. All declared, one by one, that reality is a substratum of our experience. Some unashamedly claimed: 'Reality is my ego.' 'Reality is what you create.' Such a thing would not have been possible among graduating engineers twenty-five years ago.

What took me twenty years to learn – that reality is not independent of my mind – they learned painlessly during their undergraduate education. In a sense, it seems a bit unfair. But this is how history proceeds. They arrived on the scene when the whole mind-set was changing. They simply acknowledged as obvious what was once deemed as 'the

subjective heresy', namely that reality does not exist objectively and independently of our minds.

Yet there is a price to be paid for this easy liberation from
the canons of objectivism. To say that 'reality is my creation'
is fine. However, if the statement is not thought through
deeply enough, it may lead to all kinds of murky waters and
dangerous alleys – from which there is no easy recovery.

When I challenged my students, during this revealing
session in the spring of 1990, whether there was no objective
substratum to their subjective experience of reality, they were
happy to maintain that only through our subjective experience
can we form any viable picture of reality. When I asked them
whether 'anything goes', the consensus was – yes, anything
goes.

I then came to draw epistemological consequences following from their position. If anything goes (and if one's subjective experience is the only reliable source of judgement), then
murder goes, then druggies go, then all kinds of perversion
and pathologies go. Any view of reality – sick and pathological as it may be – is then as is good as any other. It also
follows that there are no intersubjective criteria for the discernment of *quality* in art, in life, in thinking. All these conclusions
were not to the liking of my students. But they had no idea
how to avoid the 'unpleasant' consequences of 'anything
goes.'

We simply cannot defend the ideas 'reality is my ego',
'reality is my own creation.' Such ideas belong to what I call
shallow subjectivism. Their epistemological and eschatological
consequences are lethal. If anything goes, then the druggy's
and the murderer's world-views are as good as your own.

Let us be prepared to acknowledge that this last conclusion
flies in the face of the recorded history of human kind, which
is the history of human striving for *meaning*. Deny the meaning

to human history, and this history is nothing. Deny the meaning to human life, and human life becomes nothing.

Thus in order to maintain the meaning of human life and of human history, we must transcend the tenets of shallow subjectivism. How can we rescue our subjective feeling of what reality is from its nihilistic consequences? By reminding ourselves of the glories of the participatory universe in its unfolding journey.

The grandeur of evolutionary becoming is not a subjective figment of our imagination. Evolution is the canvas of our perception and the participatory universe has been the weaver that has woven this canvas. There were many contingent moments in evolution when evolution was at a turning-point and could have gone in a different direction. To that degree, there has been nothing preplanned or preordained in evolution.

But once evolution brings to being consciousness, and subsequently the human mind, including its distinctive sensitivities, we – human beings – do not perceive like frogs but like humans. We do not think like mountains but like humans. We do not value like bacteria but like humans. These processes of perceiving, of thinking, of valuing are species-specific. There is a great gamut of individual differences within the range of human thinking, valuing, perceiving. But *the whole underlying structure, the structure of the human mind, is common to us all*, is the same for the whole human species. For this reason we can understand each other. For this reason also we, humans, have a similar sense of beauty. And for this reason we share similar values.

Our common evolutionary journey through the participatory universe has assured that we are not monads drifting aimlessly in our isolated subjective universes but that we are connected strands in the tapestry of evolution. This is precisely what saves us from the nihilistic abyss of shallow subjectivism.

The universe is not the Newtonian machine cranking its deterministic laws and making the world 'as it is' independently of us. This we know. The universe is not a predetermined design in the mind of God; it is not 'as it is' because of God's Inscrutable Plan. Neither is the universe a subjective soup in which we are separate noodles of no consequence to any larger plan. This we know as well.

On the canvas of the participatory universe, we – as individuals – weave our own little universes of meaning. Our subjectivity is important and through it we express the world of human differences. But our common evolutionary bond is even more important. Through it we express the magic of being human, the values that enhance and elevate the human condition, the indelible sense that in spite of all agonies it is thrilling to be alive, to be on the journey of becoming, to have other living beings as our brothers and sisters in creation, and to have mountains and brooks and forests and clouds as our companions in the unfolding tapestry of evolutionary becoming.

The universe is not my ego, although it has been filtered through my ego. What must not escape our notice is the fact that this very filter, which is my ego, is a refined product of the whole evolutionary process. Our subjectivity is thus universal. Scratch its veneer and under its façade you will find the universality of evolutionary grandeur. Let us therefore beware of the glib expression: 'The universe is my own creation.' No, it is not! You are its creation. You are the mirror in which the universe is contemplating itself. You are the yeast out of which the universe is making thoughts. You are one of the myriad atoms out of which the universe is making its mosaics, including the mosaics of human meaning.

Glory to human subjectivity, for it is a miracle of creation. Glory to the participatory universe, for it is a trans-subjective canvas out of which human subjectivity can arise. Glory to God Who is making His footprints through the workings of our own subjectivity and through grand designs of the participatory universe.

Summary

We never think little of our minds. We are conditioned to think that our culture knows best. For these reasons, when we meet people of different cultures, conditioned by radically different spirals of understanding, our first reaction is – they must be crazy.

Until the twentieth century, Western anthropologists and Western people in general, while trying to understand other cultures, attempted to force them into the boxes of Western understanding, with the result that these other cultures have been grossly misinterpreted and impoverished. So often, we deemed those other cultures irrational as they did not conform to our criteria of rationality.

This picture has been changing in the twentieth century, particularly in the second half of the twentieth century, when we have tried to understand other cultures through *empathy* and by merging ourselves with the context of these cultures. Thus we have come to realize that different cultures may, and often are, based on different forms of rationality.

It is the invisible that controls the visible. This is so in all cultures, including our own. The quality of the invisible determines the quality of our lives. If your invisible is a benevolent god which showers blessing on you and guides your life daily, then your life is going to be more happy and connected. If, on the other hand, the controlling invisible are electrons and quarks which do not give any guidance or blessings to your life, then your life, inspired by and controlled through this invisible, is going to be less connected and happy.

The spiral of understanding not only provides the cognitive structure for our intellectual understanding. It also provides a normative matrix within which and against which things are evaluated. Taken in toto, the spiral is a normative agency. It never sits still objectively and guides us with its objective commands. *The spiral continuously pulsates with life.* For it is an embodiment of life itself. For this reason alone it is a normative agency.

An enlightened culture can imaginatively reconstruct the premises (the spiral of understanding) of other cultures and can demonstrate that the ways and paths that at first appear 'odd' and unacceptable from the viewpoint of our standards are perfectly normal and acceptable within those other cultures. Thus one of the consequences of understanding in depth the meaning of the spiral of understanding, within our own culture and across cultures, is *tolerance*. Tolerance is the fruit of understanding.

It is never easy to accept the spiral of understanding of another culture, for it requires, in a sense, renouncing the spiral of understanding of our own culture, or at least significantly altering it. Such changes are invariably seen as a threat to our identity. Therefore, such changes are vigorously if not vehemently opposed, particularly by the guardians of the status quo, who have vested interests in keeping things as they are. For this reason we should be aware that we may never be able to *persuade* the guardians of the status quo about the necessity for new departures, for they do not want to see changes and specifically *they do not want to believe in the validity of new phenomena* and new forms of knowledge which contradict the old. And if you do not want to believe, no evidence will convince you. Children are our hope. For them, magic is natural. They co-create effortlessly with the universe.

As to the claim that minds are computers, we should not fear; not yet; and not for *quite* a while. When the computers do catch up with us (if ever) we shall by that time be on a higher level of our evolutionary development. The fact that *some* people are so eager to reduce us to the machinery of electronic automata is not so much an insult to the glory of the human mind but rather a profound comment on their mentality. Who are those people who are so eager to see us as machines? What is their conception of heaven?

I did not devote much space to the findings concerning the mechanisms of the brain. But this fact in no way invalidates my findings about the mind. It is a fallacy to assume that by understanding the brain we shall understand the mind. We shall understand the mind by understanding the mind.

Concerning the predecessors of the participatory theory of mind, there were many: from Heraclitus to Bateson; from Meister Eckhart to Jean Gebser. Although I freely admit my indebtedness to Popper, I do not consider his interactionism as a predecessor of my participatory mind for the reasons I have explained. My interactionism precedes Popper's by a decade.

Bateson's ideas, on the other hand, are beautiful anticipations of the participatory mind; and partial articulations of it. The idea of healing epistemologies, the idea of the ecology of mind, the idea of the universal or the cosmic mind, the idea of relational thinking (which I prefer to call participatory thinking) are all parts and aspects of the participatory mind – although differently expressed in my philosophical system.

Jean Gebser, whom we discussed only briefly, is a friendly

soul, and we salute his cosmic quest. Although I find his programme fascinating and important, his mind I find less understandable and less attuned than the minds of Bateson and Teilhard.

Our age is one of spiritual search. With evolution truly recognized, our spirituality and our God are parts of the becoming of the universe. This is the only viable alternative that has thrust itself upon us after we have awakened to the nature of the participatory universe and the nature of the participatory mind. There are no mysteries of the universe, except for the mystery of the mind. As the mind is, so is the universe. This is the mystery of the mind as the key to the becoming of the universe.

CHAPTER 10

Participatory Truth

> Truth is that kind of error without which a certain kind
> of living being cannot live.   Nietzsche

1. The correspondence theory

Truth is a sublime subject. But also a thorny one. So much depends on the viability of truth – for if truth is abandoned, what happens to society and our concept of justice? What happens to our quest for knowledge, which is so often identified with the quest for truth?

We are now discussing truth as an intersubjective entity which holds good in transactions among people. In other words, we are discussing universal truth in contrast to personal truth which we discussed in chapter 8. From Aristotle on, we have inherited the correspondence theory of truth or the classical theory of truth, which claims that truth is the correspondence between reality and its faithful (or adequate) descriptions. These descriptions, which are faithful, or adequate, we call true. Truth resides in these descriptions. Truth is an attribute of descriptions or linguistic utterances.

A glimmer of this concept of truth can be found in Plato and Socrates, and perhaps also in their predecessors. But in Plato we find equally forcefully expressed another concept of truth – truth as a living dialogue: words and utterances are made true in virtue of the total situation, of the total context within which they are embedded at a given time. Transposed on paper, the living situation, the living truth becomes a dead truth – like a living leaf taken off a tree.

From Aristotle on the correspondence or the classical concept of truth begins to prevail. The living truth, as Plato envisaged it, becomes less important. The correspondence theory of truth becomes known as objective truth. It is this truth that is an inherent part of the rational heritage of Western man. This truth, or should we say more precisely this theory of truth, has become the backbone of Western rationality. Let us now see the hidden structure of the correspondence theory. We often do not realize that it presupposes a number of things:

(1) It presupposes the existence of an objective, unchanging reality out there.

(2) It presupposes that this reality is equally available to each of us, under the same aspects.

(3) It presupposes that language, and specifically present language, can describe this reality adequately.

(4) It presupposes that we can judge – each of us equally – the adequacy or the correspondence between our linguistic descriptions and reality itself.

(5) Finally it presupposes (if we put the matter in the language of the participatory mind) the same spiral of understanding that resides in each of us.

This is a lot to presuppose! Presupposition (5) only summarizes presuppositions (1) to (4) and makes transparently clear what they claim. Let us be acutely aware that only after the five above-mentioned assumptions are granted can the classical or the correspondence theory of truth be maintained. Historically, these assumptions have been granted without much doubt or reflection. For indeed it was *assumed* that there is one reality out there, and that our knowledge can and, does, describe it adequately or faithfully.

We should mention parenthetically that some of these assumptions have been questioned by some thinkers even within the Western intellectual tradition. Among those thinkers are those whom we call mystics. Some of them have maintained that the ultimate knowledge of reality, and thus this reality itself, cannot be known through, or cannot be rendered through, the bits and pieces of analytical knowledge that we pursue in our specialized sciences. This ultimate knowledge can be grasped only in the acts of mystic contemplation.

By and large, we have brushed aside these insights and arguments as not sufficiently rational and gone on believing in the *transparency of reality*. We have held this belief in the transparency of reality not only in science and the whole edifice of cognitive knowledge; we have also held this belief in what can be called religious knowledge – from Thomas Aquinas onward. The traditional Christian orthodoxy is that of Thomas Aquinas as grafted on to the corpus of Aristotelian philosophy. The whole body of Christian philosophy is in fact a rather rational and discursive enterprise – upholding and cherishing Aristotle's idea of the correspondence between reality and its description.

Let us now focus on another aspect of this rational enterprise that Western knowledge represents. While we adhere to the correspondence theory of truth, we assume that the universe is static, permanent, unchanging. Only when we assume the universe to be unchanging can we happily go on believing in the correspondence theory of truth. Let us put it otherwise. Given the static or unchanging concept of the universe, it is not only easy but almost inevitable to believe that since the universe is one and the same, there should be one and the same unchanging truth about it – that is, if you grant another assumption, namely, that reason is powerful enough to render reality in linguistic descriptions. What if reality can be understood only in the depth of our intuitions or in the acts of mystical insights?

Belief in the static, unchanging nature of reality has been maintained in the Western tradition throughout its major developmental stages. In antiquity, Plato and Aristotle believed in the fixed, unchanging universe. Heraclitus didn't. The knowledge of Forms was the true knowledge for the whole Platonic/Aristotelian tradition.

In medieval times the church believed in the fixed, unchanging universe – as based on God's design. The knowledge of God's design was considered the true knowledge.

In modern times science has believed in the fixed, unchanging universe – as based on the laws of science. The knowledge of these laws has been considered the true knowledge of reality.

From our point of view, it does not matter that the basis of our beliefs was different in each epoch. What does matter is the fact that an unchanging reality was assumed to be there, which we would then try to capture through our knowledge. A central point is that *in the process the correspondence theory of truth played a vital role*. And so entrenched and important has it become that we have great difficulty in relinquishing it, or even reconsidering it, in spite of the evidence which undeniably suggests that one unchanging reality, and one truth corresponding to it, has been one big metaphysical fiction.

The serious crisis in the foundations of our knowledge had started already at the end of the nineteenth century, and it has continued undiminished for at least a century. And this crisis, we must be perfectly aware of it, vitally affects the classical theory of truth as well as every objective (or universal) concepts of truth.

We all know that Newtonian physics started to totter at the end of the nineteenth century, that is with the discovery of radioactivity and other phenomena that could not be fitted or explained within the structure of Newtonian physics; and therefore within the structure of the laws of nature as envisaged by this physics; and therefore within the structure of reality as conceived by this physics. Obviously what was at stake was the established concept of truth and the established concept of reality.

Some perceptive minds, such as those of Henri Poincaré (1854–1912) and Ernst Mach (1838–1916), immediately realized the enormity of the problem and its far-reaching consequences. To 'save' reality, or at least to save traditional knowledge, they started to devise altogether new stratagems and conceptions. Thus Poincaré devised *conventionalism*, or the idea of truth by convention: you cannot describe reality as it is because there may be more than one reality out there (*Science and Hypothesis*, 1905). What you do describe (as being 'out there') is the result of your axioms, or the basic concepts that you assume as the foundation of your discipline or your branch of knowledge. The choice of basic axioms is up to you. They are admitted by *convention*. Consequently what follows is not necessarily a true description of reality but a convenient one – by virtue of the axioms and basic concepts you have assumed, and with respect to how you wish to describe reality – a different set of axioms may lead to a different description of reality. There is no compelling reason that can advise us which basic axioms or basic concepts are best or true, for the choice of these axioms and concepts is always somewhat circular and always somewhat question-begging.

We have absorbed and partly digested the insight of Poincaré and other conventionalists as a valuable correction concerning the nature of knowledge, and particularly the role of axioms while building and developing formal or deductive branches of knowledge. But we are far from accepting all the consequences of this insight, particularly concerning the correspondence theory of truth, and the notion of truth as such.

We are somewhat afraid that truth by convention may lead us to the idea of subjectivity of all truth: if the acceptance of basic axioms (basic language) is up to us, then the determination of truth is up to us. We don't like this consequence. And for good reason. For then all truths somehow become personal truths.

The idea of truth by convention may lead us in another direction: to look at all knowledge in a new way. This new direction will almost certainly lead us to revise the entire edifice of objective knowledge and the objective view of reality which we have cherished so much. We don't like this consequence either, for it gives us much to do. And we may be too lazy to rethink it all.

Indeed, philosophers have become lazy nowadays. They don't like deep, searching questions which are all-consuming and all-important. Instead they occupy themselves with little analytical, often facile problems which give them the satisfaction of doing the work really well – even if it is of a purely technical nature. They like to cling to the traditional notion of empiricism and refine it over and over again. As a result, the whole notion of empiricism has become meaningless if not ludicrous. Thus we have 'robust' empiricism, 'hypothetical' empiricism, 'good' empiricism, 'tentative' empiricism, 'plain' empiricism, 'conceptual' empiricism – you name it. All these labels indicate a sort of desperation to preserve something that is untenable. For empiricism is a doctrine based on: (1) the acceptance of the correspondence theory of truth; (2) the acceptance of reality as postulated by science.

Nearly all varieties of empiricism are based on the acceptance of the old Newtonian hat, and this hat is now worn out. It is unbelievable that so many clever and perspicuous philosophers, who can see the faults and weaknesses of any theory, and who are well acquainted with the limitations of and the cracks within the Newtonian theory, can still go on devising new empiricisms or at least being busy conceiving new labels for something the foundations of which are cracked and crumbling. In weak moments, these philosophers would say: 'If not empiricism, then what else?' A lot else, if you have the courage to think through the foundations.

Empiricism, of whatever variety, is not the only issue that is at stake. Indeed, the whole civilizational formation is collapsing – and by this I mean the philosophical foundations of the modern Western world-view. This world-view was based on the doctrine of metaphysical realism – the belief that things are as they are and science describes them best. The collapse of this metaphysical realism is now acknowledged. In its wake we have seen the emergence of pernicious cultural relativism; pernicious because it only adds to cultural confusion; pernicious because it allows the advertising man to be a maker of truth; pernicious because it absolves you from the responsibility of thinking and allows any half-wit to claim that his ideas are as good as anybody else's – because there are no longer any universal yardsticks.

Since the doctrine of (metaphysical) realism is so dear to our hearts, some have tried to rescue it *per fas et nefas*; well, if not the content of it, at least the term. Thus Hilary Putnam, a leading Harvard philosopher, recently wrote *The Many Faces of Realism*,[1] in which he advances 'a kind of pragmatic realism', a curious hybrid between old-fashioned pragmatism and old-fashioned realism. Putnam is to be applauded for trying. But the very idea of 'the many faces of realism' takes us back to the old mould, focuses our attention on a wrong image, indirectly tries to convey that realism is still right after all.

As with so many concepts of the past, so it is with

empiricism and realism. We still use them, we cling to them although their value and meaning are now questionable. They are now a counterfeit and we treat them as good currency – a peculiar act of self-deception. Putnam and others have embarked on a new notion: 'contextual relativity' or 'internal realism'. Both labels are misleading but they are groping in the right direction – towards participatory truth.

2. The coherence theory of truth

The other thinker I have just mentioned was Ernst Mach. He went in another direction (*Science and Mechanics*, 1893). He found that reality has become somewhat elusive. So he decided: 'Let us not talk about reality, perhaps we don't know what it is.' How do we save knowledge in these circumstances? By quietly abandoning the correspondence theory of truth in favour of the coherence theory of truth – whether explicitly or implicitly formulated. The coherence theory of truth maintains that it actually does not matter whether we can describe reality or not. What matters is that our knowledge is coherent, that every new theory and new description fits with the rest. Thus a new theory or proposition is true if it is coherent with the rest of our knowledge.

We have never been happy with this conception of truth, for it somehow abandons reality – which has been too precious to us for the millennia of rational inquiry. Besides, the coherence theory of truth makes it difficult to distinguish coherent fiction from coherent knowledge. (Take the tale of *Alice in Wonderland*, a wonderfully coherent fiction; so coherent in fact that you almost want to believe in the truth of its reality.) Ultimately a disturbing question arises, namely whether everything that is created by the human mind (including knowledge) that is coherent, or semi-coherent, is not one stupendous semi-coherent fiction. There is no valid answer to this question, at least one that can be legitimately derived from any acknowledged system of knowledge, for each of them is partial, question-begging, self-referential; thus each may itself be a part of this stupendous fiction.

Among the twentieth-century philosophers, Karl Popper stands out as the man who saw clearly the consequences of the disintegration of the Newtonian model of reality and who tried to build a rational model of human inquiry, and indirectly a new model of truth; as well as a new model of reality.

Popper incisively concluded that if it is the case that even such well-established theories as Newton's are limited and cannot be claimed to provide absolute and permanent knowledge, then *all knowledge is tentative*. This was an epoch-making step. The tentative or conjectural nature of knowledge, including scientific knowledge, is now almost universally accepted. The crux of the matter is that, while accepting the tentative character of all knowledge, Popper refused a possible conclusion that all knowledge is subjective or personal. He wished to maintain the fundamental assumptions of the Western rational tradition, namely (1) that reality is out there – as it is, and our knowledge, especially scientific knowledge, can describe it; (2) that the correspondence of truth holds, that we do indeed describe reality adequately in our scientific theories. The assumptions (1) and (2) would be difficult to maintain in their traditional forms, as Popper was painfully aware of the crisis in the foundations of our knowledge. And especially as Popper insisted that all knowledge is tentative. Therefore a reconstruction of some of the traditional views had to be undertaken to make the new edifice coherent and convincing.

Thus Popper invented the notion of *approximation* to truth, which tried to save – at the same time – both the traditional concept of reality as objectively existing out there, and the correspondence concept of truth. There exists objective truth, Popper held. It happens when we describe reality adequately, faithfully, thus truly. *But we never know, and we can never know whether our descriptions of reality are ultimately true or only approximately true. We, the seekers of truth, are like mountain climbers, scaling high mountains in perpetual dense fog. And the fog is so dense that we do not see our way around. Even if we are at the top of the peak, we do not know it, for there may be another peak higher up which is covered by fog.* Thus even if we had arrived at objective or absolute truth, we have no way of knowing it for certain.

This is both a romantic and a cunning concept of truth. Romantic because the image appeals to us (we are the climbers scaling high mountains in the perpetual fog – how much more romantic can you be?); cunning because it presupposes the fog is so dense that we do not see our way around, even if we are at the top. If the fog is so dense, we want to ask, how do we *ever* know what we are doing? We were once told that science is lucidity and clarity. We are now told that the search for truth in science is a journey in a perpetual fog. The notion of truth born in this fog bodes ill.

The problem of truth has been a thorny one indeed for Popper. The idea of approximation to truth was meant to be the solution in the following way. We propose theories. They are, in time, refuted. New theories represent a closer approximation to truth. Popper even tried to quantify and formalize this notion of approximation to truth. But deep conceptual difficulties have always been there. How can we know that new theories represent a closer approximation to truth if we climb in perpetual fog? Even if we travelled in luminous light, how could we know that a new theory was a closer approximation to truth *unless* we somehow knew this truth already, unless we had somehow already grasped that to which our tentative theories were approximating? And the question arises: does this whole process not involve some kind of multi-valued logic, or even perhaps the relativity of truth?

All the difficulties concerning the nature of reality and of truth are strikingly apparent in Thomas Kuhn's *The Structure of Scientific Revolutions* (1963). Kuhn hardly discusses the notion of truth. Truth is mentioned a couple of times as it were in passing. The point is that if we don't know how to talk about reality coherently, how can we talk about truth coherently? A prudent stance on the subject should induce us to avoid mentioning these subjects altogether. And many do. Kuhn vacillates. Since Kuhn attempts to reconstruct the history of science – how it proceeds and how it progresses – he cannot avoid the subject of truth altogether. For if science is about reality, then it must also be about truth. Yet reality and truth are troublesome subjects, so throughout Kuhn concentrates on *how science works, rather than what it describes and what is its truth.*

Kuhn's reconstruction of science (through the notion of the paradigm) is a two-faced affair. On the one hand, claims are made that science is about reality and somehow about truth. On the other hand (when we come to specific arguments), truth is paradigm-bound. Since reality is paradigm-bound, so must truth be.

There is no way of determining the nature of reality except through the conceptual framework which a given paradigm represents. *Reality is the paradigm.* And so is truth: intersubjectivity is coextensive with the paradigm. It goes only as far as the paradigm goes. What we obtain is not a correspondence between reality and its descriptions; *it is only a coherence within the paradigm.* Kuhn clearly opts for the coherence theory of truth.[2]

Now this entire discussion was meant to demonstrate only one point, namely that during the last several decades we have wanted to uphold the notion of universal truth (trans-subjective, trans-personal, or simply objective) but *we have been unable to do so*. In particular we have been unable to maintain the classical or the correspondence theory of truth. Thus the notion of truth needs a thorough reexamination. What follows is an outline of the participatory concept of truth.

3. Participatory truth

The participatory concept of truth does not set out to abolish truth as such, and particularly the claim that there are truths which are trans-subjective and in a sense universal. But this intersubjectivity and this universality must be delicately handled and not confused with old-fashioned objectivity, and especially with the absolute notion of truth. Thus the participatory theory claims that truth is intersubjective and in a sense universal, but not objective or absolute.

Let us first examine the characteristics of participatory truth. And let us be aware that participatory truth is not an entity in itself, but a consequence and an articulation of the whole edifice of the participatory mind, including the notion of the participatory universe. Participatory truth can be characterized as follows:

(1) It is species-specific.
(2) It is culture-specific or culture-bound.
(3) It is evolving.
(4) It is determined by the spiral of understanding.
(5) (Since it is participatory) it is a *happening*.

(1) PARTICIPATORY TRUTH IS SPECIES-SPECIFIC

If we live in the participatory universe, and if all our knowledge is participatory knowledge, then all truth must be seen
as species-specific. *If there is no species, there is no truth. If there is
no consciousness, there is no truth.* The truth of the stars or the
truth of God are quite different from ours – as their consciousness is different. Our participatory consciousness changes
with time; and so does our participatory truth.

(2) PARTICIPATORY TRUTH IS CULTURE-SPECIFIC

Truth is a specific property of the human species. Let us note,
however, that human beings live and think in specific, well-
bound and well-defined contexts. These contexts are not
whimsical or personal. They are called cultures. And cultures
determine the overall context of participation in a subtle and
yet all-pervading way. Thus truth is culture-specific. Culture
determines the rules of participation. There is no truth without
participation. Participation is determined by ritual, myths,
cognitive strategies, a variety of forms of praxis.

In a sense culture is the maker of truth – specific for a
given epoch. Let us be quite clear that this last statement is
not an admission of the subjectivity of truth or the relativity
of truth. The context of a culture is not subjective, is not
personal, is not relativistic. What this statement asserts is that
all truth occurs within human discourse. There is no truth
without language. There is no language without participation.
Language is a property of culture, a property of participation.
In outlining the boundaries and the matrix of participation,
culture also determines truth, which is bound by its context,
which is intersubjective within a given culture.

(3) PARTICIPATORY TRUTH IS EVOLVING

This characteristic seems startling – because we are conditioned to think otherwise. Our conditioned mind immediately questions the assertion: how can truth be evolving? If something is true, it is true, because it is true. But this way of looking at truth leads us back precisely to the absolutist framework within which reality is fixed and unchangeable, and our knowledge of it is a strict photographic representation of it – as based on the old idea of correspondence.

Now when Plato, then Aquinas, then Newton proposed their absolutist frameworks, they were not aware of the nature and the very existence of evolution. When we say that truth is evolving we mean to say precisely that evolution itself is evolving; as it does, so must our truth of it. But more importantly still – as our knowledge is evolving, so our understanding is evolving. If our understanding is evolving, our truth is evolving. *For our truths are only the distilled fragments of our unfolding knowledge.* Once we recognize that knowledge is not a firm static pyramid to which we add various stones as if we were masons working on the same pyramid; once we recognize that the image of the pyramid – one and the same persisting in all times – is not adequate and indeed fundamentally mistaken as a representation of the growth of knowledge; once we recognize the dynamic, fluid, dialectical nature of evolving knowledge – we are bound to recognize truth as evolving, particularly if we operate within the framework of the participatory mind.

Let us underscore the point by observing that what we have said simply follows from the very nature of evolution. We first recognized evolution in geology. With the publication of *Principles of Geology* (1830–33) by Charles Lyell, it was established that continents have been evolving. With the publication of *The Origin of Species* (1859), it was established that species have been evolving. It took us another century to realize that in a very similar sense knowledge has been evolving. What we wish to emphasize is that with the publication of Popper's *Conjectures and Refutations* (1962) and almost simultaneously of Kuhn's *The Structure of Scientific Revolutions*, we have a clear acknowledgement that all knowledge is evolving. We can thus see that the discovery of evolution has so far gone through at least three stages:

(1) Geological evolution (Lyell).

(2) Biological evolution (Darwin).

(3) Epistemological evolution (Popper, Kuhn et al.).[3]

The consequences of what I term 'the evolution of knowledge', or 'epistemological evolution', are far-reaching and not yet fully drawn. The discovery and articulation of the epistemological evolution is not only limited to Popper (all knowledge is conjectural) and Kuhn (all knowledge is paradigm-bound) or their followers and associates Feyerabend, Lakatos, et al. The articulation of this stage of evolution has been furthered by such thinkers as Ilya Prigogine ('The nature of the laws of nature changes') and David Bohm ('The known and the knower merge as the implicate order unfolds').

Actually the theory of the participatory mind developed throughout this volume is one continuous articulation of the idea of epistemological evolution. Put simply, *the participatory mind is epistemological evolution writ large*. It incorporates early insights of Popper, Kuhn, Prigogine and Bohm, and tries to justify them in a new coherent framework. One of the consequences of epistemological evolution is noetic monism (discussed earlier). *Nous* pervades the universe. At least the universe that we can reach. Any other form of universe is not the universe for us. At the very least we have to recognize that *nous* pervades all human knowledge. For *nous* is built into the very structure of this knowledge.

Now this is the context that informs us why truth is evolving. It is evolving because our mind is evolving, our knowledge is evolving, and our universe is evolving. *As the universe is evolving, so it creates more knowable minds. As the mind becomes more knowable, it begets a more intelligent universe.* In this process, truth does not remain static and frozen, but evolves with our evolving universe and knowledge.

(4) PARTICIPATORY TRUTH IS DETERMINED BY THE SPIRAL OF UNDERSTANDING

Little needs to be said on this subject. For if we remember the characteristics of the spiral of understanding, its place and role in the formation and transformation of human knowledge; if we remember the fact that the spiral is continually evolving – then it immediately follows that truth must be seen as evolving and not static; as participatory, not absolute; as determined by the characteristics of the mind and not by absolute reality existing independently of us.

(5) PARTICIPATORY TRUTH IS A 'HAPPENING'

Truth is a 'happening' – not a frozen state of being. Our language is not adequate here. By a 'happening' we usually denote a half-serious, half-frivolous affair, while truth is supposed to be a very serious affair indeed. Perhaps we are too serious in our outlook on truth. Perhaps we should be mindful of the words of Nietzsche about truth: 'Truth is that kind of error without which a certain kind of living being cannot live.' Perhaps the time has arrived when we realize that truth is one of the most playful of concepts. It always *happens* in the framework of some participation, never by itself. Even when Moses was receiving his Tablets, this was happening within the context of his alleged conversations with God.

In brief, *the context of participation determines the nature of truth.*[4] This context *may* be delineated by what we call the objective method or the scientific method. It then becomes the context of scientifically-controlled experiments. It is a participation of a kind, nevertheless.

This context may be one of conversing with God, and then bringing the truth of the Ten Commandments is the result.

This context may be one of finding the truth concerning human nature by making a portrait of a person (Rembrandt).

To maintain that the latter two contexts are illegitimate as bearers of truth, or at least as the basis of truth, is dogmatically to insist that there is only one framework of participation – that of science. When we so limit our participation, we limit the universe at large. And the consequences are disastrous.

All truth is participatory. In the strict sense, there is no such thing as *physical* truth. All truth is noetic, is a property of or an attribute of the mind. It is the human mind that makes observations. It is the mind that makes sense of deductions. It is the mind that builds patterns of coherence out of those observations and deductions that are then called descriptions of reality or simply truths.

Participatory truth is always partial, is always fragmentary, is always incomplete, for every context of participation is fragmentary and incomplete.

Even when we grant all of this, we still want to ask: is there ultimate, objective, or absolute truth? And if so, what is the most fruitful way of looking at it, of thinking about it?

Furthermore: how is this ultimate or absolute truth related to our participatory truths?

There is an answer to these questions. *There is absolute or ultimate truth. It is one gigantic truth about the whole universe, in its totality, in its unfolding, in its realization.*

Such a truth even God cannot comprehend. And yet this may be the only objective or absolute truth. We cannot even hope to grasp this total truth. Yet we can envisage that each context of participation is a fragment of this enormous evolving truth. Is this then a reassertion of the relativity of truth? No. It is an assertion of participatory truth.

4. Participatory truth as the search for the completeness of the universe

Each turn of the enormous kaleidoscope called the evolving cosmos produces a specific pattern. When we enter this pattern and participate in it, a fragment of truth is created; but not before we enter the pattern, and not before we interact with it and participate in it. The patterns in which human beings do not participate are not patterns for us. They cannot be the basis for truth. *For truth happens only within human discourse, within language, within the context and structure of participation.* This is perhaps the clearest meaning of the expression that truth happens and is not a static thing. Thus to talk about the truth of the universe as it is – independently of us – does not make any sense.

The kaleidoscopic fragments of truth created through the intervention of human imagination and human participation are real. There is nothing subjective about them. These fragments of truth are aspects of the gigantic absolute truth about the whole universe in its totality.

At this point we cannot but inquire further. How do we know that these fragments, which we entertain as partial truths, fit, that they are integral aspects of the total truth? We cannot know this for certain. For to know this would mean to have a glimpse of the total absolute truth. Are we therefore groping in darkness, from one participatory context to another, without any signpost to absolute truth which alone can vindicate our fragmentary truths? In short, is there no guiding light on the road to Truth? We cannot be sure that there is, as this absolute truth is so enormous that it exceeds the bounds of our reason and our science. Yet there seems to be a guiding light. This is the light of our intuition, the light of the special insight that so often flares up to illumine our destinies.

The light of intuition suggests that the more meaningful the participation, the more truth it reveals. The deeper the participation, the deeper you enter into the mysteries of life – until you arrive at the deepest contest of participation, which is God.

If we have the courage to follow the logic of participation, then we are ultimately bound to conclude that *Truth* (the ultimate total truth) *is the realization of God*. We need to pause here and take a breath. For we seem to have departed from the usual contexts of truth. However, we need to notice that there is nothing outrageous in our conclusions. If it is the case that some contexts of participation lead somewhere, while other contexts of participation lead nowhere, then this may be our signpost. Clearly this signpost makes us cherish the significant contexts of participation for a reason. We find that they are significant because somehow they contribute to the realization and fulfilment of the human condition. They help in the redemption of the world. When we have the courage to go a step further, we can say that they contribute to the realization of God. It is in this sense that ultimate truth is the realization of God. And it is in this sense that it is a rational proposition. And this sense has been cherished in many religious contexts. Unexpected conclusions reveal themselves to the searching mind. Let us search more deeply and see whether our conception of ultimate truth as the realization of God is a far-out idea, or whether it has some basis in human history.

When we look at it perceptively, religion can be seen as the search for paths leading to God, to the absolute reality, to that scene of the cosmic drama in which the universe is consummated and fulfilled. Religion, in addition to being a ritual (sometimes empty), a ceremony (often significant), an opiate for the masses (not entirely insignificant), has often been a profound search for the ultimate wholeness of the universe, for absolute truth, for the ultimate completeness of the universe. Although this search could not be based on empirical facts and data, it is one that does not defy reason as it expresses one of the noblest aspirations of the human psyche. In spite of the fact that we can grasp only fragments, we desire to embrace the whole. Our longing for something much greater than we are is part of our human condition, the propelling force of transcendence. Browning's words not only strike the chord, but they convey our transcendent nature:

> Ah, but a man's reach should exceed his grasp,
> Or what's a Heaven for?

Participatory truth as a search for the completeness of the universe is one that has been pursued by many illustrious seekers. We have now made a bridge to the old spiritual traditions. We are back in the universe of Pythagoras, of Plato, of the Buddha, of Zoroaster. These traditions are not concerned with mundane truths but attempt to behold the ultimate one. There is no language to express the ultimate truth, and probably there never will be. So even the most illustrious seekers, when they tried to grasp and reveal the ultimate truth, revealed only fragments.

What is important to realize is that spiritual leaders, whom we revere as law-givers and fountains of light, were not just old-fashioned misguided souls who didn't know their physics. They were after something much greater and more magnificent. They wanted to reveal to us ultimate reality and ultimate truth. They intuitively knew that there is only one truth about the whole universe. And they called this truth God.

Thus the participatory theory of truth rehabilitates religious seekers as rational beings. They had the courage to contemplate the ultimate frames of reference, the ultimate contexts of participation. They had the courage to participate in the greatest dream – the dream of reaching the absolute, of becoming one with God.

We know that Mahatma Gandhi was a rational being, and a very practical one for that matter. Yet for him truth was God; and God was truth. This identification of one with the other was not the result of Gandhi's philosophical confusion but his cunning intuitive grasp of participatory truth in its cosmic evolution – the awareness of how truth in the ultimate sense relates to the ends of human life, here on earth.

5. Truth is the consequence of the participatory context

Let us come back to our ordinary reality (if there is such a thing as ordinary reality). Our discussion of the rationality of religion as the search for ultimate contexts of participation in no way denies the rationality of our participation in other frames of reference, including that of conventional science. We need to emphasize – our truth is a consequence of the participatory context. If our universe (thus our context) is so contrived that we see in it only physical bodies moving according to certain mechanistic laws; and if our context of participation determines that we are supposed to be detached observers dispassionately recording the movement of these physical bodies through the apparatus that is given to us, which mainly photographs and classifies, *then* our participatory truths will be in the form of statements about physical facts and physical theories – which our spiral of understanding has ingeniously constructed, and which our theories mirror and merely want to confirm. And then we obtain those wonderful physical results as predicted because our frame of reference (our context of participation) ingeniously coerces us to do so. The whole affair is predictable, circular and question-begging.

Let us be crystal clear that physical truth is not a privileged kind of truth, let alone the arbiter of all truth. It is just participatory truth of one kind. There is no physical truth in itself and by itself – unless there is an appropriate context of participation. This context of participation is often clinically arranged, including the fact that some research scientists wear white coats. The Yoga of Objectivity is the yoga of a special kind of participation. But participation it is.

Physical contexts are important. But they are not the only contexts. Indeed, within the staggering variety of contexts within which we live, think and act, these contexts are a distinct minority. Let us notice that a great variety of contexts are value-laden. Their purpose is to be life-enhancing. We know that not all contexts are equally life-enhancing, or under the same aspects, or within the same time-frame. The criterion of what is life-enhancing must be delicately balanced. It should be seen against a larger panorama. What is this panorama? The liberation of life in the long run, the realization of our evolutionary potential, the realization of the God-within. Thus, those participatory truths that more clearly help us to realize the God-within, that more clearly help us to realize our cosmic potential, are preferable to those that help us less obviously and less directly.

Let us now spell out some of the important contexts of participation signifying different kinds of truth. Participatory truth, when it is envisaged in the ultimate context, in the context that is called absolute truth or complete truth, is part of the process of the realization of God, or of the fulfilment of the destiny of the universe. In this sense, participatory truth is close to *religious* truth.

Participatory truth, when it is envisaged as part of the process of the realization of human meaning within the cultural context, could be called *cultural* truth.

Participatory truth employed in the physical framework within which we search for the regularities in the physical universe – which are then recorded in the annals of science and of history of knowledge – is *physical* truth. Participatory truth in this sense is the creation of statements and theories that provide the elucidation and articulation of the physical structure of the universe – as the human mind can conceive of it.

Participatory truth that is created when we construct new logical and mathematical theorems and proofs is *formal* truth. This form of truth at first appears to be remote from everyday reality. Yet sooner or later it finds an application in this reality.

Participatory truth that emerges out of contexts in which, for example, we inquire whether DDT accumulated in sprayed crops can be harmful to human beings over longer periods of time, is what we call *practical* truth.

All these forms of truth – religious, cultural, physical, formal, practical – are intertwined with each other; are woven together in one magnificent symphony of human participation, which is continually played in this universe of becoming.

If Ultimate Truth is equal to the self-realization of the universe – which some people without apologies wish to identify with God – then *the destruction of the universe would be the ultimate falsehood*. If one could imagine a black hole, which grows exponentially, and devours the entire universe, while the human species is still present, then this would signify falsehood indeed. For then all grounds for participation would be annihilated. No universe – no species; no species – no participation; no participation – no culture; no culture – no language, and finally – no truth.

Falsehood is thus an annihilation of the participatory context that bears and enables participatory truth. Actually, the annihilation of the *whole* context prevents us from talking either about truth or falsehood. No context – nothing.

Usually falsehood occurs when there exists a violation of some features of the context, some discrepancy, some dissonance between what we expect to find, within the established and accepted context, and what we *do* find in it. This discrepancy/dissonance/violation may manifest itself in different ways, depending on the nature of the context.

Thus in the context of the theories of classical science, the discrepancy/dissonance is called the lack of correspondence between theory and facts – which do not fit the theory; the lack of fit is also the ground for calling a phenomenon false within a context. If instances (observations) clash with a theory that is considered valid and true, these instances are called falsehoods. Sometimes the whole theory needs to be scrapped when it disagrees with a more important theory (a more important context). More important contexts overrule less important ones. This is equally true of science and of life at large.

The dissonance/discrepancy/violation as a form of manifestation of falsehood reveals itself differently in religion. A false icon is one that disagrees with the accepted symbolism of a given religion. A false prophet is one who undermines the accepted faith. False gods are ones that question or undermine the authority of the established God(s).

We can also quite legitimately talk about someone's behaviour as 'false'. We often hear statements such as: 'His behaviour is so false.' Strictly speaking, behaviour cannot be false – if truth is the property of statements or linguistic utterances. Yet the above-mentioned expression can be seen as valid when we allow the notion of language to be conceived broadly. For *behaviour is a form of language that we can read with great subtlety*.

What happens in a situation where I perceive somebody's behaviour as false is something like this. I have a clear notion of the situation, and what a given person should represent in a given context. In other words, I have a clear notion of how a given person should act and behave in the context. In the case of 'false behaviour' I perceive, on the one hand, that the person makes verbal utterances as if he or she were approving of the context and in agreement with it; while I perceive, on the other hand, that his or her body language, facial expression, intonation of voice and entire demeanour disapprove of the context, of the truth he or she is supposed to be upholding. Thus this behaviour is false because I read the language of his body and this language tells me that he is only pretending and not genuinely accepting the context.[5] I feel (and am convinced of it) that inside, the person is *not truthful* to what he or she allegedly professes. It is in this sense that the person's behaviour is false.

In brief, participatory truth signifies harmony with the context within which we act/think/worship. Falsehood, on the other hand, signifies disharmony/dissonance with the aims and goals of the context given as valid and accepted. Parenthetically, we don't need to accept a context of which we disapprove. Yet social life sometimes forces us to do so. 'Hypocrisy is homage paid by vice to virtue' (La Rochefoucauld).

Truth and falsehood are a matter of life-forms, not mere thought. The arbiter of truth is life itself. Truths should be judged in accordance with their life-enhancing powers. The more significant the context, in the overall pursuit of life, the more significant truths it contains. Any given proposition, thought or action (each of them is a life-form) should be judged in accordance with how much it contributes to a given life-enhancing context. The production of nuclear bombs is the production of evolutionary lies.

Summary

With the collapse of the Newtonian world-view, we witness the collapse of the doctrine of metaphysical realism – which was its philosophical justification. Simultaneously we witness a collapse of a variety of empiricisms from Locke and Hume to Russell and Quine. These empiricisms have been merely more refined versions of metaphysical realism.

On another level, the collapse of the Newtonian worldview signifies (at least a partial) collapse of the correspondence theory of truth – which in modern times has been uniquely bound to the scientific world-view. The correspondence theory of truth did not originate with the Newtonian world-view and therefore does not need to be entirely tied to it. Yet modern Western philosophy is inconceivable without the tie between the correspondence theory of truth and the scientific world-view.

Some have tried to rescue the correspondence theory while forgoing the notion of permanent knowledge which Newton's physics stipulates. Among the bravest of these was Karl Popper who introduced the notion of approximation to truth – an ingenious idea but ridden with the irresolvable difficulties: if we don't know truth, how can we ever handle an approximation to it? What is the meaning of an approximation if we don't know that which it approximates to?

Others have tried to replace the correspondence theory of truth with truth by convention (Poincaré, early Quine). Yet others have tried to find an escape in the coherence theory of truth (Mach, Kuhn). Others again have opted for the pragmatic theory of truth – American pragmatists on the one hand, and Marxists in the communist world on the other. Although I have not discussed the pragmatic theory of truth in any detail, it is fair to say that this theory (as a replacement of the correspondence theory) does not fare any better than other new candidates for truth. The pragmatic theory of truth can be a social disaster when it becomes a weapon of advertising men and of politicians.

As we reconstruct the cosmos and the meaning of this illusive term called 'reality', so we need to revise our old idea of what truth is, or what is the most judicious way to use the term. Participatory philosophy outlines the participatory concept of truth, which is neither objective nor subjective; neither absolute nor relative but intersubjective and universal – within the boundaries of the species (truth is species-specific); within the boundaries of culture (truth is culture-bound and language-bound); within the boundaries of the spiral of under-standing. As evolution unfolds so does the mind unfold, so our knowledge unfolds, so our truth unfolds. By saying that truth is unfolding we are saying that truth is a *happening* or simply that truth is participatory.

The concept of participatory truth enables us to recognize the validity of the religious concept of truth – which is determined by the specifically religious context of partici-pation. By recognizing religious truth, we are able to shed a new light on spiritual seekers, the Illustrious Ones, who gave us religions and the moral law, and who, at times, identified God with truth. They were not half-baked, confused philoso-phers but envisaged truth as the realization of God, as the consummation of the destiny of man.

Yes, there is absolute or ultimate truth. It is the truth about the whole universe, in its totality, in its unfolding, in its realization. This may be God's truth; or the truth that even God cannot comprehend. Some simply say that ultimate truth is God.

We human beings must be satisfied with partial truths – always fragmentary. Fragmentary truths are not relative or subjective. Each turn of the kaleidoscope called the evolving cosmos produces a specific pattern. When we enter this pattern and participate in it, a fragment of truth is created. Truth does not exist before we enter the cosmos or kaleido-scopic configurations of it, but only within human language, within the context of participation.

It is difficult to live with truth. It is impossible to live without truth. As a human species we need guidance as to what is right and what is wrong; what is justice and what is injustice. Truth has historically served as the basis of justice, as the yardstick of goodness – even if it was so in an indirect way. We now know that the only truth we can know is human truth – man-made truth. The human condition is frail but not arbitrary. And so is our truth.

No species – no truth! Participatory truth does not describe things as they are. Participatory truth is a vehicle of becoming. Participatory truth is the Promethean fire of transformation.

CHAPTER II

Grand Theory in the Participatory Key

1. The return of grand theory

In 1959 the American sociologist Wright Mills published his celebrated book *The Sociological Imagination*, in which he tried to bury and to ridicule what is called Grand Theory. Grand theory insists that framework is more important than particular facts. For facts receive their meaning from an underlying framework – a general theory, or a paradigm. Mills and his followers thought otherwise. They advocated the 'scientific' study of human nature, and of human institutions, in which particular empirical facts – their analysis and detailed examination – predominate, and are the only important thing.

This was, of course, positivism applied to social science. This was the era in which not only social scientists became captive to positivism. The whole epoch was in the clutches of narrow, atomistic, positivist thinking. Thirty years later, grand theory is flourishing again. If not flourishing, at least alive and making a significant comeback. There are, of course, many contenders to grand theory and quite a bit of confusion concerning the meaning of the term, as the schools of hermeneutics and deconstructionism quarrel with each other.

What is important is not the differences between various schools but the fact that large normative thinking has returned. It is again clearly perceived that our frameworks *do* determine the nature of facts we examine, that the meaning of the whole determines the meaning of the parts. Thus holistic thinking is in, while atomistic thinking is waning, at least among prominent grand theorists of the last decade.

The new developments concerning the reemergence of grand theory are well documented in Quentin Skinner's *The Return of Grand Theory in the Human Sciences* (1985). Skinner and the scholars who contributed to the book attempt to make us aware that in spite of the growing fragmentation of knowledge that we have witnessed in our time, a process of synthesis is going on.

Some of the main characteristics of grand theory are:

(1) It attempts to meet the challenge of the problems of the epoch.

(2) It attempts to offer an original interpretation of the multitude of phenomena, while at the same time it is capable of maintaining the value of tradition.

(3) It attempts to serve as a model or a paradigm for other fields of inquiry.

(4) It attempts to be consistent with scientific progress, or more generally, with the progress of knowledge.

I will now offer participatory philosophy as a candidate for a new grand theory. Participatory philosophy as developed throughout this book meets the above-mentioned criteria, with the proviso that scientific progress must be interpreted broadly – not as a progress within a given paradigm, especially of Newtonian mechanics, but a progress of human understanding, of which scientific understanding is but one aspect.

Thus in this chapter I shall sketch an outline of Grand Theory in the Participatory Key. More specifically, I shall provide some of the missing links of the participatory grand theory which has been implicitly developed throughout this volume.

We shall first reconstruct the process of reality-experience-knowledge when we make a transition from one reality to another. Let me put it otherwise. We wish to make explicit the process of *reality-making*, whereby we transform reality by co-creatively participating in it, so that – to express it in colloquial language – we move from one picture of reality to another. A more exact way of saying this would be: *when our mind moves from partaking in one reality to partaking in another reality – while being in the same universe.* We shall need to reflect on the following:

(1) The relationship of reality (R_1) to experience.

(2) The nature of experience itself.

(3) The relationship of experience to knowledge; how knowledge arises out of experience, and how it in turn shapes and moulds experience.

(4) How new knowledge is possible, and what is the role of new insights and new illuminations in the creation of new knowledge.

(5) How this new knowledge creates in its wake a new reality (R_2).

We have travelled now from one reality (R_1) to another reality (R_2). The journey from R_1 to R_2 I call the Great Circle of Knowledge. This circle is not closed, but open; actually in the nature of a spiral. We can represent our basic notions expressed in points (1)–(5) by means of a diagram (Fig. 1).

The movement around this Great Circle is what I call the process of *reality-making*. I will use conventional language to describe this process. Reality (R_1) impinges upon experience. Experience, in its turn, gives rise to knowledge. Knowledge bursts with new insights. New insights change the nature of existing reality, and create a new reality (R_2). Now let us trace the process in some detail. How can we account for this process in participatory terms?

Let us first examine the nature of experience. The Greek poet Archilochus of the seventh century BC wrote: 'Life is short.

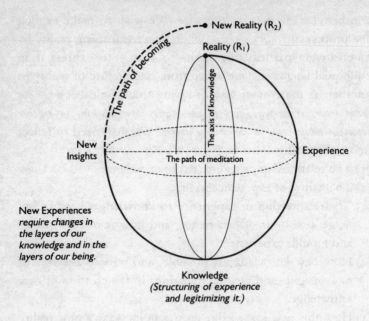

Fig. 1 *The Great Circle of Knowledge*

Art is long. Experience is difficult.' And indeed experience is difficult. The concept itself is at once extremely simple and extremely complex. We all know what experience is. We are but bundles of experiences. Experience and experiences accompany us whatever we do. On one level it is all simple. Since they are our daily companions, we know our experiences well. But this knowledge by acquaintance is rather superficial.

Our brain cells and our muscle cells are our daily companions too. We can hardly say however that we know the nature of their exquisite labour – unless we study the subject intentionally. It is similar with experience. We need to study it in depth to know its nature. For what is experience? A very simple question. But not so simple to answer. I sip my tea. It goes down my throat. It warms me. It gives me some energy. This is an experience. Or is it? I drink four cups of tea daily. After I have done it for several years, it is not an experience any more, but 'just a cup of tea'. Both forms of expression are justified. So that a cup of tea is an experience, and not an experience.

I drink a glass of wine in the company of a beautiful young woman. While sipping my wine I realize that I am falling in love with her. By the time I have finished this glass, I realize she is reciprocating. Drinking this glass of wine *is* an experience – which stays in my memory for many years. I marry the woman, and we have a glass of wine with dinner every day. After several years, drinking the wine with her is *not* an experience any more (although sometimes it is).

I participate in an archaeological dig. Shovel after shovel, I dig up rubble and dirt. The work is beginning to wear me down – sweat and dirt are covering me all over. 'It is not a great experience,' I murmur to myself. The archaeologist who is in charge of the dig, an expert on the culture we are trying to reconstruct, comes by. He stops and is immediately arrested by what he sees in the rubble I have dug out. He calls me a 'moron' and tells me that I am butchering his site by being so incredibly insensitive to what is there – rare treasure in the rubble I have dug out. There are, in my pile, recognizable bits of pottery and other artifacts of the old culture that he is trying to reconstruct. My pile of rubble makes the other man ecstatic. We look at the same mound of dirt. For him it is a great experience. For me it is sweat and dirt.[1]

I visit a glacial lake in the higher reaches of the Tatra Mountains. I am mesmerized by the total silence that almost sings. I see the rugged peaks surrounding me as magnificent cathedrals. I almost hear the angels singing in them, except that their music is silence. I am overwhelmed by the experience. Upon my return to the valley, where the buses and people are, I recognize a man whom I saw at the glacial lake. He is asked by his companion, who stayed behind: 'What have you seen?' He responds, 'Eh, nothing, a heap of rocks.' I cannot believe my ears. But there it is: a great experience for me; a pile of rocks for him.

The singing of the silent cathedrals and the beauty of the desolate scene of the Tatra Mountains haunts me in days to come to the point that I finally write a poem. The more I work on the poem, the more significant it becomes. The more significant is my poem, the more significant becomes the experience which has given rise to it; until it becomes one of the most significant experiences of my life. This experience leads me to the realization that all creation is sacred – if and when we are in an appropriate reverential frame of mind . . . as I was while listening to the silence amidst the cathedrals of the Tatra Mountains.

Experience. What is it? Let us try to sort out the various meanings of the term (in the experiences I have mentioned) in order to distinguish significant experiences from insignificant ones. My ten-thousand-seven-hundred-and-thirty-fourth cup of tea, drunk in ordinary circumstances, is a mundane and thus an insignificant experience. I hardly want to talk about it as an experience. The glass of wine I was drinking while I was falling in love with the young woman was an experience. Even more so was the writing of the poem about my experiences of the silent cathedrals. This experience has actually stretched over a period of time: the more my poem has developed, the more vivid and *significant* the experience of the glacial lake has become.

2. Significant experiences

Experience includes at least three components:

'Reality' out there.

Psychic dispositions to experience it.

Appropriate sensitivities to articulate the experience.

'Reality' is usually indispensable as the basis of an experience, or of experiences. But not always. Some of the greatest experiences we experience inwardly. They are the soul-trips or the mind-trips, not derived from or inspired by the outside reality.

There are some experiences that appear as beautiful or at least pleasant at the time you experience them. However, they seem to be in the nature of a cloud. They float through us and disappear. Once the time of a given experience is over, nothing remains of it but a vague memory of a mist. These are not significant experiences.

Significant experiences are *memorable* – like the glass of wine I drank at this memorable dinner. Furthermore, significant experiences are *articulate*, or at least articulable: we can recall and express them in words, or by some other means – maybe through dance, maybe through body language. Thirdly, significant experiences are *transformative*. After they have occurred, something has happened to us.

Let us express these characteristics of the nature of significant experience in the language of the participatory mind. *Significant experience is that kind of event, or that series of events, which leads to recognizable transformations of the spiral of understanding – either personal or universal (cultural).*

Wishy-washy experiences do nothing to our spiral of understanding. Drinking the ten-thousandth cup of tea in ordinary circumstances does nothing to our spiral of understanding.

But we can make the act of drinking the ten-thousand-and-first cup of tea a beautifully significant experience if, for instance, we transform the mere drinking into some Zen ritual, or if we imagine the tea to be the blood of Christ, or pure energy of the Buddha – and we drink this sacramental tea with such a gravity and with such a holy and reverential attitude that our entire being is transformed in the process. This experience then *becomes* significant because it is transformative. Since our entire being has changed, our spiral of understanding has changed.

Knowledge and experience are deeply but subtly connected. Sometimes new experience leads to changes in our knowledge. After we have undergone some experiences, we know differently. Our knowledge has been somehow rearranged.

The converse is also true. Not infrequently, new knowledge that we have acquired changes the nature of our experience. If I suddenly (or perhaps not so suddenly) learn that my wife has been unfaithful to me, this may significantly alter the way I experience the act of love-making with her. To take another example, which many people have experienced, if I suddenly learn that I have an incurable cancer, and that I have no more than fifteen months left to live, this knowledge may significantly alter all my future experiences.

Obviously we seek experiences that are not banal or humdrum but enriching and ultimately transformative. These are what we call new and significant experiences. These are the experiences that are *meant* to be new experiences. I propose to call this form of experience, which is significant and which is meant to be an experience, *S-experience* ('S' standing for significant).

Let us relate the present discussion to our earlier discussion of the spiral of understanding. The first point. The spiral of understanding can only change through S-experience. Only those experiences that are significant can affect and change our spiral of understanding, the logos of our being. Humdrum experiences only reinforce the existing logos.

The second point. New experiences or S-experiences require courage, openness, making oneself vulnerable. All these attributes of the human psyche are the preconditions of creativity. Indeed, *courting an S-experience is a creative act*.

To participate in any creative venture is to become open, to loosen one's armour, to take risks. The creative process is one open to the S-experience. On the other hand, if we are not prepared to loosen our armour and to become open, we are inadvertently closing the gates of experience, at any rate, the gates of S-experience.

Why are some people so lucky in encountering new, transformative experiences? Because they invite these experiences by being open and vulnerable. Why are some other people rather unlucky in encountering significant experiences? Because they keep these experiences at bay by being too guarded and closed up, and not wishing to be vulnerable. Vulnerability is a precondition of all creative experience; and of most S-experiences.

The third point is this. Deterministic and mechanistic systems, such as science, subtly coerce us to close up, to cling to what is predictable, what includes no risk. But safe gambits do not lead to new experience. On the contrary, they lead to stale forms of life – dull, repetitive, predictable. No risks, no vulnerability – no new experiences, and little creativity.

Let us try to summarize some of the main points of our discussion. There is experience, and there is *experience*. In our language: there is experience and there is S-experience. *Unarticulated experience is a mist*. Mist is pleasant to experience but it does not leave any worthwhile residue. We must open the gates of our being to new experiences.

Significant experience is one that somehow changes our being. Sometimes it changes the core of our being – in the process it changes our spiral of understanding, our logos. But the converse is true as well: significant changes in the spiral of our understanding (which is the filtering structure of all our experience) signify changes in the nature of our experience. The nature of our logos and the nature of our experience are twin sisters.

In this entire picture we must not forget about sensitivities. They are ultimately the artists that give a distinctive shape to our experiences. They are the sculptors of our experiences. Why was I called a 'moron' at the archaeological dig? Because I did not possess the appropriate sensitivities to see the clues of a great culture that was lurking behind the rubble I was digging out on the site. Why was I so moved by the silent singing cathedrals at the glacial lake? Because I possessed appropriate aesthetic sensitivities to transform the mere granite rocks into the metaphysical *mysterium tremendum*.

The role of the mind is all-important in shaping the nature of experience and in bringing out those distinctive forms that we sometimes call the delight of life, sometimes revelatory illuminations. By the mind, of course, we do not mean the abstract brain, but the entire universe of sensitivities. What senses and sees and thinks is the entire body – not just the abstract brain. Our body, as the repository of the sensitivities of evolution, is doing the knowing and the thinking. This clearly follows from the idea of the participatory mind.

The role of 'reality' is not denied here. The role of sensory inputs is not denied here. But sensory inputs as such are dumb. The whole Candillac model of the transformation of pure sensations into refined modes of knowledge is dumb itself. The French eighteenth-century philosopher Candillac imagined, along with many other empiricists, that mind is a *tabula rasa*, a white sheet of paper on which experience writes its designs. A newly born babe could be compared to a human statue made of glass – all transparent and containing nothing inside. As experience writes on us, we become articulated persons. For the empiricists, of whom Candillac was one, there is nothing in the mind that has not been previously in the senses. As it was put in Latin: *Nihil est in intellectu quod non prius fuerit in sensu.*

The participatory theory of mind reverses this dictum by claiming that *there is nothing in the senses that has not previously been in the structure of our sensitivities, thus the structure of our (evolutionary) mind.* We make sense of what is in the senses through the refined working of the mind.

To emphasize, the very idea of the senses is not a sense datum, but a refined product of the mind. There are no sense data in the strict sense, for *the sense datum itself is not a datum of the senses but a product of the mind.* Even if there were 'pure sense data' or the raw data of the senses, they could not possibly have been able to transform themselves into refined knowledge, for 'pure sense data' are dumb, mute and incoherent. Only by the power and mercy of our sensitivities could they be transformed into articulate experience and articulate forms of knowledge.

The web of our sensitivities is all-pervading. It touches and refines everything that enters our being, whether through the senses, whether through intuition, whether through divine revelation. Divine revelation cannot descend upon the mind that is not sensitive enough to receive it, and somehow make sense of it. Glory to the sensitive mind, for it is the maker of all knowledge, of all experience.

3. Experience and knowledge

Let us now consider the relationship between experience and knowledge. At what point does experience become knowledge? By experience we do not mean the raw data of the senses. Indeed, as we have emphasized, within the participatory mind there are no *raw* data of the senses. When they become the data of the senses, these data are already processed.

Let us note that what is beyond your experience does not exist for you. What is beyond the experience of the species does not exist for the species. We are reiterating in a new setting the statement that unless there are appropriate sensitivities to experience a given phenomenon, or a given aspect of reality, it is beyond us, and doesn't exist for us.

We all know that there is a difference between experience and knowledge. At which point does experience become knowledge? Or what kind of experiences qualify as knowledge? I want to propose that knowledge is:

a significant experience;

an articulate experience;

a distilled experience (and a significantly filtered one);

a communicable experience;

a sharable experience;

a linguistically structured experience;

a repeatable experience.

These are some of the main characteristics of experience that is transformed into knowledge. *Knowledge is a significant transformation of experience*. Not all of the characteristics mentioned above can be found in all species of knowledge. Playing the violin is one kind of knowledge. Doing experimental physics is another kind of knowledge. Doing theoretical physics is another kind of knowledge. Introducing a new vision – for example, of the impressionist way of viewing reality, as expressed in the first impressionist pictures, is another kind of knowledge.

Let us try to put these insights together. *Knowledge is a structuring of the significant and distilled experience; which we subsequently legitimize by expressing it in sharable and intersubjective patterns and forms.* Sometimes we share it in linguistic forms, especially within discursive knowledge. Sometimes we share it by doing it, as in dancing or playing the violin. No amount of words on how to play the violin can teach you how to play. The real knowledge comes from the imparting of skills from the master to the pupil. This imitative-demonstrative way of learning may be the basis of most of our learning.

True knowledge is a refined and sharable experience. But it is also something else. *Knowledge is light. Knowledge is igniting sensitivities that can see*, in the manifold senses of the term 'see'. When your bow and your fingers can finally play a difficult passage in a Paganini caprice, and you are one with the music, then it can be said that your knowledge sings.

We can go only so far in expressing what knowledge is in 'objective' terms. The rest is seeing that *knowledge is seeing*; that knowledge is light. We can thus say that *knowledge consists of significant new experiences that lead to new illuminations*.[2]

Knowledge is a peculiar light which illumines other things. Knowledge is a torch which (if it is to define itself) wants to illumine itself. It is through knowledge that we must define knowledge, even if we do it imperfectly. The problem of self-reference cannot be avoided. The whole edifice of knowledge is very frail stuff; nevertheless, it is magnificent in spite of its frailty.

We cannot define the human condition because this condition defines us. We cannot define knowledge because knowledge is doing the defining. We cannot explain the nature of the mind because the mind is itself the source of all explanations. Being fragmentary and incomplete beings is the source of many of our agonies. But also of some of our ecstasies – that is, when, through our own work, through new illuminations, we become less fragmentary and more complete.

4. *From new illuminations to new realities*

We are moving along the Great Circle of Knowledge (see Fig. 1). From reality (R_1) we arrive via experience (and S-experience) at knowledge of this reality. But our mind does not remain static or frozen. In its explorations it conceives new ideas, is haunted by new insights or new flashes of imagination. How these flashes occur and why we do not know. But we know that they do occur, particularly to open-minded and venturesome spirits.

The emergence of a new insight is usually preceded by the following three dialogues: of the mind with the existing reality; of the mind with the existing knowledge; and of the mind with one's own experience. At first, there is a tendency to subsume the new insights under the existing categories of knowledge and integrate them into the existing framework of reality. Only after a while does it become apparent that these new insights constitute new knowledge.

This knowledge may be a small extension of the existing one; or may be a major breakthrough. In the latter case it may even lead to a new picture of reality. This new picture of reality is what we call, in our Great Circle of Knowledge, another reality (R_2).

We have travelled on the path of becoming from one reality (R_1) to another (R_2). *Nothing has changed except our mind*. It is precisely in these terms that the participatory mind co-creates with reality. *It is at the point of new illuminations or new insights that the closed system of reality-knowledge becomes an open system*. By charting for itself a new path, the mind enters what I call the *path of becoming* (Fig. 1) which leads to a new reality, and which transcends the closed system of the previous reality.

The difficulties of seeing a new insight or a new illumination for what it is – when we travel in the Great Circle – are similar to those that we experience when our spiral of understanding pierces through the walls of the existing cosmos. These difficulties are not only similar. They are the same. We are talking about the same phenomenon in two different frames of reference.

At this point, it is only a matter of patience to translate all the arguments about the spiral of understanding (and the cosmos corresponding to it) into the language and categories of the Great Circle of Knowledge. Why is the process of discovery, of invention and of creation always so messy? Because at the time it happens we are in no man's land – our spiral of understanding is dislocated, and our cosmos begins to totter.

Why is absolute knowledge (whether of religion or of physics) a threat to our freedom? Because – although it gives us a sense of security – it imprisons us in the static and frozen universe.

On the existential level, absolute knowledge is a severe stumbling block to new experiences, and S-experiences. For if reality is completely fixed and known, then there is nothing to be known beyond it. In such circumstances, we are not supposed to have new insights, new revelations (new experiences). Thus at one point, cognitive absolutism becomes a denial of human freedom on existential grounds: our path of becoming is blocked at the outset.

To recapitulate, if there is becoming, then we can accept no absolute framework which formulates us. On the other hand, if there is an absolute framework to define us, then there is little room for becoming.

Let us move to another question: why is the notion of experience, and particularly new experience, so difficult to handle via objective knowledge? Why, in general terms, this tension and uneasiness between solid, articulated knowledge and fluid, volatile experience? Because knowledge is the guardian of the status quo, is the servant of the existing cosmos; whereas *experience is an inspired agent of becoming*, is the harbinger of the things to come, a herald of the new world which by its very nature is unsettling to the status quo. Ultimately, being and becoming have to accommodate each other. In our language this means that the existing cone of the cosmos on the one hand, and the changing spiral of understanding on the other, have to accommodate each other so that they are a coherent unity.

And so it is with the pair knowledge-experience. Ultimately they have to recognize each other as siblings. But some problems will always remain. For it is in the nature of things that when new experiences outstrip the capacity of the established knowledge (of a given culture) to handle them, then, in self-defence, the existing knowledge (through the actions of the guardians of the status quo) 'defines' these experiences as crazy, lunatic, or at least irrational.

We have seen the wrath of judgement pronounced by the guardians of the status quo upon dissenters quite often in our times. From the standpoint of the people who are the leading actors in the drama of becoming, those high-handed judgements of the existing knowledge are a clear indication that this knowledge has become stale, dogmatic, petrified, ossified, at least inadequate to help us to see the value of new S-experience.

This situation can be clearly seen within the structure of the present Western universities. While its guardians, the top administrators, deans and presidents try to pretend that all is well, that the existing knowledge is the yardstick of all knowledge, the critics who see the inadequacies of present structures consider these guardians the blind priests of a stale religion.

Thus, while the guardians of the status quo within the universities consider the innovators crazy, rash, irrational and irresponsible, the innovators think that these guardians are slaves to vested interests, insensitive to new realities, petrified in their reason, and ultimately irresponsible. So who is responsible? And by what yardstick shall we measure this responsibility? Obviously we have two different spirals of understanding clashing with each other. We have the realm of being – established reality and established knowledge. And corresponding to them: form, structure, immanence, intersubjectivity, established language. On the other hand, we have the realm of becoming. And corresponding to it: new illuminations flourishing amidst creativity, fluidity, change, questioning, transcendence. This is the old eternal conflict between being and becoming.

5. The axis of reality and the axis of meditation

We have travelled around the Great Circle of Knowledge, exploring its outside boundaries. We shall now enter the inside of the circle, and try to explore its inner forces. Let us call the line connecting the points of reality and of knowledge (the solid line) the *axis of knowledge*. This axis is well articulated in the existing theories of knowledge, particularly those that enshrine the importance of scientific knowledge. In fact, this axis is so well articulated and so well recognized, and so much attention is being paid to it, that other points on the Great Circle and the Circle itself are neglected to the extent of being invisible.

Every scientist knows, and especially every philosopher knows, that knowledge does not generate itself, that there is a human agent involved in the process; that the human mind and the human experience are a necessary interface between reality and knowledge. However, the history of knowledge, and particularly of scientific knowledge, is often presented as if reality were having a direct intercourse with knowledge. Reality, as it were, lays its eggs in the basket of knowledge, which in its turn produces little chickens called scientific theories. In this model of direct liaison between reality and knowledge, the human mind, and especially human experience, seem to be dispensable.

The objective model of knowledge, which is still dominant in our culture, is precisely of this sort. The objective method, which is often called the scientific method, seeks to remove the observer from the alliance reality-knowledge. The human observer, the white-coated, detached scientist, is supposed to be there *only* to help reality and knowledge mate with each other successfully. His business is to record the results of this intercourse; in quantitative terms, if possible.

If this rendering appears a bit of a caricature, it at least vividly portrays what we mean by saying that 'science impartially records the behaviour of nature, while excluding the subjective aspects of the observer.' Statements like this are a part of the myth of objectivity. They are themselves a caricature of what happens, although they sound so right and so unbiased.

The myth of objectivity has been so powerfully perpetuated that we often think that knowledge is a realm unto itself, with its own imperatives and regardless of our role in the process of acquiring knowledge. Some myths are false but fruitful. Some myths are false and harmful. The myth of objectivity belongs to the latter category. In pushing itself on us, it distorts our conception of what knowledge is. It distorts our concept of reality. It distorts the meaning of experience and its role in creating knowledge. How many more deficiencies do you need to record to recognize the myth as harmful?

Let us admit that the same myth may play different roles in different periods of history. I am prepared to acknowledge that in the seventeenth century the myth of objectivity may have been fruitful – while science was a force of liberation against the petrified dogmas of the church. But this is no longer so. This myth has become a part of the petrified dogma and a part of the petrified church.

Let us see a more complete picture. Let us realize that experience *always* mediates between reality and knowledge, regardless of how much we want to diminish, neglect and negate its role. The direct axis between reality and knowledge is a fiction. The two never commune, never cohabit; they never have an affair with each other. Only we, through the versatility of our experience, have endless affairs with each.

The first conclusion is: *do not deify or reify (or objectify) the reality-knowledge axis as if it were something existing out there independently of us*. This axis is one of the expressions of the myth of objectivity.

Let us now consider the horizontal axis which I call the *axis of meditation* (the dotted line in Fig. 2). It often happens that new insights or new flashes of imagination spring, as it were, from our inner experience. New illuminations seem to be visiting us regardless of reality, and of existing knowledge we possess.

This meditative process so struck Edmund Husserl (1859–

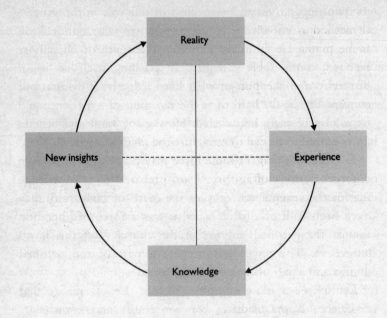

Fig. 2 *The reality-knowledge axis and the axis of meditation*

1938) that he deified it and wove around it his new method of inquiry, which he called the *phenomenological method*, otherwise called 'the direct intuition of essences'. According to Husserl and other phenomenologists, this method is far more reliable in reaching the core of things, the heart of matters, than the usual scientific method, which only *explores surfaces*. Husserl's phenomenological method has in time become the basis for a new grand theory which ties truth, particularly of the human world, with the exploration of our inner selves.[3]

What is striking in Husserl is the boldness of imagination. Against the aggressive tide of empiricism, which was riding high, and the scientific method, claiming its supremacy, he delegated to the human intuition, and to the inner contemplation of essences, the power to discover truth and to generate new knowledge. Since Husserl enshrines the phenomenological method *as objective in its own right*; and since this method can be pursued only in the solitude of the individual mind, there is a considerable friction between these two demands, objectivity and the pursuit of solitude. How can a solitary *individual mind* be the basis of an *objective method*?

It is not the place here for a discussion of the demerits and merits of the phenomenological method. What is to be emphasized is the following. Although the process of contemplation or meditation, resulting in new insights, may be a deep individual journey, this journey always takes place in the larger context of a culture: in the context of past and present knowledge, and of the existing images of reality. These contexts may be invisible. But they guide our imagination, our intuitions, our processes of contemplation and meditation.

The second conclusion is: *do not deify the axis of meditation as if it were independent of knowledge and reality*. For in the acts of illumination, whether you call them the phenomenological intuition of essences or by some other names, our knowledge and our reality are firmly embedded.

We are now moving to a new trajectory, which is the *path of becoming*. It is this path that incorporates, explains and redeems both the axis of knowledge and the axis of meditation. This path becomes quite clearly visible after new illuminations attempt to find for themselves a new expression in terms of a new reality (R_2). But this path is actually there all the time, embodied in the path of knowledge and in the path of meditation – it uses them for its purposes.

The path of becoming ultimately illumines all the paths of the Great Circle of Knowledge including its crystallized points – experience, knowledge, new insights and a new reality. Only from the inside, from the standpoint of the path of becoming as it unfolds itself, and brings about new vistas and new perspectives, can we understand the vicissitudes of our experience and the true progress of knowledge: why are certain experiences trivial and others significant? How is experience distilled into forms of knowledge? What do these forms of knowledge attempt to express, codify, denote? What are the new insights of, and why are they new?

The path of becoming may seem to be nebulous. But in elucidating those points through which it has travelled, we can see it as luminous: it is light that wants to become more luminous. Becoming is a benevolent god which devours being as it is and transforms it into new forms. Becoming is a continuous fire of creation which changes and destroys in the process of its transmutation. Becoming is the Heraclitean *Pantha Rhei*; it is the dancing Shiva of unending change. Becoming is a perpetual Prometheus. Becoming is the founder of new orders. Always restless, it is a positive demon which strives for perfection but never achieves it.

6. Knowledge as power and knowledge as liberation

The whole of Western civilization is power-crazy. This craze for power affects not only little individuals and big politicians, but also philosophers, who, although they should have been a critical mirror confronting the shortcomings of society, have succumbed to the lure of the myth of power. This process has also distorted our perspective on knowledge. Thus Jürgen Habermas talks about the production of knowledge. *Production* of knowledge? What on earth is that? Do we have factories for the production of knowledge? If we do have such factories, then they surely do not produce *new knowledge*, but something of an inferior nature.

You can have factories for producing tractors and other technological gadgets. But you cannot have factories for producing knowledge. Full stop.

Our civilization, alas, has succumbed to the ogre of instrumentalization. That this is pathological and deplorable, there can be no doubt. If such eminent philosophers as Jürgen Habermas and Michel Foucault think that they must legitimize this pathology in their philosophies, then they are themselves a part of this pathology of power.

Foucault talks about Knowledge-Power. He is so taken by the Baconian-Faustian syndrome of 'knowledge as power' that he no longer sees knowledge as illumination.

An altogether different perspective follows from the discussion of this chapter. The production of knowledge is a *vulgar* endeavour. The knowledge-power quest is a pathological venture. Knowledge is illumination and there is no better term for describing its nature than that. Knowledge is not a hatchet for destruction or an instrument of domination, but a torch of light. An instrumental approach to knowledge is mere *techne*. Perhaps the ancient Greeks were right in holding *techne* in contempt. Perhaps in the depth of their souls they knew that if they elevated *techne* to a superior position, the quest for enlightenment would have been reduced to the quest for manipulation.

Knowledge as liberation is not only an attribute of ancient knowledge, whether of the Greeks or of the Hindus. This kind of knowledge is the foundation of our individual existence. As we grow, we acquire knowledge. As we acquire knowledge we are gradually liberated – from the bondage of babyhood, from the bondage of our original egotism. And this liberation is proportional to the depth of knowledge we acquire. *We grow through the knowledge we acquire. And through knowledge we are liberated.* Thus knowledge is liberation. This is also true of societies. As societies grow and mature, they are liberated – from old taboos, fears, restrictions, hang-ups of various sorts.

This also holds for the human species at large. As the species becomes more knowledgeable (in the true sense of the term 'knowledgeable', not in its pathological, instrumental sense) so it becomes more enlightened. As it becomes more enlightened, it becomes more liberated. Is there any other path than this? If there is, we haven't discovered it yet.

As we travel on the wheel of unfolding evolution, we sharpen our sensitivities, which enable us to make new sense of old experiences. New significant experiences give rise to illuminations and new forms of knowledge. As new forms of knowledge unfold and articulate themselves, they unveil to us new shapes of reality, they become new realities.

In this journey we are occasionally led astray; as we have been by the phenomenon of power. So intoxicated have we become by its enticing potency that like an alcoholic, we became addicted to it. But this addiction to power is only a temporary aberration; a strange epicycle in our Great Journey, whereby not for the first time we have temporarily lost ourselves and our bearings.

To reduce knowledge to power is to challenge evolution at its very core, is to challenge the ascending spiral of understanding, is to challenge the spiritual heritage of humankind. Doctor Faustus accepted this challenge . . . and he ended in Hell. Even if we do not wish to accept the biblical version of Hell, it is quite clear – at least to those who see knowledge as a ladder to enlightenment – that to reduce knowledge to power is to create existential Hell on earth.

But new travellers will embark on the Great Journey. They will bypass the old power-crazy epicycle and will go on to unfold new dimensions of reality by pursuing the quest for knowledge-illumination. Such is our evolutionary destiny. Those mesmerized by the epicycle of power may be too dazed to notice that the new travellers have gone beyond them. Like heroin addicts, they will refuse to see, or will be unable to see, completely blinded and incapacitated by their addiction.

But evolution goes on. The unfortunate addicts will be left on the side. And there they will remain, on the sidewalks of history. This prophecy of doom is not a fantasy but a realistic reading of evolution. It simply follows that the offshoot from the tree of knowledge called knowledge-power and the power-crazy fringe of civilization are not pursuing a realistic evolutionary policy. The idea that 'the reality of power is the only reality' is a somnambulist intoxication of those who have lost their souls. The addicts of power are pursuing a lunatic course. They are stuck in a self-destructive epicycle. The pursuit of power ultimately destroys those who pursue power.

Summary

Grand theory is as old as human knowledge. When Moses brought his Tablets from the top of Mount Sinai, this was one example of grand theory. When Thales declared that all is water, this was another. When Plato insisted that Forms explain all, this was another. When Newton formulated his Laws of Nature, this was yet another. To be coherent, our thinking must follow some patterns. The master-patterns determine the meaning of particular words and events – whether we call these patterns grand theories or not.

The Participatory Grand Theory reveals and analyses the process of reality-making. In trying to understand this process, we need to reflect on the nature of experience; and on the relationship between knowledge and experience.

Experience is such a difficult term to define – yet such an easy phenomenon to acknowledge on the existential level. We float in the endless sea of experience. However, unarticulated experience is but a mist. Articulated experience leads to knowledge, art, philosophy. Each of these great realms of the human universe – knowledge, art, philosophy – is but a *crystallized form* of human experience. But how exquisitely crystallized! Let us be aware – this power of crystallization or articulation of experience is a form of experience itself. But it is a second order experience. Though a vital one. Without this form of experience – ordering and structuring all other experiences (the first order experiences) – we would live in a perpetual fog. Intuition would not help us.

Significant experience is that kind of event, or that series of events, which leads to recognizable transformations of the spiral of understanding – either personal or cultural. Those experiences that are significant and have far-reaching consequences I call *S-experiences*. Courting an S-experience is a creative act. The creative act requires courage, openness and vulnerability. Those are the very attributes and also preconditions of new experiences. Playing for safety does not lead to new experiences. On the contrary, it leads to stale forms of life – dull, repetitious, predictable. No risks – no S-experience.

Knowledge is structuring of the significant cognitive experience. We legitimize this experience by expressing it in intersubjectively sharable patterns. Yet on another level, knowledge is light. Knowledge is igniting sensitivities that can see. Knowledge consists of new significant experiences that lead to new illuminations. The incompleteness of our definitions of knowledge does not come from the deficiency of our linguistic or intellectual resources. Rather, it comes from the incompleteness of our being, the incompleteness of our truth.

Traditional theories of knowledge postulate, if only implicitly, that there is a firm axis reality-knowledge. Knowledge reflects reality, while reality feeds into (and tests!) existing knowledge. The presumption is that it is the same knowledge and the same reality that feed into each other in a circular way. This whole picture is fundamentally inadequate. The direct axis between reality and knowledge is a fiction. The two never commune, except through us. We are the point of connection. We are the point of communion. Therefore, we should not deify the reality-knowledge axis, as if it existed independently of us. To unduly stress the importance of this axis is to perpetuate the myth of objectivity.

Neither should we deify the axis of meditation, as if it were independent of knowledge and reality. In the acts of our illumination – whether we call them the phenomenological method or not – our knowledge and our reality are subtly embedded. Intuition should be recognized, but not deified.

The path of becoming is all-important. It integrates the axis of reality-knowledge with the axis of meditation; and creatively transcends them. Becoming is a benevolent god that devours being and transforms it into ever more effervescent forms. Becoming is a continuous fire of creation. Becoming is an endless transcendence, for only in this way does the world realize itself.

CHAPTER 12

The Promise of Participatory Philosophy

I. *Philosophy as the pursuit of a life-style of grace*

God is dead, announced Nietzsche. Philosophy is dead, announced Heidegger. Are consumerism and philistinism the only things alive? Far from it! Philosophy is not dead. It has been a vital force – even during our times. The pity of it is that we have allowed such a shallow and one-dimensional philosophy to dominate our horizons – the philosophy that has eliminated man's spiritual concerns from its scope.

Our times call for a new holistic philosophy, integrative par excellence and not shy of spirituality; capable of addressing far-reaching cosmological problems concerning the origin of the universe and existential problems concerning the destiny of mankind – all in the same framework.

Philosophy feeds on its past, as does the human soul. It may be of some value to remind ourselves of some forms of philosophy practised in the past – very different from our discursive philosophy; yet very nourishing to the soul.

When we examine the lives of the illustrious ones, such as the Buddha, Jesus or Socrates, we realize that something strange is at work. Some great alchemy is taking place.

They knew. They possessed knowledge. They were philosophers. Or should we say, they could have been philosophers, if they had chosen to be. But they didn't. They opted for something else, something much higher. Or rather were chosen for something much higher. In each case we see philosophy abandoned, as it were thrown out. The illustrious ones seem to be saying: if you live aright, you don't need philosophy.

Philosophy is very important. It gives a structure of support to your life; that is, if you cannot do it otherwise. If you can do it otherwise, you don't need philosophy. In the lives of the illustrious ones, philosophy is *transcended* in favour of living in effortless grace.

The art of living is second to none. The art of living is a form of philosophy. However, the art of living in effortless grace is ultimate philosophy. How many have been able to practise this kind of philosophy? How many have been able to make their lives a living torch of this philosophy? Perhaps a few dozen. Perhaps a few hundred.

In one sense living one's life as a continuous act of effortless grace is transcending all metaphysics; and denouncing it. The Buddha was famous for keeping his golden silence, and for remonstrating with his disciples when they indulged in too much metaphysics. The Buddha was once asked by a disciple: 'So, Sir, are you saying that there is no God?' And the Buddha responded: 'Did I say that there is no God?' And the disciple pressed: 'So, Sir, are you saying that there is a God?' And the Buddha responded: 'Did I say that there is a God?'

Jesus was not a metaphysician either. In fact there is surprisingly little metaphysics in Jesus's teaching. It was different with Socrates. But we don't truly know where Socrates ends and Plato begins.

At one time the Western tradition was close to the Eastern tradition. I contend that Socrates was perhaps more of a Buddhist than he was a Platonist. He was chagrined by those spurious metaphysical inquiries concerning the nature of physical reality pursued by the early cosmologists, such as Thales and Anaximander. These inquiries, according to Socrates, do not help us to live. We need not therefore bother about them, particularly if they make us deviate from the path of enlightenment. The Buddha too, as we have seen, kept his golden silence about those metaphysical questions that were likely to confuse the mind of his disciples rather than to help them on the path.

However, in Socrates' time the dice was already loaded. So much cosmological reflection had gone on (including the paradoxes of the Eleatics), so much discursive thinking had been used to enshrine the newly established logos, that this discursive thinking began to dominate the Greek mind. It is at this point that we witness the rise of the supreme architect of human thought, Plato.

Why do we call him a supreme architect? Because he was able to construct a system of thought of staggering beauty, lucidity and depth. While doing this he was able to accomplish a rare thing: to combine what was sayable and what was unsayable. Plato wanted to have it both ways: to appease the discursive reason and, at the same time, to fly with the angels beyond the realm of logic and reason – on to the land of Enlightenment and spiritual salvation.

Let us be quite clear that Plato's is a philosophy of liberation, a form of *moksha* (an Indian term for liberation via philosophy). The Eastern philosophies, particularly those originating in India, emphasize the supreme importance of *moksha*. Plato's philosophy as a path to Enlightenment is in complete congruence with major Hindu and Buddhist traditions. Plato insisted that philosophy is a training for death.

But there is much more in Plato than a philosophy of liberation. There is, in fact, so much more that even if you forget the quest of liberation, you can happily roam through the chambers of Plato's philosophical palace to your heart's content. This is exactly what the Western mind has done. It forgot about the *moksha* aspects of Plato. Instead it has pursued his cognitive and intellectual opus. Logos has been severed from Eros. The hard intellect has suppressed compassion and empathy. Cognition has become a form of salvation.

True enough, Plato's philosophy follows from that of Socrates. Aristotle's philosophy follows from that of Plato. But there is a disjunction in the process. Socrates' quest is unmistakably that of liberation. Plato wants to have it both ways – liberation as the spiritual salvation and the discursive satisfaction.

Aristotle clearly abandons the idea of liberation. His ideal is the possession of knowledge. Aristotle wants to *know* everything (where is the wisdom we have lost in knowledge?), he wants to classify all phenomena, put them in boxes, label them. This was the beginning of the analytical disease.

If we look at the pair Socrates–Plato, it is somewhat similar to the pair Jesus–Paul. Socrates and Jesus were ineffectual dreamers. Socrates never wrote, never earned any money, never wore sandals; he always went barefoot. Jesus's life-style is very similar. Now, Plato formalized Socrates. While Paul formalized Jesus.

What has been bequeathed to us as Christianity is Paulinism rather than the teaching of the Gentle Jesus. Paulinism versus Christianism means: the sense of organization, empire, insignia of outward glory, edicts, explicit formulations vs gentleness, living by the heart and in utter simplicity. The friction between Paulinism and Christianism has been continuous throughout the history of Christianity, particularly since the time of Saint Francis, who truly confronted the Imperial Roman Catholic Church with the gospel of simplicity and total solidarity with all living beings. The Franciscan challenge is still with us, and is especially relevant in our technological age which has so thoroughly twisted our relationships with the rest of creation.

Let us return to the main theme of this section: the illustrious ones as expressing their ultimate philosophy through their lives. We comprehend these lives. We comprehend them best in total silence.

The problem starts when we attempt to extricate from these lives, lived dynamically and radiantly, some metaphysical truths which are supposed to be their foundation. If we push this venture far enough, we then translate these radiant lives into frozen, stilted truths. What we receive in the process is a stillborn baby called 'philosophy'. Indeed *philosophy is a mental substitute for our inability to live our life in continuous grace*. The actual act of living in effortless grace is the only convincing ultimate philosophy.

Therefore it should not surprise us that the illustrious ones did not write. They knew that there is a special form of truth which is *the living truth*, and which can only be conveyed and expressed through the light that emanates through one's life. For this living truth emanates; especially if one succeeds in dwelling in the space of grace. Hence 'the life-style of effortless grace' is the right description of this ultimate philosophy which has left words and dwells in light.

In the Western tradition, Pythagoras, Socrates and Plato knew the meaning of the living truth. Plato was actually apprehensive that his written philosophy was a betrayal of the living truth. He wrote with misgivings, as if apologetically, pointing out that his written philosophy was a form of entertainment, diversion rather than an expression of the living truth. In his famous Seventh Letter Plato writes: 'Owing to the inadequacy of language . . . no intelligent man will ever dare to commit his thoughts to words, still less to words that cannot be changed, as is the case with what is expressed in written characters.'[1]

The underlying assumption is that philosophy put on paper is dead. The only way of practising philosophy is the living dialogue. And this living dialogue can be carried out only with living beings. In the *Phaedrus* Plato says (through the mouth of Socrates): 'In the past, dear boy, people were content to listen to an oak or a rock, provided it spoke the truth.' We do not know now how to read these words, and whether to take Socrates seriously. Yet deeper down we know that all kinds of dialogue are possible. The methodology of participation informs us that dialogue with our cells, and even with oaks and rocks, may not be far-fetched – if we release and activate appropriate sensitivities.

2. From perennial philosophy to scientific philosophy

The history of philosophy follows a meandering path. From the mystical exaltations this path has led *some* philosophers in the twentieth century to the realm of ruthless logic, which alone was meant to secure reliability and respectability for philosophy.

Since Descartes philosophy has been fixated upon method. Descartes was discontented with the amorphousness of philosophy and its often contradictory results. Hence he introduced his famous analytical method (in his *Discourse on Method*, 1632) which proposes to divide and subdivide every single problem until we arrive at problems which are so simple and rudimentary, and so clearly defined, that we can indubitably resolve them without any ambiguity.

This method has brilliantly succeeded in the exact sciences, but not in philosophy. For philosophy dies when it is reduced to minute, specific, exact problems. Yet the lure of the 'assured method' has been at times irresistible. Now with the introduction of powerful tools of modern mathematical logic, especially from Gottlob Frege (1848–1925) on, philosophers and logicians thought that at last they had obtained language and conceptual apparatus powerful and precise enough to tackle all philosophical problems and resolve them to their logical minds' content.

Thus in 1910 Bertrand Russell announced the idea of scientific philosophy. This was an indirect result of his work (together with Alfred North Whitehead) on mathematical logic. The fruit of their joint venture was the monumental work in three volumes (1910–13) entitled *Principia Mathematica*.

From this point on we witness wave after wave of the new philosophy, which attempts to be as sharp as a knife and as dry as a bone. First Wittgenstein, in *Tractatus Logico-Philosophicus* (1921), with his Logical Atomism, which was a metaphysical application of the logical tools of the *Principia*. Then the programme of scientific philosophy of the Vienna Circle with Rudolf Carnap's *The Logical Structure of the World* (1928) as a forerunner of other similar ventures. Almost simultaneously we witness the emergence of the Polish school of logic and of analytical philosophy,[2] Jan Lukasiewicz announcing his programme of scientific philosophy in 1927.

Then the centre moved to England, first to Cambridge, then to Oxford. And then, with the refugees fleeing from Austria and Germany, analytical or scientific philosophy reached the United States, particularly after Carnap, Hempel and Reichenbach settled there. A new philosophical orthodoxy was established in the United States under the inspiration of the ex-philosophers of the Vienna Circle who settled in America. It was philosophy in the image of logic.

This orthodoxy is still controlling the departments of

philosophy in major English and American universities. However, these departments are a pale reflection of the original glory of analytical philosophy of the 1930s. After it emerged, this new philosophy (call it scientific, analytical or linguistic) was meant to be a revolution in philosophy. It was meant to settle all philosophical problems – once and for all. It was also meant to provide right, rational foundations for our lives. In this sense it was meant to be *ultimate philosophy*.

This whole alleged revolution turned out to be a mountain bearing a mouse. Analytical philosophy has failed to help culture and to be a genuine part of culture. Analytical philosophy is indicative of the barrenness of the Western philosophical mind over the last century, when Western philosophy has been brilliant and sometimes dazzling in its formal virtuosity but not creative.

What does it mean to say that a given philosophy has been creative or a given philosopher has not been creative? When we look at the great philosophical systems, those singular expressions of the philosophical mind that were both novel and that have survived, at least three criteria offer themselves for a philosophy to be called creative.

(1) A given philosophy must be novel; better still, original.

(2) A given philosophy must offer a new interpretation of the cosmos and/or life.

(3) A given philosophy must prove sustaining to the culture from which it has grown, and to succeeding cultures.

It is the third criterion that is quite crucial. Philosophy must be like yeast. It must enable other things to grow. If nothing grows out of it, then it is not a creative philosophy.

This kind of philosophy has a peculiar power to inspire, to fecundate, to renew, to sustain, and the great philosophical systems of the past, both in the East and in the West, possess this kind of power.

Philosophy is part of culture. It expresses and sustains culture. Great philosophy sustains not only the culture that engendered it but also succeeding cultures as well. A philosophy cannot be creative if it does not sustain a culture; or worse still – if it contributes to the atrophy of a culture.

The anaemia of present-day analytical philosophy shows itself with luminous clarity in the triviality of the problems it investigates. Here we are, in one of the most momentous periods of human history, with tremendous problems in front of us which cry out for a philosophical reflection. But those analytical philosophers play games, oblivious of the tremors and agonies of the world. Performing endless empiricist epicycles, they are engaged in a game of appearances – for the sake of pleasing the three hundred other initiated minds. This alone shows a lamentable lack of moral responsibility.

Who are we if we do not assume and cherish moral responsibility? Less than human. Through its methods of philosophizing, analytical philosophy has contributed to the value vacuum which is pervading the campuses of the Western world. And this value vacuum is proving to have devastating existential and social consequences. A culture not guided by intrinsic values is like a ship without a rudder. And indeed Western culture has been drifting.

At this point an astute analytical philosopher may take me to task and say: prove that there is a value vacuum, that it is devastating, and that the methods of analytical philosophy are partly responsible for that. What am I to say? Only that this kind of question is characteristic of the mind that is as clever as it is uncaring. We cannot prove everything in life. Most of the important things we, indeed, cannot. If we were to wait until we can prove everything, we should have to wait until our extinction.

The fundamental error of Descartes has been compounded

by the brilliance of our minds. Analytical philosophers are neither dim nor obtuse. They are often brilliant. And sometimes, alas, too clever for their own good. They can defend their analytical-linguistic paradise rationally. They tell us that their rational minds do not permit them to tackle problems for which there is no assured solution. This is, at best, the indication of the narrowness of their rationality. At worst, it is an expression of hypocrisy – for they know how severe the present predicament of human kind is. The forest is burning and they themselves, as human beings, are feeling the heat.

The whole Western culture, or at least a significant portion of it, is devastated by the clinical objectivity with which the Western mind has punctured the products of older, spiritually inspired cultures. Present academic philosophy is an epitome of this clinical objectivity. Instead of becoming the guardian of values, of humanity, of wisdom, present philosophy has become a part of the destructive process. Big business, which is, alas, geared to greed, profit and exploitation, could not be more pleased when professional philosophers announce that there are no permanent or intrinsic values; that all is relative; that values are not so important, after all.

This moral detachment is immoral. It gives a dispensation for continuous exploitation of the earth and carte blanche for further pursuit of individual greed. It is not a coincidence that clinically oriented analytical philosophers are so well regarded by the Establishment. They are not a threat to but actually a support of the existing structures. They don't rock the boat. They mind their own business. In so doing, they perpetuate the sickness of our present society.

Many young university students choose to take courses in philosophy as a part of a search for understanding and enlightenment. So often they find analytical philosophy 'dreadful'. They feel betrayed. They cannot articulate their feelings and exactly put their finger on what is wrong. But they know that philosophy is failing them. They are not stupid. They want enlightenment. Instead they receive rules for transformation of formal languages ... and moral indifference which verges on contempt for the human.

Philosophers of the present time are not the causes of our plight. Just as we are, they are sad victims. Being brought up in a morally desensitized environment, being simply brainwashed by the ideology of technicism, they suppress their moral impulses and the spiritual aspects of their being – only in this way could they have completed their studies and obtained their PhDs. Who is to be blamed? Our crass materialist culture. Which simply must be changed. This materialist pig of a world must go!

3. Philosophy as courage

At the beginning was courage. And courage has begotten all other attributes that made us into human beings. Courage has brought about art, religion, philosophy. The emergence of philosophy has been one continuous act of courage.

In the Homeric universe gods ruled supreme. Not only did they determine the general laws according to which human beings lived, but they constantly intervened in the daily affairs of ordinary humans. Fate was inscrutable and the blows of outrageous fortune could befall poor humans at any time. Events often happened by the intervention of a *deus ex machina*. And gods at times were whimsical. This kind of universe does not appear rational to us. But it was deemed rational by the Greeks of the time. The gods were responsible for the rationality of the world. It was perfectly rational to assume that gods were in command and responsible for the vicissitudes of human destiny. From generation to generation myths formed the underlying structure of explanations of the world and of the human struggle for meaning. Greek tragedies of the fifth century BC supremely exemplify the strengths and shadows of the mytho-poetic world-view.

A new breed of men appeared; or should we say a new form of mind emerged. It started in earnest with Thales (634–546 BC), who speculated that all is water. Then came Pythagoras (585–495 BC), who postulated that all is number. Then came Heraclitus (535–475 BC), who was possessed by the idea of *pantha rhei* – all is changing, wearing out. These thinkers started to think in a new way. In the process of the new thinking a new form of explanation evolved. No longer were the new thinkers satisfied with the constant intervention of gods in man's daily affairs. They now wished to explain both the visible and the invisible in the cosmos through natural reason.

Thus the translucent logos was born. This is a momentous and revelatory occasion. For it marks the beginning of philosophy. It also marks the beginning of the liberation of man from the bondage of myths; at any rate from the bondage of myths as conceived in Greek mythology.

Where is the place of courage in all this? Indeed, it took tremendous courage to conceive of an altogether new way of looking at the universe, and a new way of thinking about it, particularly from inside a cocoon of myths. *Every new philosophy that breaks away from the cocoon of the established orthodoxy is an act of courage.*

The early Greek philosophers possessed little knowledge in our sense of the term – systematic, well ordered, well defined knowledge. But what resources of imagination they possessed! What power they had in conceiving new ideas! And what courage in articulating and expressing them!

Ideas are elusive things – not clearly expressed, they are

lost. New ideas are a gift of God. But to convey them in such a way that they can be understood by others requires skill and courage. For new ideas invariably go against the grain of established orthodoxies. The guardians of the status quo are forever watchful and always ready to pounce on the new eagles, always ready to intimidate those who dare to deviate from the norm. Thus to announce new ideas that challenge the foundations of the existing order requires strength and courage. In so far as great philosophy is a continuous challenge to the established order – as philosophy continuously reinvents reality, the existence and continuation of great philosophy is a monument to human courage. It is in this sense that philosophy is courage.

Sri Aurobindo, a great twentieth-century Indian thinker, who attempted to fuse the Western idea of evolution with the tradition of the Upanishads,[3] once said that reading Upanishads is like travelling from light to light. This is the feeling that one experiences while reading early Greek philosophy; and indeed, while reading the works of all great philosophy; especially of philosophers who engage in the act of reinventing reality. Such an act of philosophical creation is an event of cosmological significance.

When I first read those words of Aurobindo, it immediately struck me that reading present-day philosophical treatises is like *travelling from footnote to footnote*.

Now, not all philosophy that is recognized as great is the expression of courage in the sense we have discussed. There are some outstanding philosophers who made their lasting contribution to human thought by rearranging the existing pieces. We should therefore distinguish two kinds of philosophy:

philosophy as creation;

philosophy as justification.

To the former category belong the early Greek philosophers we have mentioned; and Socrates and Plato, as well as Berkeley, Descartes, Galileo, Kant, Hegel and Marx, to name just a few. They all attempted to redesign reality. They all combined exemplary courage with exemplary imagination. Indeed, the two must be combined, for exemplary courage without inspired imagination may lead us to the land of lunacy, as happened with Adolf Hitler. On the other hand, exemplary imagination without the corresponding courage produces anaemic private flowers which are lost to the world.

Philosophy of justification is of a different kind. It serves the existing order rather than attempts to change it. In addition to the inspired moments of illumination, there is something plodding about Aristotle, painstakingly classifying, sorting out, justifying. Aristotle is the beginning of the reign of the discursive reason that got the better of the Western mind, particularly during the last three centuries. There is no question that from Aristotle on, the Western mind is split, is caught between the desire for rational explanation and the desire (suppressed but still existing) for illumination and liberation.

Yet so strong has the desire become for rational explanation that we have created the myth of reason, according to which to understand (and explain things intellectually) is a form of liberation. Our yoga is the intellectual yoga. We grind everything into the powder of atomistic concepts and then somehow hope that the process of analytical scrutiny is liberation itself. But it isn't. And we know it.

The philosophy of justification is represented by such giants as Augustine and Thomas Aquinas – both saints of the Roman Church. The context within which they toiled for the glory of God makes us immediately aware why it was necessary for them to become the philosophers of justification; and in a sense impossible otherwise.

In modern times the philosophy of justification is represented by such thinkers as Locke, Mill, and all the variety of empiricists. Present-day analytical philosophers, needless to say, are philosophers of justification. They endlessly justify, often quite forgetting what it is that they set out to justify. Theirs is philosophy without courage and without imagination. But so convinced are they about the rationality of their endeavours, and so righteous about it, that they do not perceive how narrow their turf is, and how thoroughly they have been duped to serve the interests of the status quo – a peculiar form of blindness. Theirs is not a journey from light to light, but rather a journey from footnote to footnote. Thus philosophy today is in a slumber – 'Newton's Sleep'; William Blake recognized it.

4. Participatory philosophy

The early Greek philosophers achieved greatness not only because they had courage and imagination but also because they discovered the secret of participation. They redesigned their world by co-creatively participating in it. This is what great philosophy always does – it assumes, if only subconsciously, that the world is neither static nor given to us. It assumes furthermore that the mind is not a simple mirror but an active force co-creating with reality. The very idea of *reinventing* reality, or at least *redefining* it, implies and necessitates the two notions that we have discussed – namely that reality is not given to us as something unalterable, and that the mind has an important role to play in the process of co-creation of reality.

Let us put it otherwise: if it is the case that reality has been continuously redefined and redesigned, then it simply means that philosophers must have assumed that it is not static and given to them once and for all.

Participatory philosophy, which emerges as the result of our search for the philosophy of renewal, is not just a nice label. Participatory philosophy is a potential powerhouse of ideas and energies. To begin with, it implies a rediscovery of participation – as the vital process of being in this world, of having a mind in this world, of creatively contributing to this world – and thereby shaping one's meaning and one's destiny in this world.

The idea of participation is a true gift. It opens the gate to a new metaphysical paradise. When you follow the idea to its ultimate conclusions, it reveals a new world and new, exciting dimensions of our individual lives.

Participatory philosophy implies a rediscovery of courage – the courage to be, and the courage to become: the courage to behold one's destiny without a grudge and with dignity; the courage to uphold the rational mind and at the same time to admit its limits in this mysterious universe; and above all, the courage of having a mind – so illustrious and so frail an instrument, which is our torch, our delight, our only bridge connecting us with God.

The courage of having a mind in this context simply means a rediscovery of the mind itself, as the maker of our destiny and of our freedom, as the facilitator of all things in heaven and on earth. It is a curious facet of our techno-logical society that while releasing so much new power, we have been reducing the significance of the mind. Indeed *the consumerist society is a mindless society*. It continuously replaces our ingenuity with expertise, our self-reliance with new gadgets, our capacity to govern ourselves with technological crutches. The destiny of the human species requires releas-ing more and more of the resources of the mind, not the mindless consumption that reduces the potency of our mind.

Fortunately, the mindless society has not yet become a reality, and there is courage to behold and celebrate. This courage I see first of all among physicists. In our time, they are indeed men of courage. To have conceived of those new entities (so strange, so invisible, so untouchable – as the ultimate explanation of the visible reality) has been an act of courage bordering on the insane. Imagination as the mother of truth has been amply confirmed in the outreach of contemporary physics. Here is the discipline that is not afraid of the power of the mind. Here is the discipline that uses the mind creatively.

There is an enormous gap between the wonderfully fluid but penetrating new concepts of the New Physics and the stilted forms of learning pursued in our schools and academia. This gap can be bridged only by right philosophy. Perhaps the name of this philosophy is after all Participatory Philosophy.

What is the specific content of participatory philosophy, and how does this philosophy differ from other philosophies? This whole volume is the answer to that question. The subject of participatory philosophy has been revealed, bit by bit, as we have gone from chapter to chapter.

To understand the role of the participatory mind in the participatory universe is to receive the key to participatory philosophy. To apply the participatory mind while we converse with the universe is to weave new ontological designs out of the half-given cosmos; is to outline new epistemological strategies, as well as elicit and sharpen new sensitivities – our windows on reality – through which we can gaze at the universe more clearly and converse with it more meaningfully.

We thus announce participatory reality, the co-creative

mind, the spiral of understanding, the repertoire of sensitivities, the Evolutionary Telos, the methodology of participation, participatory research programmes, participatory truth, participatory space of grace, participatory sense of experience, courage to be and courage to become – to be specific concepts of participatory philosophy.

Yet participatory philosophy does not seek to be just a store of ready-made concepts, formulated once and for all. For participatory philosophy is first and foremost a *process philosophy*. It outlines a framework and a strategy. It liberates the mind to fly high and to explore deep – without constraining this mind by determining what it ought to find.

We readily admit that we have not tackled, let alone resolved, all the major philosophical problems in this volume. Nor did we mean to. For, to say it once more, participatory philosophy outlines a process, a programme, a strategy – which we can then apply to any problem, and to all problems. For example, we haven't discussed ethics at any length so far. Let us therefore ask: what kind of ethics does the participatory mind presuppose and imply?

5. Participatory ethics

Where do we begin? With the idea of *participation*, which immediately provides the focus and the point of departure. It spells out our obligations as well as our behavioural strategies, on at least three levels:

(1) on the interpersonal level (person to person relationships);
(2) on the interspecies level (person to other species relationships);
(3) on the cosmic level (person to God relationships).

(1) PARTICIPATORY ETHICS ON THE
INTERPERSONAL LEVEL

What kind of precepts and strategies follow from participatory ethics in the realm of human relationships? From our earlier discussion we remember that the deep meaning of participation implies: empathy, reverence and responsibility.

To be a person in the participatory universe entails the recognition of the bond of participation. If we don't recognize this bond, we have relinquished our rights to live in the participatory universe. If we recognize this bond, then we ipso facto recognize empathy for other persons, reverence for other persons, responsibility for other persons. Thus in minimal terms, participatory ethics implies reverence for other persons and responsibility for the well-being of other human beings. And this is so by virtue of the very meaning of participation. Genuinely to partake in the meaning of our humanness is to act out the bond of empathy with the other. To treat the other with reverence is to take the responsibility for the whole context in which the well-being of the other resides.

After we acknowledge reverence as the foundation of participatory ethics, the question is how should we view the variety of selfish ethics, which extols individual greed and individual satisfaction at the expense of the well-being of others? This is non-participatory ethics. It appears appealing on the surface. Yet ultimately it makes the individual estranged from the larger context of participation and, in the end, deeply unfulfilled within his/her inner core. Non-participatory ethics satisfies the ego, but leaves the soul and the inner person deeply unsatisfied. Such ethics cannot be a path to genuine happiness, let alone serve as a foundation for social justice. When selfish ethics prevails for a long time, social injustices build up and then explode with vengeance and violence.

(2) PARTICIPATORY ETHICS ON THE
INTERSPECIES LEVEL

On this level participatory ethics becomes a form of ecological ethics. We participate in the glories and riches of nature, for nature is us and we are it. Nature is of intrinsic value, as much as we are. Both nature and we ourselves are parts of the seamless web. 'Whatever befalls the earth befalls the sons of earth. Man did not weave the web of life, he is merely a strand in it. Whatever he does to the web he does to himself.'[4]

Reverence for natural systems is a consequence of our participation in nature's project. To encourage and maintain diversity is a part of the ethical imperative of participating in the riches of creation. In the very idea of participation are contained ethical signposts concerning how we should treat all other forms of life. They are part of the family, part of ourselves. They are our brothers, sisters, cousins; part of the same blood system.

Thus reverence for all life, and for all creation, is part of the ethical imperative of participating in life at large, and of recognizing all creation as a part of our larger being. Let us remind ourselves: if we recognize the nature of the participatory mind, we thereby recognize our larger being, as coextensive with the cosmic consciousness; or at least as coextensive with the consciousness of the human species. The idea of the cosmic consciousness may worry some as too grand and not quite warranted. But who are we, if not cosmic creatures? How can we *not* participate in the cosmic consciousness, while we have been formed by all the changes of the cosmic evolution?

Thus the very notion of our existence, if we consider ourselves evolutionary beings (and how can we *not* recognize that we are a part of unfolding evolution?), implies profound consequences. It implies that we live in the participatory universe and that we are the agents of participation. To be agents of participation, on a deeper ethical level, implies reverence and responsibility for all human beings and non-human beings.

Ecological ethics based on reverence for life,[5] conceived within the larger panorama of the participatory mind, does not necessarily imply species egalitarianism. Species egalitarianism is a misconceived notion. Egalitarianism is a term that belongs properly to the vocabulary of political thought of the nineteenth and twentieth centuries. It is a weak concept to make a basis of interspecies ethics. We need something much stronger, much deeper and more fundamental than the mere recognition of all other species.

I recognize my enemy as my equal – and then I kill him. The idea of equality does not contain any ethical imperative. Even if we recognize all species as equal, there is nothing in the idea of equality that would prevent stronger species smashing weaker species. We need strong concepts, such as reverence and compassion, to safeguard the safety of the weak against the strong; and particularly against the fiendishly clever species Homo Sapiens.

Let us consider some examples that demonstrate why egalitarianism and equality are insufficient for any strong, enduring ethics. I contemplate the last sample of a rare aquatic life. I consider it equal to me. And then I let it wither. And perhaps persuade myself in the process that it was not equal to me after all. For what is there in the idea of equality itself that can act as an inspiring *ethical* impulse?

On the other hand, I contemplate the same last sample of a rare aquatic life. I marvel over its uniqueness. I revere it as an extraordinary form of life. My *reverence* for it is my motivating ethical principle which makes me protect it, take responsibility for it – even if I do not consider it equal to my life. And why should I – while my evolutionary consciousness tells me otherwise?

Participatory ethics as ecological ethics is neither anthropocentric nor anti-anthropocentric. It is *evolution-centric*. Some people would consider the term 'bio-centric' preferable to my term 'evolution-centric'. But I find the term 'bio-centric' not far-reaching enough; it only indicates the distinction between living systems and dead ones; it leaves out the extraordinary dynamic complexity of life unfolding, which evolution suggests.

Anti-anthropocentrism has been propounded as a part of a larger movement called Deep Ecology. Although Deep Ecology has a very worthy agenda and worthy aspirations, it has overstated its positions. One of these overstated positions is the condemnation of all forms of anthropocentric thinking. By implication it is a condemnation of almost all forms of evolutionary thinking. Deep Ecology is quite incoherent when it becomes virulently anti-anthropocentric.

Let us notice that Deep Ecology itself is a form of anthropocentrism! Why so? Because whatever assertions it makes about anthropocentrism, and anti-anthropocentrism, these assertions are made through the agency of the human mind, not through the agency of the mind of a wolf or of a mountain. These are anthropocentric assertions. Let us probe this issue further.

I am told that we must think like a mountain, which Aldo Leopold has recommended.[6] I am quite in sympathy with what he *wanted* to say, but not with what he actually *did* say. Unfortunately, we cannot think like a mountain; nor can we even assume that the mountain would like to *think*; like a mountain, or otherwise. When we ponder the matter in some depth, we realize that the idea of thinking like a mountain sets for us a dreadful anthropocentric trap. If we are careful enough, the most we can say is that we should *mountain* like a mountain. Now this is quite a different proposition from Leopold's. We are in a different ontological and psychological situation when we say that we must *mountain* like a mountain, contrasted with the situation when we say that we must *think* like a mountain. The idea that we should mountain like a mountain is an appealing one, except that we don't exactly know what it means! Perhaps the ordinary meaning is not important; but then again perhaps it is. This is only the beginning of the difficulties.

A more important point is this. All those claims that we make on behalf of others – the trees, the brooks, the mountains, the fields, the foxes, the whales, and last but not least, the dying cultures being decimated in the Amazonian forests – by *whom* are they made? With what kind of mandate? By whom is this mandate given and to whom? If a mountain were to speak on behalf of all others, she might just as well shrug her shoulders and say nothing. It is very likely that the mountain would not want to talk on behalf of others. It is *our* peculiar propensity to do so. It is our peculiar moral burden to have to do so. We care for others because we feel that we must. This is our human predicament, part of the glory of our species. We do not know whether other species, with their consciousness and sensitivities developed as they are, would wish to (and indeed could) take the responsibility for all others.

Let us be clear: all claims made on behalf of the biotic community are made by human beings. They are filtered by human sensitivities and by human compassion. They are based on our human sense of justice, on our human recognition of how things are and *how they ought to be*. They are pervaded with human values. In brief, *all these claims are deeply and profoundly embedded in our anthropocentrism*, whether we care to recognize this or not.

It is simply naïve to assume that we can escape our anthropocentric predicament. We cannot be wolves. We cannot be mountains. We cannot be angels. But through our acts of empathy, which stem from our deep participation in all there is, we can, because of the characteristics of the human consciousness, so identify with the well-being of other beings that this empathy becomes an act of reverence. This reverence stemming from the idea of participation becomes an assured ethical path of tolerance, of protection, of preservation, of care and of love.

Our reverential consciousness is part of our anthropocentric legacy. We should be proud of it. The very meaning of the term *anthropos* is intricately complex. For who is the *anthropos*? A bio-machine? An egotistic, selfish, greedy, parasitic individual? Or the Buddha? The meaning of *anthropos* can be sublime and can be despicable. If we articulate our consciousness in the image of the Buddha, we can be proud of the *anthropos* in us.

(3) PARTICIPATORY ETHICS ON THE COSMIC LEVEL

We have analysed the first two levels of participatory ethics – interpersonal and interspecies. The third, the cosmic level, is the level that connects us with things unseen; or one which relates us to God – if we allow ourselves to use the term. How does participatory ethics spell out our relationship with God? If we remember what we have said about the power and the role of the participatory mind, while it is acting in the participatory universe, then our relationship to God becomes immediately clear. In the simplest possible terms it could be expressed as follows:

Live as if you were God.

To enunciate this principle is not an act of human arrogance but an act of human courage. This principle clearly follows from the architecture of the participatory universe which, in its unfolding, creates the participatory mind. The participatory mind enables the universe to articulate God which is latent in it. Even if God is conceived as the prime mover, we need the participatory mind to discover God's nature.

The idea of man reaching out to heaven to become God is not strange to Eastern cultures, notable the Hindu and the Buddhist. The glory of man sung in the Upanishads is the glory of man who becomes God. This idea is expressed in Buddhism in a more subtle way. Each of us has a Buddha hidden in us. To fulfil our destiny is to become a Buddha, is to release the Buddha from within us. To become a Buddha is to live like a God.[7]

The time has come to realize that the Eastern spiritual traditions are part of our tradition. We can incorporate these traditions into our belief systems. We can indeed conceive of ourselves as God-in-the-process-of-becoming without feeling sacrilegious or unduly arrogant. For what can be our destiny if not to become God?

The glory of God is infinite. We are part of this glory. This is what all religions teach. Christian religion teaches that we are the children of God. One day the children of God will become adults. And that means God!

Participatory ethics does not claim to be entirely novel or unrelated to other ethical systems. Its first component – reverence in interpersonal relationships – is closely related to Kantian ethics, based on the moral imperative: '*Act in such a way that you always treat humanity, whether in your own person or in the person of any other, never simply as a means, but always at the same time as an end.*'[8]

The second component of participatory ethics – reverence for natural systems and for all beings – partly overlaps with Buddhist ethics, and partly with a variety of ecological ethics proposed in recent times; especially those that attempt to elevate bio-centric communities to the level of ethical entities.

The third component of participatory ethics: *live as if you were God*, coincides with the teachings of the Upanishads and with other spiritual traditions. This component of participatory ethics has a distinctly religious connotation. Indeed, most ethical systems are disguised forms of religion. Whether we take it as a religion or ethics, a clear imperative for our times, and for our evolutionary destiny, is as follows. Act in such a way as if you were God, Who is powerful but compassionate, Who has the courage of acting and the vision of seeing the consequences of His action.

Summary

Philosophy is a quest of liberation. All philosophies seek to elevate man, release him from bondage, bring him closer to Nirvana, to heaven, to the inner god.

Some philosophies deliberately attempt to be a path joining man with God. In this quest, they become akin to religion. Eastern philosophies have never renounced the ambition of delivering man to heaven. They have tried to be liberators in the spiritual sense. In this role they are close to religion. In our language, these philosophies have not yet separated themselves from religion. Nor did they mean to. This is the source of their strength – they address themselves to the total person; and this is the source of their weakness – they are intellectually and rationally less rigorous than Western philosophies.

In the West, philosophy has become more and more instrumental. The business of philosophy is to liberate reason, which in turn will liberate man. In this process of the liberation of reason we have surely gone too far. Reason has now become an autonomous agency which has the power to control and often to oppress. Reason has alienated itself from the overall quest of the liberation of man. Instead of liberation and enlightenment our physical knowledge has brought us *power*, in terrifying degree. We are a power-hungry civilization which at the same time is scared of the power it has accumulated.

The time for a new liberating philosophy has arrived. Proposed in this volume is an outline of participatory philosophy which, by liberating the mind, liberates our destiny, and in a sense the destiny of the cosmos.

Participatory philosophy is the ultimate courage of man to surprise himself by creating realities surrounding him/her; the ultimate courage to realize that all is a web of dreams, but dreams so tangible and lucid that we cannot distinguish them from reality because they are reality. Participatory philosophy is the realization that we create the universe in our own image – as we are in the image of the universe which, by creating us, wants to reflect itself in that which it has created.

Among the great spiritual traditions of the past, the Upanishads expressed the glory and mystery of the becoming of man through the mind unfolding in the most luminous and persuasive manner. 'Mind is indeed the source of bondage, but also the source of liberation.' The Buddhist tradition is also supremely aware of the importance of the mind. We read in the *Dhammapada:* 'What we are today is the result of our thoughts of yesterday. And our thoughts of today pave the way to what we shall become tomorrow.'[9]

Participatory philosophy is the courage of flying . . . flying in control. There is a sense of wonderful exhilaration when you ski down a demanding slope, almost flying, and yet in perfect control. Take another example: the sense of freedom and adventure when you let your mind wander in front of an audience. You explore a new territory. You know that you may get stuck and perhaps make a fool of yourself. Yet you are inwardly assured that *somehow* your imagination will carry you through. This is flying in control. *Flying in control is living in freedom and in dignity.*

This mode of our being that we describe as flying in control is a psychological consequence of genuinely accepting the notion of the participatory universe and the participatory mind. There is no co-creation without courage and without flying. Great artists have always known this simple and magnificent truth.

This process of flying in control is a precondition of following a spiritual path, a path to Enlightenment. Following such a path entails fearlessness resulting from the realization that when your inner essence is intact, then your life is in balance; then you can fly in control in whatever circumstances you find yourself. Flying in control is a central aspect of participatory philosophy: it is a description of the participatory mind on its journey of fearless exploration, on its journey of perpetual becoming.

Participatory philosophy heralds hope as an inherent part of our being: as a part of our ontological structure; and also as a part of our psychological structure which sustains us daily. Hope is trans-rational. And yet hope is a precondition of all human rationality. To live in hope is to live in grace.

Participatory philosophy declares that to be a person in the participatory universe entails the recognition of the bond of participation. If we don't recognize this bond, we have relinquished our rights to live in the participatory universe. This simple insight, when spelled out, unveils the notion of participatory ethics – based on reverence and responsibility as aspects of participation in the deep sense.

Participatory ethics contains three levels: interpersonal, interspecies, God-man relationships. The three levels are all united by the notion of participation and its consequences. To participate is to be responsible. The larger the reach of our participation the larger the scope of our responsibility. Thus participatory ethics should be seen as an integral aspect of the participatory mind; both its consequence and its articulation.

Participatory philosophy is an act of courage: to live as if you were God, for what else is left to man if he takes his destiny seriously? To live as if you were God is both a principle of participatory ethics and a principle of human understanding.

The universe has created many wonders. Among these wonders was the creation of the mind – which was no less spectacular than the creation of any galaxy. Perhaps more spectacular. For the mind has become the eye through which the universe can look at itself. This is one of those rare truths: *through the human mind, the universe appreciates itself.* Without the mind, all the glory of the universe would be mute. When there is no mind to comprehend, there is no universe to behold. What a marvel it was when the universe created the mind to celebrate itself!

What I have described in this book is one sublime journey. The question may be asked: is such a sublime journey possible in our times? Yes, it is; because it is the only journey worth travelling. Embarking on this journey is a creative and necessary response to the forces of disintegration and darkness. The light will prevail because we shall prevail.

Let us end with a prayer to the universe.

Be benevolent to us, o universe
So that we can worship your glory.
As you have made us
So we reflect your splendour.
Allow us to become more splendid
So that you become more splendid.
Allow us to become more compassionate
So that the whole universe breathes more compassionately.
Be generous to us, o universe
So that we can be generous to you.

Out of the void of darkness
The light of understanding appeared.
We thank you, o universe
For the light of the mind
Which can illumine the immensities
Including your own nature.
We are aware that when we think of you
You are thinking about yourself through us.
We are an instrument of thy glory.
We are delighted and grateful that in creating us
You made us your seeing and thinking eye.
We have no doubt that you have created us
To celebrate yourself.
May we have enough wisdom and courage
To celebrate your depth and mystery
In the grandeur that it requires.

Notes

CHAPTER 1: Outlining the Participatory Mind

1 See especially Teilhard's *The Phenomenon of Man*, London and New York, 1959 (first published in French, 1957), certainly one of the most important books of the twentieth century.

2 It is safe to say that without Bergson there would be no Teilhard. Teilhard's indebtedness to Bergson is enormous. Yet paradoxically, Bergson's name is only briefly mentioned in Teilhard's oeuvre. What we witness in the pair Bergson–Teilhard is not plagiarism, but the later thinker creatively building on the earlier.

3 The existence of ESP and other 'powers', which are latent in us or emerging, is a subject of heated controversy. For some ESP is already there, present in us, and only needs to be practised and individually developed. For others, in whom this sensitivity is much less developed, and who see it as outside the range of their powers, ESP is a form of unwarranted magic – not acceptable by sane and rational minds. It is similar with other powers which are emerging in us and are being refined within the species and within individuals. Moral holism, a sense of empathy and compassion for all, is practised as a matter of course in some communities, for example among Tibetan Buddhists. Among them, universal compassion is considered the most important attainment of a person on his or her way to Buddhahood. It is not so in other cultures, particularly those eaten up by hedonism and excessive selfishness. When in the mid-1980s (the Reagan era of selfishness) I discussed universal compassion with my students in the United States, they thought I was talking fairy tales. So as to which sensitivities we choose to elicit, much depends on the climate of the epoch; but also on individual natural endowment.

4 Perhaps the term 'monism' is not entirely adequate. The Sanskrit term *advaita* may be more felicitous, as it suggests that it is neither this nor that but both at the same time. *Advaita* asserts a seamless unity of things which, however, can be organized in different compartments, and then named with different labels such as material, mental, spiritual. Yet I hesitate to use a new term 'advaitism' or 'New Advaita' for it would be odd to the Western philosophical ear. The question – an ancient metaphysical question – is: how to name that which comprises all?

CHAPTER 2: Mind in History

1 Alfred Tarski, *Pojecie Prawdy w Jezykach Nauk Dedukcyjnych* (The Concept of Truth in Formalized Languages), Warsaw, 1933.

2 See especially Karl Popper, *Conjectures and Refutations: The Growth of Scientific Knowledge*, Routledge & Kegan Paul, 1963.

3 It should be mentioned at this point that Popper has grappled valiantly with the notion of truth – which he tried to save at all costs. But there have always been great difficulties with this. Now, if all knowledge is tentative, then it would seem to follow that all truth is relative. Relativism of truth was the last thing Popper wanted to admit. Consequently, he invented a new concept, that of approximation of truth: newer theories that refute older ones are preferable because they more closely approximate the truth. The notion of approximation to truth has been ridden with difficulties which Popper never resolved, in spite of some attractive semi-formal formulations he found for the concept. How can we know that we 'approximate' the truth if we do not know the truth; this something we approximate? Popper has never explicitly given up the classical notion of truth: for this would mean that scientific knowledge is not superior to other forms of knowledge. Why? Because the cornerstone of scientific theories is empirical refutability, in other words, the assumption that there is an empirical reality out there which science faithfully describes; and because it does so, we can compare our theories with nature itself. The meaning of refutability rests on the assumption that science does describe reality in an unequivocal and faithful way. Although Popper did not give up the classical notion of truth explicitly, he did give it up implicitly. As a result of Thomas Kuhn's reconstruction of science, Popper seemed to agree with Kuhn that theories are not refuted in actual scientific practice, but rather like old soldiers, fade away.

4 See P.W.Bridgman, *The Logic of Modern Physics*, New York, 1927; *The Nature of Some of our Physical Concepts*, New York, 1952.

5 See B.F.Skinner, *The Behavior of Organisms*, New York, 1938; *Science and Human Behavior*, New York, 1953.

6 J.B.Watson, *Psychology from the Standpoint of a Behaviorist*, New York, 1919.

7 Gilbert Ryle, *The Concept of Mind*, 1949, p. 7.

8 See Henryk Skolimowski, 'Evolutionary Rationality', in *Proceedings of Philosophy of Science Association*, 1974, ed. R. S. Cohen et al., Reidel, 1976.

9 Paul Feyerabend, 'A Plea for the Hedonist', in *Criticism and the Growth of Scientific Knowledge*, ed. Imre Lakatos and Alan Musgrave, Cambridge University Press, 1970.

10 See Imre Lakatos, op. cit., and his subsequent writings.

11 For further discussion of Popper's philosophy, particularly his conjecturalism and his metaphysics of World 3, see my essay 'Karl Popper and the Objectivity of Scientific Knowledge' in *The Philosophy of Karl Popper* (*The Library of Living Philosophers*), ed. Paul Schilpp, Open Court, La Salle, Ill., vol. 14, pp. 483–508, 1974.

12 *The Dhammapada*, trans. Juan Mascaro, Penguin Books, 1973 (1).

13 Ibid. (89).

14 Ibid. (36).

15 Ibid. (37).

16 The Chandogya 8. 7–12 in *The Upanishads*, trans. Juan Mascaro, Penguin Books, 1970.

17 The Maitri Upanishad 6.24, ibid.

18 The Maitri Upanishad 6.24, ibid.

19 Boruch Spinoza, *Ethics*, part V, prop. XLII.

CHAPTER 3: The Spiral of Understanding

1 At the turn of the century there were some eminent scientists and philosophers (Ernst Mach among others) who did not believe in the existence of the atom. While opposing the existence of this illusory entity they would ask their opponent: 'Have you seen any of them?' We still haven't, but the existence of the atom is now part of our ABC of science. However what can be accepted as existing and what can be questioned is not an obvious matter.

2 For further discussion of this point, see chapter 4 section 2 on the views of Willis Harman regarding the way in which we can validate metaphysics.

3 For further discussion of this issue, see Henryk Skolimowski, 'Quine, Ajdukiewicz and the predicament of 20th Century Philosophy' in *The Philosophy of W. V. Quine* (*The Library of Living Philosophers*), ed. Lewis Edwin Hanh, Open Court, La Salle, Ill., 1986; see also Skolimowski, *Polish Analytical Philosophy*, especially the chapter on Ajdukiewicz, Routledge & Kegan Paul, 1967.

CHAPTER 4: Teilhard's Story of Complexity

1 See *Studies in the Philosophy of Biology: Reduction and Related Problems*, ed. Francisco Ayala and Theodosius Dobzhansky, University of California Press, 1974.

2 Actually the term 'noosphere' was used for the first time most probably by Leroi in Bergson's seminar in Paris around 1925. Teilhard adopted the term and incorporated it in his magnificent structure. See Skolimowski, 'Reconstructing Teilhard's Background: A Note About the Origin of the Term "Noosphere",' *The Teilhard Review*, vol. 21, no. 3, 1986.

3 For further discussion of this point, see Henryk R. Skolimowski, *The Theatre of the Mind*, especially chapter 2, 'Science and Evolution', Theosophical Publishing House, 1984.

4 Richard Dawkins, *The Blind Watchmaker*, Oxford University Press, 1986.

5 The idea of punctuated evolution is most closely associated with Stephan Gould who has been its most vigorous champion – see his various books. The terminology 'punctuated evolution' is Gould's. But the idea itself is much older. It goes back to Bergson and Teilhard. Before Gould christened it with his own label, the view of evolution as discontinuous was subscribed to by many scientists, notably Szent Gyorgyi and Ilya Prigogine. Actually, Gould's stepping stones to fame were his vociferous attacks on Teilhard. Basing his charge on circumstantial evidence, Gould accused Teilhard of consciously and knowingly participating in the Plaiston Man hoax. The evidence is only circumstantial. Teilhard should have spoken out. He didn't. Sometimes silence is not golden.

For a man of Stephan Gould's intellect and abilities it is demeaning and unworthy to have attacked Teilhard (while he could not defend himself), make a scandal of it, and capitalize on it – without providing any substantial evidence. Men of great abilities should build their careers on their positive achievements and not by finding faults – real or imaginary – in others.

6 We should have no qualms in using the term 'miracle', for the process of transcendence occurring within evolution which brought about such staggering novelty and variety makes reason speechless and gasping for explanation. The idea of gradualism (unless it is used idiosyncratically as denoting the creative process) is impotent even to begin to explain the nature of transcendent processes.

7 An anticipation of this idea, specifically as applied to human growth and development, can be found in the work of the Polish psychologist K. Dabrowski, who used the term 'positive disintegration' (*Personality Shaping through Positive Disintegration Processes*, J. and A. Churchill, Edinburgh, 1968). See Skolimowski, *The Theatre of the Mind*, chapter 18, 'Prigogine and Dialectics – Uphill from Entropy'.

8 See especially Thomas Kuhn, *The Structure of Scientific Revolutions* (1963), University of Chicago Press, 1970. However, many crucial ideas showing how discontinuous science is were proposed and articulated by Karl Popper; see especially *The Logic of Scientific Inquiry* (1934), 1959 and *Conjectures and Refutations: The Growth of Scientific Knowledge*, Routledge & Kegan Paul, 1963.

9 Willis Harman, 'Scientific Positivism, The New Dualism, and the Perennial Wisdom', *Scientific and Medical Network Newsletter*, Fall 1986.

CHAPTER 5: The Four Great Cycles of the Western Mind

1 J.L. Austin, *Philosophic Papers*, Oxford University Press, 1981.

2 The categories of knowledge, particularly those developed under the auspices of empiricist epistemology, are brittle and exclusive. They do not recognize any merging of things. They are based on either/or logic. This logic is characteristic of the Western mind at large. We don't like shades of grey. Everything must be either this or that. Western two-valued logic reinforces this habit of mind. Western man does not do well in situations of ambiguity. The Hindu mind, on the other hand, is very much at ease in the world of ambiguity.

3 We should be aware that cognitive understanding has been in a sense monopolized by what is called (within empiricist epistemology) cognitive knowledge, which is based on cognitive claims. But what exactly is cognitive knowledge and what exactly are cognitive claims? This question is not so easy to answer; unless we *arbitrarily assume* that cognitive knowledge is physical knowledge and logical tautologies. Then, of course, we are question-begging; actually on behalf of a worn-out and outdated metaphysics, the metaphysics based on Newtonian mechanics. One wonders whether the philosophers who are so proud of pursuing cognitive knowledge are actually aware what a shoddy metaphysical edifice they are supporting.

4 Leonardo da Vinci, *Notebooks*, ed. and trans. E. Maccurdy, Jonathan Cape, London, 1956.

5 Gregory Bateson, see especially the last chapter of *Mind and Nature; A Necessary Unity*, E. P. Dutton, 1979.

CHAPTER 6: The Methodology of Participation and its Consequences

1 Ludwig Fleck, see especially *Genesis and Development of a Scientific Fact*, University of Chicago Press, 1979; German original published in 1935.

2 Joseph Chilton Pearce, *Magical Child*, E. P. Dutton, 1977; Paladin, 1979.

3 Paul Feyerabend, 'Consolation for the Specialist' in *Criticism and the Growth of Knowledge*, ed. Imre Lakatos and Alan Musgrave, Cambridge University Press, 1970, p. 228.

4 Karl Popper, *Conjectures and Refutations: Growth of Scientific Knowledge*, Routledge & Kegan Paul, 1963.

5 Lakatos's scientific bias is quite flagrant, particularly in the section 'Science: Reason or Religion' of his work on research programmes ('Falsification and the Methodology of Scientific Research Programmes' in *Criticism and the Growth of Knowledge*). In the old-fashioned manner of Marxist commissars he puts down religion and elevates science to a religious pedestal, claiming, among other things, that *commitment* is an

outright crime while he himself unequivocally expresses *his* commitment to scientific research programmes.

6 The Polish phenomenologist Roman Ingarden is of special relevance for us here as he has painstakingly described the conception of art as an intentional object. For further discussion of Ingarden's views see H. Skolimowski, 'Roman Ingarden', *The Encyclopedia of Philosophy*, ed. Paul Edwards, Collier-Macmillan, vol. 4, 1967, pp. 193–95.

7 Evelyn Fox Keller, *Reflections on Gender and Science*, Yale University Press, 1985, p. 165.

8 See especially Patsy Hallen, 'Making Peace with Nature: Why Ecology Needs Feminism', *The Trumpeter*, vol. 4, no. 3, summer 1987; as well as Keller, op. cit. and her other works.

9 For further discussion of the inherent difficulties in objectivity justifying itself objectively, see H. Skolimowski, 'Problems of Rationality in Biology', chapter 13 in *Studies in the Philosophy of Biology: Reduction and Related Problems*, ed. F. Ayala and T. Dobzhansky, University of California Press, 1974.

10 Brian Swimme, *The Universe is a Green Dragon*, Bear, 1984, pp. 138–39.

11 For a summary of this debate see Jeremy Bernstein, 'Personal History – The Life It Brings', *The New Yorker*, 2 February 1987, p. 60.

12 Milton, *Paradise Lost*, book i, lines 254–55.

13 F. D. H. Kitto, *The Greeks*, Penguin Books, 1951, p. 169.

CHAPTER 7: Structures, Symbols and Evolution

1 Herbert Simon, *Sciences of the Artificial*, MIT Press, 1970, p. 108; see in particular the chapter 'The Architecture of Complexity'.

2 Figs 1–3 and much of the accompanying text appeared in my previous book *Living Philosophy*, 1992, pp. 192–94.

3 In presenting objects of art as intentional objects, I follow the line of analysis initiated in the 1930s by the Polish phenomenologist Roman Ingarden (1893–1970).

4 The idea of symbolic forms seems to have been initiated by Goethe, although the term was not used by Goethe. The germ of the idea was developed by Schelling within the realm of aesthetics. When it was well developed, the aesthetician Friedrich Theodor Vischer made symbolic form the foundation of aesthetics itself. From him, particularly his essay 'Das Symbol' published in 1887, Cassirer took the idea, and then developed it into a philosophy of his own.

It should be mentioned that aesthetics was not the only inspiration for Cassirer. The essential meaning of symbolic form was derived by Cassirer both from his reflections on past aesthetics and on Einstein's theory of relativity. Actually the term 'symbolic form' is used by Cassirer in his essay 'Einstein's Theory of Relativity' (1921). Cassirer's desire was to subsume under symbolic form all varieties of knowledge: cognitive (including scientific), aesthetic, ethical, religious. He wrote that philosophy 'has to grasp the whole system of symbolic forms, the application of which produces for us the concept of an ordered reality . . .' Once this is accomplished, then an orderly picture of reality would be obtained whereby the right place would be found 'for each of the particular forms of the concept and of knowledge as well as of the general forms of the theoretical, ethical, aesthetic and religious understanding of the world.' In *Substance and Function of Einstein's Theory of Relativity*, 1923, p. 447, Cassirer does not seem to be fully aware of the different nature of scientific symbols, as contrasted with religious symbols. These two realms of symbols have different sets of meanings in the human universe, as I argue in section 5 of this chapter.

5 R. Panikkar, 'The Destiny of Technological Civilization: An Ancient Buddhist Legend of *Romavisaya*', *Alternatives*, no. 2, 1984, p. 240.

6 Shantideva, *A Guide to Boddhisattva's Way of Life* (*Library of Tibetan Works and Archives*), 1979, p. 180.

7 The idea was put forward by James E. Lovelock, first in an article, then in a book entitled *Gaia, A New Look at Life on Earth*, Oxford University Press, 1979.

8 See especially the writings of Thomas Berry who has been most lucid and most far-reaching in articulating the new myth cum theology cum eco-philosophy.

9 Henry P. Stapp, 'Mind, Matter and Quantum Mechanics', *Foundations of Physics*, vol. 12, no. 4, April 1982, p. 396.

CHAPTER 8: The Individual Spiral of Understanding

1 Let us note that even if this reality is assumed not to be physical in character (as is the case with Plato's system, where the underlying Forms constitute the ultimate and true reality), the presumption is nevertheless upheld: we can capture this reality in our (intersubjective) knowledge.

2 In the ancient Chinese tradition, inspired by Confucius, the individual is seen as a circle surrounded by a larger concentric circle which is the family; which is surrounded by a larger circle – that of society; which is surrounded by a larger circle still – that of the cosmos. The participatory model of the self retains the identity of the self while it participates in other realms.

3 Abraham Harold Maslow, *Motivation and Personality*, Harper & Row, 1970.

4 Gregory Bateson, *Mind and Nature*, E. P. Dutton, 1979, p. 213.

5 For further discussion, see Henryk Skolimowski, *The Sacred Place to Dwell: Living with Reverence upon the Earth*, Element Books, Shaftesbury, Dorset, 1993.

CHAPTER 9: The Universal Spiral of Understanding

1 On culture as the mesmerizer, see especially the works of Willis Harman.

2 See especially *The Oxford Companion to the Mind*, Oxford University Press, 1987; a stupendous work, and stupendously biased in favour of the brain at the expense of the mind.

3 As Dr Anders Munk has put it: 'During the tremendous development of biochemistry not a single phenomenon has appeared to speak against a strictly mechanistic *description* of life. But mark the difference between "description" and "explanation"! The mind hypothesis brings everything together.' (Personal communication, December 1987.)

4 Henryk Skolimowski, 'Epistemology, the Mind and the Computer', subsequently published in *Biology, History and Natural Philosophy*, ed. A. D. Breck and W. Yourgrau, Plenum Publishing, 1972.

5 John Archibald Wheeler, 'The Universe as Home for Man', *The Scientific American*, November/December, 1974.

6 *The Philosophy of Karl Popper*, ed. Paul Arthur Schilpp, in series *The Library of Living Philosophers*, Open Court, La Salle, Ill., 2 vols, 1974.

7 Ibid., vol. 1, pp. 507–8.

8 Ibid., vol. 2, pp. 1066–7.

9 Karl R. Popper and John C. Eccles, *The Self and Its Brain: An Argument for Interactionism*, Springer-Verlag, Berlin, 1977.

10 Ibid., p. 35.

11 Ibid., p. 48.

12 Ibid., p. 551.

13 Ibid., pp. 548–61.

14 Ibid., p. 554.

15 Jean Gebser, *The Ever Present Origin*, Ohio University Press, 1985.

16 Georg Feuerstein, *Structures of Consciousness: the Genius of Jean Gebser: An Introduction and Critique*, Integral Publishing, 1987.

17 Ibid., p. 61.

CHAPTER 10: Participatory Truth

1 Hilary Putnam, *The Many Faces of Realism*, Open Court, La Salle, Ill., 1987; really not a continuous treatise but four different lectures.

2 Thus the whole concept is opaque in Kuhn, and in Popper, and in most thinkers that have followed them. It is opaque because we have lost the firm referent called 'reality' to which all truth was supposed to correspond. The debate on the nature of science which Feyerabend and Lakotos continued, following in the footsteps of Popper and Kuhn, only adds to confusion and obfuscation. We no longer know what is what within the universe of science, let alone what truth is.

3 I have distinguished the fourth stage of evolution, theological evolution, or the evolution of God, in my booklet *Eco-theology* (1985); see also my book *The Sacred Place to Dwell: Living with Reverence upon the Earth*, Element Books, Shaftesbury, Dorset, 1994.

4 This idea is much more potent and epistemologically more significant and more promising than the idea of either 'contextual relativism' or 'internal realism' which Putnam and others seem to favour.

5 For further discussion of the language of being, see chapter 13 of my book *The Theatre of the Mind*, Theosophical Publishing House, 1984.

CHAPTER 11: Grand Theory in the Participatory Key

1 Actually the philosopher Collingwood, who was a part-time archaeologist, was making a similar point when he said that what turns up on your shovel depends on the quality of your imagination, of your knowledge, of your expectations.

2 Now it would seem possible that a computer may come up with a new proof or theorem, thereby contributing to knowledge, while bypassing the human experience. However, it takes the human mind to recognize a given series of formulae as a coherent proof, let alone an original one. So the imprimatur of the mind is on the proof at the point at which it is recognized as such. Human experience inevitably and ineluctably enters – even if it is in an indirect and subtle way. Unless something happens to the mind, nothing can happen on paper in terms of the formal structure of the proof. Even if the computer comes up with spectacular results, 'the computer does nothing – it is the human mind that recognizes the spectacular results' and makes them 'spectacular' by its recognition. 'Spectacular results' unrecognized and unacknowledged are nothing. The computer cannot recognize results – spectacular or otherwise – for it is a dummy.

3 The English translation of *Logische Untersuchungen* by J. N. Findlay, *Logical Investigations*, Routledge & Kegan Paul, 2 vols, 1970.

CHAPTER 12: The Promise of Participatory Philosophy

1 Plato, *Phaedrus and Letters VII and VIII*, trans. Walter Hamilton, Penguin Books, 1973, p. 343.

2 For detailed discussion see Henryk Skolimowski, *Polish Analytical Philosophy*, Routledge & Kegan Paul, 1967, especially chapter 3.

3 See chapter 10 of my book *The Theatre of the Mind*, Theosophical Publishing House, 1984.

4 From the great speech of Chief Seattle, delivered in 1854.

5 For further discussion of ecological ethics, see chapter 8, 'Eco-ethics

and the Sanctity of Life' of my book *Living Philosophy: Eco-philosophy as a Tree of Life*, Penguin Books (Arkana), 1992.

6 Aldo Leopold, *Sand Country Almanac*, Oxford University Press, New York, 1969; new ed. Ballantine, 1986.

7 For further discussion of Man-as-God-in-the-process-of-becoming see H. Skolimowski, *Eco-Theology: Toward a Religion for Our Times* (Eco-Philosophy Publications no.2), 1985; and *The Sacred Place to Dwell: Living with Reverence upon the Earth*, Element Books, Shaftesbury, Dorset, 1993.

8 Immanuel Kant, *Groundwork of the Metaphysics of Morals*, trans. H. J. Paton, Harper & Row, 1964, II.17, p.96.

9 *The Dhammapada*, trans. Juan Mascaro, Penguin Books, 1975, p. 35.